# ITALIAN RENAISSANCE POETRY

GARLAND REFERENCE LIBRARY
OF THE HUMANITIES
(VOL. 712)

# ITALIAN RENAISSANCE POETRY
## A First-Line Index to
## Petrarch, Ariosto, Tasso and Others

Maureen E. Buja

GARLAND PUBLISHING, INC. • NEW YORK & LONDON
1987

**Library of Congress Cataloging-in-Publication Data**
Buja, Maureen E., 1958–
Italian Renaissance poetry.

(Garland reference library of the humanities ;
vol. 712)
Bibliography: p.
1. Italian poetry—To 1400—Indexes.
2. Italian poetry—16th century—Indexes.  I. Title.
II. Series: Garland reference library of the
humanities ; v. 712.
PQ4210.B8   1987      016.851      86-33522
ISBN 0-8240-8581-7 (alk. paper)

Printed on acid-free, 250-year-life paper
Manufactured in the United States of America

# CONTENTS

# ACKNOWLEDGEMENTS

I would like to thank the following people for their encouragement and support: James Haar of the University of North Carolina at Chapel Hill; Margaret Lospinuso, Kathryn Logan and Stephen Lurie, all formerly of the University of North Carolina; Christopher Buja, formerly of Princeton University; and Maria Koba of Booz Allen and Hamilton and Frederick Nesta of PaineWebber for their technical support. I would also like to thank the Library of Congress and the Newberry Library for supplying microfilm necessary for this project.

# INTRODUCTION

Though there exist concordances to the major Italian poets, access to some of the major Renaissance poetic works has always been difficult because of the lack of adequate line–by–line indexes. In the case of the five poets selected here, Petrarch, Tasso, Ariosto, Bembo and Strozzi, complete indexes have not been available, and, in some cases, modern editions have not been available either. For music scholars, the Einstein and Marocco checklists have provided some access to musical settings, although in cases where the text was not recognized to be by Ariosto, Tasso or Petrarch, the checklists cannot help. Through these indexes, I am seeking to make accessible these large works as well as aid the task of the scholars seeking to trace the authorship of unknown texts. The poets included in this volume were chosen from an examination of the index of *Il Nuovo Vogel* where these were the poets who were set the greatest number of times.

Although he was of the fourteenth century, Francesco Petrarch (1304 - 1374) can in many ways be considered the first of the Renaissance poets. His themes are the conventional ones of medieval literature, yet it is his unique and characteristic treatment of them that removes him from the medieval circle and places him into the Renaissance. Throughout the *Canzoniere*, his collection of 366 poems dedicated to Laura, Petrarch plays on the theme of love; not the medieval topos of the love of God but the secular theme of unrequited love.

The influence of Petrarch can be seen in the innumerable poems in both his century and the following that couch their language so closely on his. The *Canzoniere* was used as a source of inspiration not only by minor poets but also by those who had their own fame. Einstein, in the *Italian Madrigal*, called Petrarch the "most frequently composed poet not only of the time of the madrigal but of world literature." (200). Petrarch's poems were set to music by composers from Dufay to Schoenberg, and had their greatest flowering of settings in the music of the sixteenth century. The rise of humanism and the need for literary texts led scholars back to the great writers of the fourteenth century: Dante, Boccaccio and Petrarch. Few of the works of Dante or Boccaccio were set to music, it was Petrarch who captured the imagination of composers. This is particularly evident in the change in Italian secular song between the frottola and the madrigal. Where the composers of the frottola were content to use light contemporary poetry, the madrigalists felt compelled to return to Petrarch as well as demand poetry of comparable quality from their contemporaries.

In the sixteenth century, the new epic poets came to the fore. Ludovico Ariosto's *Orlando Furioso* (the continuation of the earlier *Orlando Immamorato* by Boiardo) and Torquato Tasso's *Gerusalemme Liberata* both used a background setting as big and wondrous as the world itself. The poems detail the wars of the Christians and the Pagans and proceed in seemingly endless streams of ottave rime. Both works proved to be virtual goldmines for texts appropriate for musical setting.

Neither Pietro Bembo nor Giovanni Battista Strozzi the Elder wrote the epics of their contemporaries but their poems, in works such as Bembo's *Rime* and Strozzi's *Madrigali*, lent themselves quite well to music setting. Bembo, considered the arbiter of poetics, as Castiglione was the arbiter of social manners, published the first edition of his *Rime* in 1530, and then continued to change and rewrite the texts in the later editions of 1535 and 1548. Although Strozzi's work was not yet published until 1593, 22 years after his death, his poems obviously were in circulation much earlier. We can find settings by the composer Francesco Corteccia as early as 1547.

Luigi Cassola, although hardly mentioned in the standard reference works on Italian literature, was considered a significant poet by composers in the middle of the sixteenth century. The first setting of a poem of his dates from 1530 in a work by Marco Cara; his first and only printed collection of poems was gathered in the 1544 in a collection entitled: *Madrigali del Magnifico Signor Cavallier Luigi Cassola Piacentino*. One of the last settings is by Andrea Gabrieli in the 1570s. Cassola wrote a very specific kind of poem: sentimental ones that finished with an epigrammatic "point," on the models of Bembo in *Asolani*. These poems are also filled with Petrarchan quotations and for composers, this added to the attraction. Nearly all of the poems in this book are, as the title says, madrigals. These differ from the Petrarchan model of three line verses: sixteenth century madrigals are poems with seven and eleven syllable lines in one or two stanzas with varying numbers of lines in each stanza. The collection ends with two sonnets and an set of stanzas in ottava rima dedicated to Charles V. In addition to the 1544 collection, there also exists a manuscript collection of his works in the Fondo Capponiano in the Vatican Library.

Giovanni Della Casa, the papal nuncio to Venice in 1544 through 1550, wrote only a few poems. Scattered in various sources, these works were collected in 1558, two years after Della Casa's death, by his secretary, Erasmo Gemini. Despite the small number of poems, one of his poems is most famous in its setting by Rore, "O sonno, o de la queta umida, ombrosa."

Because of problems specific to each collection of poems, some of the indexes differ in their organization. In every case, however, the line of poetry is followed by two numbers: the first, a Roman numeral, indicates the number of the poem, or, in the case of the Ariosto and Tasso indexes, the canto; the second number following as slash (/), an arabic number, indicates the position of the stanza within that poem or canto. Thus, for Tasso,:

A costei la feretra e 'l grave incarco, XI/28

XI/28 means that this is stanza twenty-eight of canto eleven. For Petrarch:

Ben debbio io perdonare a tutt'i centi, LXVI/6

LXVI/6 means that this is stanza six of poem sixty-six. If a poem does not have more than one stanza, the arabic number is not used.

The *Canzoniere* of Petrarch contains 366 poems in five poetic forms: sonnets, canzonas, sestinas, ballatas, and madrigals. I have indexed the first and ninth lines of the sonnets, the beginning lines of the two principal parts; and the first line of every stanza for the other forms. The numbers following each poem indicate the number of the poem (1-366) and the stanza.

The epic poems *Orlando Furioso* and *Gerusalemme Liberata* were written entirely in the poetic form ottava rima and I have indexed the first line of each stanza. The numbers following each entry first indicate the canto and then the stanzas.

Problems arose with the Bembo index because of the evolving nature of his work. This index is based on the first edition of Bembo's *Rime* (1530). This was then checked against the 1966 edition of his *Prose e Rime* and it transpired that many poems had changed from the 1530 edition and more poems had been added in the third edition in 1548. I have indexed both the original lines from the 1530 edition and their variants and the additions.

The original lines from the 1530 edition are followed in the index by roman numerals for each poem and arabic numbers indicating the stanzas. Since there is no standard numbering system for Bembo's *Rime*, as there was for Petrarch, Ariosto and Tasso, I have numbered the poems according to their position in the 1530 edition, i.e., the first poem is poem I, the second, poem II, etc. The 1966 edition follows a slightly different order from the 1530 edition; the numbers follow, in general, very closely and users should have little difficulty in using the index in conjunction with this later edition. The lines that were changed in later editions are cross-reference by number. (See below the criteria for determining changed lines.) These lines are listed with the roman/arabic numbering established for the original edition followed by a lower case roman/arabic numbering corresponding to the 1966 edition's. Poems that were added in later editions, and which therefore would not appear in the 1530 edition, are indexed followed only by a lower case roman/arabic number corresponding to the 1966 edition's numbering.

Changed lines are those that have significantly different words or word order. For example, the first line of poem I in the 1530 edition appears as:

Piansi e cantai la perigliosa guerra, I/1

but is rendered in the 1966 editions, following the 1535 edition, as:

Piansi e cantai lo stazio e l'aspra guerra, I/1, i/1

and is therefore listed twice.

Differences in spelling, such as the use of the letter H in the 1530 edition (hor, or / huomo, uomo) are not modernized in this index. Missing apostrophes have been added where necessary:

> Porto sel valor vostro arme et perigli, XIV/1

will appear as

> Porto se 'l valor vostro arme et perigli, XIV/1.

If the differences between the lines are such that the alphabetic order would be affected, the line is listed twice, once in its original form and again in its later spelling:

> Et tanto in quel sembiante ella mi piacque, V/2

will also appear as

> E tanto in quel sembiante ella mi piacque, V/2, xi/2.

The Strozzi and Cassola indexes could not be checked against any modern editions. In general, I have done little in the way of modernizing the text: capitalizations remain as presented in the 1593 edition, and old spellings have not been modernized. Diacritical marks have been added as needed. In places where the first lines of the poems appears elsewhere, I have added the second line after a slash (/) in the text, For example, in the Strozzi index, Occhi, piangete, poi, is the first line for poems LXXXII and LXXXIII, therefore, I have added the second line in both cases:

> Occhi, piangete, poi/Hor come spesso pur mi riconforta, LXXXVII
> Occhi, piangete, poi/Che di pinto di pasce, e si nodre, LXXXVIII.

The numbering of the poems for the Strozzi and the Cassola, as for the Bembo, proceeds directly from the order of the poems in the first edition, the first poem is poem I and so on. Four poems in the Cassola appear in two places; I have indicated these by placing the comment [Duplicate] after the two poem numbers.

The Della Casa index is based on the modern edition edited by Daniele Ponchiroli. I have followed the numbering present in that volume.

Maureen Buja
1 December 1986

Introduction

Bibliography:

Ariosto, Ludovico. *Orlando Furioso.* edited by Cesare Segre. Vicenza: Arnoldo Mondadori, 1976.

Bembo, Pietro. *Rime.* Venice: Giovan Antonio et fratelli da Sabbio, 1530. Copy held in the Library of Congress: PQ4608.A15 1530

Bembo, Pietro. *Prose e Rime.* edited by Carlo Sionisotti. Turin: Unione Tipografico–Editrice Torinese, 1966.

Casa, Giovanni Della. *Rime.* edited by Daniele Ponchiroli. Torino: Giulio Einaudi, 1967.

Cassola, Luigi. *Madrigali del Magnifico Signor Cavallier Luigi Cassola Piacentino.* Venice: Gabriel Giolito de Ferrari, 1545. copy held in The Newberry Library, Chicago: Case.Y712.C255.

Petrarch, Francesco. *Petrarch's Lyric Poems: The Rime Sparse and Other Lyrics.* edited by Robert Durling. Cambridge, MA: Harvard University Press, 1976.

Strozzi, Giovanbatista (Giovanni Battista Strozzi, the Elder). *Madrigali.* Firenze: Sermartelli, 1593. Copy held in the Library of Congress.

Tasso, Torquato. *Gerusalemme Liberata.* edited by Anna Maria Carini. Milan: Feltrinelli Editore, 1961.

Tasso, Torquato. *Gerusalemme Liberata.* edited by Claudio Varese and Guido Arbizzoni. Milan: Mursia, 1972.

Related material:
Einstein, Alfred. "Orlando Furioso and La Gerusalemme Liberata as set to Music during the 16tb and 17th centuries." *Music Library Association Notes*, 2nd series, VIII/4 (September 1951), p. 624 - 630.

Einstein, Alfred. *The Italian Madrigal.* translated by Alexander H. Krappe, Roger H. Sessions, and Oliver Strunk. Princeton, J: Princeton University Press, 1949/1972.

Marrocco, W. Thomas. "A checklist of the music settings on the poems of Francesco Petrarch." *Quadrivium*, XV/1 (1974), p. 115 - 136.

Vogel, Emil, Alfred Einstein, François Lesure, and Claudio Sartori. *Il Nuovo Vogel: Bibliografia della musica Italiana profane pubblicate dal 1500 al 1700.* Pomezia: Saterini - Minkoff, 1977.

# I.
## Francesco Petrarch
### *Canzoniere*

A
A l'ultimo bisogno, o misera alma, CCXXXIX/5
A la dolce ombra de le belle frondi, CXLII/1
A le pungenti ardenti et lucide arme, CCCXXV/3
A me pur giova di sperare ancora, CCLI/2
A pie' de' colli ove la bella vesta, VIII/1
A qualunque animale alberga in terra, XXII/1
Ad una ad una annoverar le stelle, CXXVII/7
Ahi bella libertà, come tu m'ài, XCVII/1
Ahi dispietate Morte, ahi crudel vita!, CCCXXIV/2
Al cader d'una pianta che si svelse, CCCXVIII/1
Alfin ambo conversi al giusto seggio, CCCLX/11
Alfin vid'io per entro i fiori et l'erba, CCCXXIII/6
Allor errai quando l'antica strada, XCVI/2
Allor fui preso, et non mi spiacque poi, CVI/3
Allor mi stinrsi a l'ombra d'un bel faggio, LIV/3
Allor riprende ardir Saturno et Marte, XLI/2
Allor saranno i miei pensieri a riva, XXX/2
Alma felice che sovente torni, CCLXXXII/1
Almo sol, quella fronde ch'io sola amo, CLXXXVIII/1
Altr'amor, altre frondi, et altro lume, CXLII/7
Amor che 'ncende il cor d'ardente zelo, CLXXXII/1
Amor, che meco al buon tempo ti stavi, CCCIII/1
Amor, che nel penser mio vive et regna, CXL/1
Amor, che vedi ogni pensero aperto, CLXIII/1
Amor co la can destra il lato manco, CCXXVIII/1
Amor con sue promesse lusingando, LXXVI/1
Amor e 'l ver fur meco a dir che quelle, CLVIII/2
Amor et io, sì pien di meraviglia, CLX/1
Amor, Fortuna, et la mia mente, schiva, CXXIV/1
Amor fra l'erbe una leggiadra rete, CLXXXI/1
Amor, i'ò molti et molt'anni pianto, CCCXXXII/10
Amor, io fallo et veggio il mio fallire, CCXXXVI/1
Amor m'à posto come segno a strale, CXXXIII/1
Amor mi manda quel dolce pensero, CLXVIII/1
Amor mi sprona in un tempo et affrena, CLXXVIII/1
Amor, Natura et al bella alma umile, CLXXXIV/1
Amor piangeva et io con lui tal volta, XXV/1
Amor, quando fioria, CCCXXIV/1
Amor s'è in lei con onestate aggiunto, CCXV/2
Amor, se vuo' ch'i' torni al giogo antico, CCLXX/1
Amor, senno, valor, pietate, et doglia, CLVI/2
Amore, tu 'l senti, ond'io teco mi doglio, CCLXVIII/2
"Ancor, et questo è quel che tutto avanza, CCCLX/10
Ancor io il nido di penseri eletti, CCCXXXVII/2
Anima bella, da quel nodo sciolta, CCCV/1
Anima che diverse cose tante, CCIV/1
Anzi tre dì creata era alma in parte, CCXIV/1
Anzi un sole. Et se questo è, la mia vita, CCLIV/2
Apollo, s'ancor vive il bel desio, XXXIV/1
Arbor vittoriosa triunfale, CCLXIII/1
Aspro core et selvaggio et cruda voglia, CCLXV/1
Aura che quelle chiome bionde et crespe, CCXXVII/1
Aventuroso più d'altro terreno, CVIII/1

B
Basti che si ritrove in mezzo 'l campo, XCVIII/2
Beata s'è che po beare altrui, CCCXLI/2
Beato in sogno et di languir contento, CCXII/1
Ben ch'i' non sia di quel grand'onor degno, CCXLIV/2
Ben debbo io perdonare a tutt'i venti, LXVI/6
Ben mi credea dinanzi agli occhi suoi, XXIII/6
Ben mi credea passar mio tempo omai, CCVII/1
Ben poria ancor pietà con amor mista, CCII/2
Ben provide Natura al nostro stato, CXXVIII/3
Ben riconsoco in voi l'usate forme, CCCI/2
Ben sai, canzon, che quant'io parlo è nulla, CXXVII/8
Ben sai che sì bel piede, CXXV/5
Ben sapeva io che natural consiglio, LXIX/1
Ben, sì i' non erro, di pietate un raggio, CLXIX/2
Ben torna a consolar tanto dolore, CCLXXXIII/2
Ben veggio io di lontano il dolce lume, CLXIII/2
Benedette le voci tante ch'io, LXI/2
Benedetto sia 'l giorno e 'l mese et l'anno, LXI/1
Benigne stelle che compagne fersi, XXIX/7


C
Caduta è la tua gloria, et tu nol vedi, CCLXVIII/3
Candido leggiadretto et caro guanto, CXCIX/2
Cantai, or piango; et non men di dolcezza, CCXXIX/1
Canzon, chi tua ragion chiamasse oscura, CXIX/8
Canzon, i' non fu' mai quel nuvol d'oro, XXIII/9
Canzon, l'una sorella è poco inanzi, LXXII/6
Canzon mia, fermo in campo, CCVII/8
Canzon, qui sono ed ò 'l cor via più freddo, CCLXIV/8
Canzon, s'al dolce loco, XXXVII/8
Canzon, s'uom trovi in suo amor viver queto, CCCXXXI/6
Canzon, se l'esser meco, L/6
Canzon, tu non m'acqueti, anzi m'infiammi, LXXI/8
Canzon, tu puoi ben dire, CCCXXIII/7
Canzone, i' sento già stancar la penna, LXXIII/7
Canzone, io t'ammonisco, CXXVIII/8
Canzone, oltra quell'alpe, CXXIX/6
"Cara la vita, et dopo lei mi pare, CCLXII/1
Carità di signore, amor di donna, CCLXVI/2
Caro, dolce, alto et faticoso pregio, CCXIV/3
"Cercar m'à fatto deserti paesi, CCCLX/4
Cercato ò sempre solitaria vita, CCLIX/1
Cesare taccio, che per ogni piaggia, CXXVIII/4
Cesare, poi che 'l traditor d'Egitto, CII/1
Ch'a me la pastorella alpestra et cruda, LII/2
Ch'i' non son forte ad aspettar la luce, XIX/2
Ch'i' non vo' dir di lei, ma chi la scorge, CCX/2
Ch'i'ò cercate già vie più di mille, CCVII/3
Ch'or mel par ritrovar et or m'accorgo, CCXXVII/2
Che, come i miei pensier dietro a lei vanno, CCLXXVIII/2
Ché d'Omero dignissima e d'Orfeo, CLXXXVII/2
Ché dal destr'occhio--anzi dal destro sole--, CCXXXIII/2

Che debb'io far? che mi consigli, Amore?, CCLXVIII/1
Che è fermato di menar sua vita, LXXX/1
"Che fai, alma? che pensi? avrem mai pace?, CL/1
Che fai? che pensi? ché pur dietro guardi, CCLXXIII/1
Che fanno meco omai questi sospiri, CXLIX/2
Ché gentil pianta in arido terreno, LXIV/2
Ché già 'l contrario era ordinato in Cielo, CCCXXIX/2
Ché l'altro à 'l Cielo, et di sua chiaritate, CCCXXVI/2
Che la mia nobil preda non più stretta, CCI/2
Ché non bolle la polver d'Etiopia, XXIV/2
Ché non du d'allegrezza a' suoi dì mai, CCXCVI/2
Che parlo, o dove sono, et chi m'inganna, LXX/4
Ché piangon dentro, ov'ogni orecchia è sorda, CCXCIV/2
Che porà dir chi per amor sospira, LX/2
Ché quella voce infin al ciel gradita, CXCIII/2
Chi nol sa di ch'io vivo, et vissi sempre, CCVII/5
"Chi pon freno a li amanti o dà lor legge?", CCXXII/2
Chi spiasse, canzone, CXXXV/7
Chi vuol veder quantunque po Natura, CCXLVIII/1
Chiara fontana in quel medesmo bosco, CCCXXIII/4
Chiare fresche et dolci acque, CXXVI/1
Chiaro segno Amor pose a le mie rime, CCCXXXII/5
Chiunque alberga tra Garona e 'l monte, XXVIII/3
Chiusa fiamma è più ardente, et se pur cresce, CCVII/6
Chiuso gran tempo in questo cieco legna, LXXX/3
Cieco et stanco ad orgni altro ch'al mio danno, CCXII/2
Cieco non già, ma faretrato il veggo, CLI/2
Come 'l candido pie' per l'erba fresca, CLXV/1
Come 'l sol volga le 'nfiammate rote, L/2
Come a corrier tra via, se 'l cibo manca, CCCXXXI/2
Come a forza di venti, LXXIII/4
Come donna in suo albergo altera vene, CCLXXXIV/2
"Come'ella venne in questo viver basso, CCCXXV/6
Come fanciul ch'a pena, CXXV/4
Come già fece allor che' primi rami, CCLV/2
Come lume di notte in alcun porto, LXXX/4
"Come Natura al ciel la luna e 'l sole, CCXVIII/2
Come talora al caldo tempo sòle, CXLI/1
Come va 'l mondo! or mi diletta et piace, CCXC/1
Con lei foss'io da che si parte il sole, XXII/6
Con quella man che tanto desiai, CCCXLII/2
Conobbi (quanto il Ciel lo occhi m'aperse, CCCXXXIX/1
Consumendo mi vo di piaggia in piaggia, CCXXXVII/4
"Così 'l mio tempo infin qui trapassato, CCCLX/2
Così davanti a' colpi de la morte, XVIII/2
Così di ben amar porto tormento, CCVII/7
Così LAU-dare et RE-verire insegna, V/2
Così lo spirto d'or in or ven meno, CLXXXIV/2
Così lungo l'amate rive andai, XXIII/4
Così mancando vo di giorno in giorno, LXXIX/2
Così mi sveglio a salutar l'aurora, CCXIX/2
Così potess'io ben chiudere in versi, XCV/1
Così sol d'una chiara fonte viva, CLXIV/2
Così vo ricercando ogni contrada, CCCVI/2

Credete voi che Cesare o Marcello, CIV/2
Crudele, acerba, inesorabil Morte, CCCXXXII/2


# D

D'un bel chiaro polito et vivo ghiaccio, CCII/1
Da l'altra parte un pensier dolce et agro, CCLXIV/4
"Da lei ti ven l'amoroso pensero, XIII/2
Da me son fatti i miei pensier diversi, XXIX/6
Da ora inanzi ogni difesa è tarda, LXV/2
Da quali angeli mosse et di qual spera, CCXX/2
Da' be' rami scendea, CXXVI/4
Da' più bolli occhi, et dal più charo viso, CCCXLVIII/1
Dal laccio d'or non sia mai chi me scioglia, CCLXX/5
Datemai pace, o duri miei pensieri!, CCLXXIV/1
De l'empia Babilonia onde'è fuggita, CXIV/1
De' passati miei danni piango et rido, CV/6
Deh, non rinovellar quel che n'ancide, CCLXXIII/2
Deh, or foss'io col vago de la luna, CCXXXVII/6
"Deh, perché inanzi 'l tempo ti consume?", CCLXXIX/2
Deh, porgi mano a l'affannato ingegno, CCCLIV/1
Deh, qual pietà, qual angel fu sì presto, CCCXLI/1
Del cibo onde 'l signor mio sempre abonda, CCCXLII/1
Del lito occidental si move un fiato, XLII/2
Del mar tirreno a la sinistra riva, LXVII/1
Del vostro nome se mie rime intese, CXLVI/2
Dentra pur foco et for candida neve, XXX/6
Deposta avea l'usata leggiadria, CCXLIX/2
Detto questo, a la sua volubil rota, CCCXXV/8
Di dì in dì spero omai l'ultima sera, CCXXXVII/2
Di dì in dì vo cangiando il viso e 'l pelo, CXCV/1
Di mia morte mi pasco et vivo in fiamme, CCXII/4
Di mie tenere frondi altro lavoro, CCCXXII/2
Di pensier in pensier, di monte in monte, CXXIX/1
Di quanto per amor giamai soffersi, XXIX/3
Di queste pene è mia propia la prima, CLXXXII/2
Di sé nascendo a Roma non fe' grazia, IV/2
Di tempo in tempo mi si fa men dura, CXLIX/1
Dicemi spesso il mio fidato speglio, CCCLXI/1
Dicesette anni à già rivolto il cielo, CXXII/1
Dico ch'ad ora ad ora, LXXI/6
Dico le chiome cionde e 'l crespo laccio, CXCVII/2
Dico: se 'n quella etate, LXXIII/3
Dir se po ben per voi, non forse a pieno, CLIII/2
Discolorato ài, Morte, il più bel volto, CCLXXXIII/1
Divino sguardo da far l'uom felice, CCCLI/2
Dodici donne onestamente lasse, CCXXV/1
Dolce mio caro et prezioso pegno, CCCXL/1
Dolci durezze et placide repulse, CCCLI/1
Dolci ire, dolci sdegni et dolci paci, CCV/1
Dolci rime leggiadre, CXXV/3
Dolor, perché mi meni, LXXI/4
Donna che lieta col Principio nostro, CCCXLVII/1
Donne, voi che miraste sua beltade, CCLXVIII/6

Dormit'ài, bella Donna, un breve sonno, CCCXXVII/2
Due gran nemiche inseme erano agiunte, CCXCVII/1
Due rose fresche et colte in paradiso, CCXLV/1
Dunque ch'i' non mi sfaccia, LXXI/3
Dunque ora è 'l tempo da ritrare il collo, XXVIII/5
Dunque perché mi date questa guerra?, CCLXXV/2
Dunque s'a veder voi tardo mi volsi, XXXIX/2


E

E 'l chiaro lume che sparir fa 'l sole, CLXXXI/2
E 'l fiero passo ove m'agiunse Amore, C/2
E ciò non fusse, andrei non altramente, CLXXIX/2
E i naviganti in qualche chiusa valle, L/4
E veggio ben quant'elli a schivo m'ànno, CXLI/2
E' mi par d'or in ora udire il messo, CCCXLIX/1
E' questo 'l nido in che la mia fenice, CCCXXI/1
"Ei sa che 'l grande Atride et l'alto Achille, CCCLX/7
Ella 'l se ne portò sotterra, e 'n Cielo, CCCXIII/2
Ella parlava sì turbata in vista, XXIII/5
Ella si tace et di pietà depinta, CCCLVI/2
Ella, contenta aver cangiato albergo, CCCXLVI/2
Era il giorno ch'al sol si scoloraro, III/1
Era un tenero fior nato in quel bosco, CCXIV/2
Erano i capei d'oro a l'aura sparsi, XC/1
Et ben m'acqueto, et me stesso consolo, CCCXLV/2
Et certo ogni mio studio in quel tempo era, CCXCIII/2
Et certo son che coi diceste allora, LXXXVII/2
Et che' pie' miei non son fiaccati et lassi, LXXIV/2
Et co l'andar et col soave sguardo, CLXV/2
Et col terzo bevete un suco d'erba, LVIII/2
Et come vero prigioniero afflitto, LXXVI/2
Et così aven che l'animo ciascuna, CII/2
Et così tristo standosi in disparte, XLIII/2
Et io, da che comincia la bella alba, XXII/2
Et io nel cor via più freddo che ghiaccio, LXVI/2
Et io pur vivo, onde mi doglio et sdegno, CCXCII/2
Et l'imagine lor son sì cosparte, CVII/2
Et le rose vermiglie infra la neve, CXXXI/2
Et lei seguendo su per l'erbe verdi, LIV/2
Et m'ài lasciato qui misero et solo, CCCXXI/2
Et mi condusse vergognoso et tardo, XLVII/2
Et non tardar, ch'egli è ben tempo omai, CCCLVIII/2
"Et per dir a l'estremo il gran servigio, CCCLX/9
Et per pianger ancor con più diletto, XXXVII/7
Et per prendere il Ciel debito a lui, CCLII/2
Et per vertù de l'amorosa speme, XXXIV/2
Et perché un pco nel parlar mi sfogo, L/5
Et poi che 'l fren per forza a sé raccoglie, VI/2
Et qual cervo ferito di saetta, CCIX/2
Et que' belli occhi che i cor fanno smalti, CCXIII/2
Et quel lor inchinar ch'ogni mia gioia, XXXVIII/2
Et s'io 'l consento, a gran torto mi doglio, CXXXII/2
Et sarebbe ora, et è passata omai, CCCLV/2

Et se cosa di qua nel ciel si cura, LIII/4
Et se non fosse esperienzia molta, CCLXXI/2
Et se non fusse il suo fuggir sì ratto, CXCI/2
Et se put s'arma talor a dolersi, XXIX/2
Et se talor da' belli occhi soavi, CCLIII/2
Et se tornando a l'amorosa vita, XXV/2
"Et se' begli occhi ond'io me ti mostrai, XCIII/2
Et senti che ver te il mio core in terra, CCCXLVII/2
Et sol ad una imagine m'attegno, CXXX/2
Et son di là sì dolcemente accolti, CXVII/2
Et tutti voi ch'Amor laudate in rima, XXVI/2
Et veggio ben che 'l nostro viver vola, CCCLXI/2
Et viene a Roma, seguendo 'l desio, XVI/2


**F**

Fa' ch'io riveggia il bel guardo ch'un sole, CCLXX/4
Fama, onor, et vertute et leggiadria, CCXXVIII/2
Fammi sentir de quell'aura gentile, CCLXX/3
Far mi po lieto in una o 'n poche notti, CCCXXXII/13
Far potess'io vendetta di colei, CCLVI/1
Fera stella (se 'l cielo à forza in noi, CLXXIV/1
Fiamma dal Ciel su le tue treccie piova, CXXXVI/1
Fondata in casta et umil povertate, CXXXVIII/2
Fontana di dolore, albergo d'ira, CXXXVIII/1
Forse ancor fia chi sospirando dica, CCV/2
Forse ch'ogni uom che legge, non s'intende, CV/4
Forse i devoti et gli amorosi preghi, XXVIII/2
Forse sì come 'l Nil d'alto caggendo, XLVIII/2
Fresco ombroso fiorito et verde colle, CCXLIII/1
Fu forse un tempo dolce cosa amore, CCCXLIV/1
Fuggendo la pregione ove Amor m'ebbe, LXXXIX/1
Fuggi 'l sereno e 'l verde, CCLXVIII/8
Fuggito è 'l sonno a le mie crude notti, CCCXXXII/6
Fuor di man di colui che punge et molce, CCCLXIII/2
Fuor tutt'i nostri lidi, CXXXV/6


**G**

Gentil mia Donna, i' veggio, LXXII/1
Gentilezza di sangue et l'altre care, CCLXIII/2
Geri, quando talor meco s'adira, CLXXIX/1
Già desiai con sì giusta querela, CCXVII/1
Già fiammeggiava l'amorosa stella, XXXIII/1
Già mi fu col desir sì dolce il pianto, CCCXXXII/4
"Già sai tu ben quanta dolcezza porse, CCLXIV/3
Giovene dona sotto un verde lauro, XXX/1
Giunto Alessandro a la famosa tomba, CLXXXVII/1
Gl'idoli suoi sarranno in terra sparsi, CXXXVII/2
Gli animi ch'al tuo regno il cielo inchina, CCLXX/7
Gli occhi di ch'io parlai sì caldamente, CCXCII/1
Gloriosa Columna in cui s'appoggia, X/1
Grazie ch'a pochi il Ciel largo destina, CCXIII/1

Guarda 'l mio stato a le vaghezze nove, CCXIV/6
Guinto m'à Amor fra belle et crude braccia, CLXXI/1


I

I begli occhi ond'i' fui percosso in guisa, LXXV/1
I dì miei più leggier che nesun cervo, CCCXIX/1
I dolci colli ov'io lasciai me stesso, CCIX/1
I pensier son saette, e 'l viso un sole, CXXXIII/2
I' che 'l suo ragionar intendo, allora, LXVIII/2
I' da man manca, e' tenne il camin dritto, CXXXIX/2
I' dicea fra mio cor: "Perché paventi?", CX/2
I' dico che dal dì che 'l primo assalto, XXIII/2
I' die' in guarda a san Pietro, or no più, no, CV/2
I' era in terra e 'l cor in paradiso, CCCXXV/4
I' fuggia le tue mani et per camino, LXIX/2
I' l'ò più volte (or chi fia che mi 'l creda?), CXXIX/4
I' mi riscossi, et ella oltra parlando, CXI/2
I' mi riscuoto, et trovomi sì nudo, CCXCVIII/2
I' mi soglio accusare, et or mi scuso, CCXCVI/1
I' mi vivea di mia sorte contento, CCXXXI/1
I' nol dissi giamai, nè dir poria, CCVI/6
I' non ebbi giamai tranquilla notte, CCXXXVII/3
I' non poria giamai, LXXIII/5
I' non so se le parti sarian pari, CCCLIII/2
I' pensava assai destro esser su l'ale, CCCVII/1
I' piango; et ella il volto, CCCLIX/7
I' piansi, or canto; ché 'l celeste lume, CCXXX/1
I' pur ascolto, et non odo novella, CCLIV/1
I' son pregion, ma se pietà ancor serba, CXXI/3
I' temo di cangiar pria volto et chiome, XXX/5
I' vidi Amor che' begli occhi volgea, CXLIV/2
I' vidi in terra angelici costumi, CLVI/1
I' vo pensando, et nel penser m'assale, CCLXIV/1
I' vo piangendo i miei passati tempi, CCCLXV/1
"I' volea demandar," respond'io allora, CCCLIX/5
"I' vostri dipartir non so sì duri, CCXCI/2
I' volea dir: "Quest'è impossibil cosa,", CXIX/5
"I' vostri dipartir non so sì duri, CCXCI/2
I'ò pien di sospir quest'aere tutto, CCLXXXVIII/1
I'ò pregato Amor, e 'l ne riprego, CCXL/2
Il cantar novo e 'l pianger delli augelli, CCXIX/1
"Il dì che costei nacque, eran le stelle, CCCXXV/5
Il dì s'appressa et non pote esser lunge, CCCLXVI/11
Il figliuol di Latona avea già nove, XLIII/1
Il mal mi preme et mi spaventa il peggio, CCXLIV/1
Il mio adversario con agre rampogne, CCCLX/6
Il mio adversario in cui veder solete, XLV/1
Il sonno è 'n bando et del riposo è nulla, CCXXIII/2
Il sonno è veramente, qual uom dice, CCXXVI/2
Il successor di Carlo, che la chioma, XXVII/1
Il tempo passa et l'ore son sì pronte, XXXVII/2
Imaginata guida la conduce, CCLXXVII/2
In atto et in parole la ringrazio, CCCLIX/2

In dubbio di mio stato, or piango or canto, CCLII/1
In mezzo di duo amanti onesta altera, CXV/1
In nobil sangue vita umile et queta, CCXV/1
In picciol tempo passa ogni gran pioggia, LXVI/3
In qual parte del Ciel, in quale Idea, CLIX/1
In quel bel viso ch'i' sospiro et bramo, CCLVII/1
In quella parte dove Amor mi sprona, CXXVII/1
In questa passa 'l tempo, et ne lo specchio, CLXVIII/2
In ramo fronde o ver viole in terra, CXXVII/3
In rete accolgo l'aura e 'n ghiaccio i fiori, CCXXXIX/7
In silenzio parole accorte et sagge, CV/5
In tale stella duo belli occhi vidi, CCLX/1
In te i secreti suoi messaggi Amore, CCLXXIV/2
In un boschetto novo i rami santi, CCCXXIII/3
In una valle chiusa d'ogn'intorno, CXVI/2
Indi per alto mar vidi una nave, CCCXXIII/2
Io amai sempre, et am forte ancora, LXXXV/1
Io avrò sempre in odio la fenestra, LXXXVI/1
Io canterei d'Amor sì novamente, CXXXI/1
Io mi rivolgo indieto a ciascun passo, XV/1
Io penso: se là suso, LXXII/2
Io sentia dentr'al cor già venir meno, XLVII/1
Io son de l'aspettar omai sì vinto, XCVI/1
Io son fu' d'amar voi lassato unquanco, LXXXII/1
Io son già stanco di pensar sì come, LXXIV/1
Io son sì stanco sotto 'l fascio antico LXXXI/1
Io temo sì de' begli occhi l'assalto, XXXIX/1
Ir dritto alto m'insegno, et io, che 'ntendo, CCLXXXVI/2
Italia mia, ben ch'l parlar sia indarno, CXXVIII/1
Ite, caldi sospiri, al freddo core, CLIII/1
Ite, rime dolenti, al duro sasso, CCCXXXIII/1
Ivi 'l parlar che nullo stile aguaglia, CCLXI/2
Ivi è quel nostro vivo et dolce sole, CCVIII/2


      L
L'acque parlan d'amore, et l'òra e i rami, CCLXXX/2
L'aere gravato et l'importuna nebbia, LXVI/1
L'aere percosso da' lor dolci rai, CLIV/2
L'alma ch'è sol da Dio fatta gentile, XXIII/7
L'alma, cui morte del suo albergo caccia, CCLVI/2
L'alma mia fiamma oltra le belle bella, CCLXXXIX/1
L'alma nudrita sempre in doglia e 'n pene, CCLVIII/2
L'alto et novo miracol ch'a' dì nostri, CCCIX/1
L'alto signor dinanzi a cui non vale, CCXLI/1
L'altre, maggior di tempo o di fortuna, CCXXXVIII/2
L'amoroso pensero, LXXI/7
L'antiche mura ch'ancor teme et ama, LIII/3
L'arbor gentil che forte amai molt'anni, LX/1
L'ardente nodo ov'io fui, d'ora in ora, CCLXXI/1
L'arme tue furon gli occhi onde l'accese, CCLXX/6
L'aspettata vertù che 'n voi fioriva, CIV/1
L'aspetto sacro de la terra vostra, LXVIII/1
L'atto soave, e 'l parlar seggio umile, CCXCVII/2

```
L'aura celeste che 'n quel verde lauro, CXCVII/1
L'aura che 'l verde lauro et l'aureo crine, CCXLVI/1
L'aura et l'odore e 'l refrigerio et l'ombra, CCCXXVII/1
L'aura gentil che rasserena i poggi, CXCIV/1
L'aura mia sacra al mio stanco riposo, CCCLVI/1
L'aura serena che fra verdi fronde, CXCVI/1
L'aura soave a cui governo et vela, LXXX/2
L'aura soave al sole spiega et vibra, CXCVIII/1
L'aura soave che dal chiaro viso, CIX/2
L'auro e i topacii al sol sopra la neve, XXX/7
L'avara Babilonia à colmo il sacco, CXXXVII/1
L'erbetta verde e i fior di color mille, CXCII/2
L'oliva è secca, et è rivolta altrove, CLXVI/2
L'ombra che cade de quell'umil colle, CLXXXVIII/2
L'opra fu ben di quelle che nel cielo, LXXVII/2
L'oro et le perle e i fior vermigli e i bianchi, XLVI/1
L'ultimo, lasso, de' miei giorni allegri, CCCXXVIII/1
L'un penser parla co la mente, et dice:, CCLXIV/2
L'una piaga arde et versa foco et fiamma, CCXLI/2
Là 've cantado andai di te molt'anni, CCLXXXII/2
La bella donna che cotanto amavi, XCI/1
La donna che 'l mio cor nel viso porta, CXI/1
La gola e 'l sono et l'oziose piume, VII/1
La guancia che fu già piangendo stanca, LVIII/1
La mansueta vostra et gentil agna, XXVII/2
La qual tu poi, tornando al tuo Fattore, CCCLII/2
La sera desiare, odiar l'aurora, CCLV/2
La testa or fino, et calda neve il volto, CLVII/2
Là ver l'aurora, che sì dolce l'aura, CCXXXIX/1
La vita fugge et non s'arresta un'ora, CCLXXII/1
Lagrima dunque che dagli occhi versi, XXIX/5
Lagrime omai dagli occhi uscir non ponno, LXXXIII/2
Lagrime triste, et voi tutte le notti, XLIX/2
Lasciato ài, Morto, senza sole il mondo, CCCXXXVIII/1
Lassare il velo per sole o per ombra, XI/1
Lasso me, ch'i' non so in qual parte pieghi, LXX/1
Lasso, Amor mi trasporta ov'ir non voglio, CCXXXV/1
Lasso, ben so che dolorose prede, CI/1
Lasso, ch'i'ardo et altri non mel crede, CCIII/1
Lasso, che disiando, LXXIII/6
Lasso, che mal accorto fui da prima, LXV/1
Lasso, che pur da l'un a l'altro sole, CCXVI/2
Lasso, nol so, ma sì conosco io bene, LVI/2
Lasso, quante fiate Amor m'assale, CIX/1
Lasso, se ragionando si rinfresca, XXXVII/4
Le chiome a l'aura sparse et lei conversa, CXLIII/2
Le città son nemiche, amici i boschi, CCXXXVII/5
Le donne lagrimose, e 'l volgo inerme, LIII/5
Le fraile vita ch'ancor meco alberga, LXIII/2
Le lode, mai non d'altra et proprie sue, CCCVIII/2
Le quali ella spargea sì dolcemente, CXCVI/2
Le stelle, il cielo, et gli elementi a prova, CLIV/1
Le treccie d'or che devrien fare il sole, XXXVII/6
Lei ne ringrazio e 'l suo alto consiglio, CCLXXXIX/2
```

Levan di terra al ciel nostr' intelletto, X/2
Levommi il mio penser in parte ov'era, CCCII/1
Li angeli eletti e l'anime beate, CCCXLVI/1
Li occhi belli, or in Ciel chiari et felici, CCCXXVIII/2
Li occhi sereni et le stellanti ciglia, CC/2
Li occhi soavi ond'io soglio aver vita, CCVII/2
"Liete et pensose, accompagnate et sole, CCXXII/1
Lieti fiori et felici, et ben nate erbe, CLXII/1


                    M
Ma 'l cieco Amor et la mia sorda mente, CCXC/2
Ma 'l suon che di dolcezza i sensi lega, CLXVII/2
Ma ben ti prego che 'n la terza spera, CCLXXXVII/2
Ma ben veggio or sì come al popol tutto, I/2
Ma benigna fortuna e 'l viver lieto, CCCXXXII/1
Ma chi pensò veder mai tutti insieme, LXXXV/2
Ma del misero stato ove noi semo, VIII/2
Ma gli spiriti miei s'agghiaccian poi, XVII/2
"Ma io che debbo altro che pianger sempre, CCCLIX/4
Ma io sarò sotterra in secca selva, XXII/7
Ma l'ora e 'l giorno ch'io le luci aspersi, XXIX/4
Ma la forma miglior che vive ancora, CCCXIX/2
Ma la sua voce ancor qua giù rimbomba, LXXXI/2
Ma la vista, privata del suo obietto, CCLVII/2
Ma lagrimosa pioggia et fieri venti, CCXXXV/2
Ma, lasso, a me non val fiorir di valli, LXVI/4
Ma, lasso, or veggio che la carne sciolta, CCXIV/4
Ma mia fortuna, a me sempre nemica, CCLIX/2
Ma non me 'l tolse la paura o 'l gelo, CXIX/3
Ma per me, lasso, tornando i più gravi, CCCX/2
Ma perché vola il tempo et fuggon gli anni, XXX/3
Ma però che mi manca a fornir l'opra, XL/2
Ma poi ch'i' vengo a ragionar con lei, LXXVIII/2
Ma poi che 'l dolce riso umile et piano, XLII/1
Ma quell'altro voler di ch'i' son pieno, CCLXIV/5
Ma s'io nol dissi, che sì dolce apria, CCVI/5
Ma s'io v'era con saldi chiovi fisso, XLV/2
Ma se consentimento è di destino, CCLXIX/2
Ma tropp'era alta al mio peso terrestre, CCCXXXV/2
Ma tu prendi a diletto i dolor miei, CLXXIV/2
Ma voi, che mai pietà non discolora, XLIV/2
Mai non fui in parte ove sì chiar vedessi, CCLXXX/1
Mai non poria volar penna d'ingegno, CCCVII/2
Mai non vedranno le mie luci asciutte, CCCXXII/1
Mai non vo' più cantar com'io soleva, CV/1
Mai questa mortal vita a me non piacque, CCCXXXI/3
Mas non fuggio giamai nebbia per venti, LXVI/7
Menami al suo Signor; allor m'inchino, CCCLXII/2
Mente mia, che presaga de' tuoi danni, CCCXIV/1
Mentr'io portava i be' pensier celati, XI/2
Mentre 'l novo dolor dunque l'accora, CIII/2
Mentre ch'al mar descenderanno i fiumi, LXVI/5
Mentre che 'l cor dagli amorosi vermi, CCCIV/1

Mia ventura et Amor m'avean sì adorno, CCI/1
Mie venture al venir son tarde et prige, LVII/1
Mille fiate, o dolce mia guerrera, XXI/2
Mille piagge in un giorno et mille rivi, CLXXVII/1
"Mio ben non cape in intelletto umano, CCCII/2
Mira 'l gran sasso donde Sorge nasce, CCCV/2
"Mira quel colle, o stanco mio cor vago, CCXLII/1
Mirando 'l sol de' begli occhi sereno, CLXXIII/1
Misera, che devrebbe esser accorta, LXXXVI/2
Morte à spento quel sol ch'abagliar suolmi, CCCLXIII/1
Morte m'à morto, et sola po far Morte, CCCXXXII/8
Morte m'à sciolto, Amor, d'ogni tua legge, CCLXX/8
Morte po chiuder sola a' miei penseri, XIV/2
Movesi il vechierel canuto et bianco, XVI/1
Muri eran d'alabastro e 'l tetto d'oro, CCCXXV/2


         N
Né altro sarà mai ch'al cor m'aggiunga, CCCXII/2
Né così bello il sol giamia levarsi, CXLIV/1
Né del vulgo mi cal, né di Fortuna, CXIV/2
"Né di Lucrezia mi meravigliai, CCLXII/2
Ne l'estremo occidente, CXXXV/3
Ne l'età sua più bella et più fiorita, CCLXXVIII/1
Ne la stagio che 'l ciel rapido inchina, L/1
Né mai pietosa madre al caro figlio, CCLXXXV/1
Né mai stato gioioso, LXXII/3
Né mi lece ascoltar chi non ragiona, XCVII/2
Né minacce temer debbo di morte, CCCLVII/2
Né per sereno ciel ir vaghe stelle, CCCXII/1
Né però che con atti acerbi et rei, CLXXII/2
Né pur il mio secreto e 'l mio riposo, CCXXXIV/2
Né so che spazio mi si desse il cielo, CCLXIV/7
Né spero i dolci dì tornino indietro, CXXIV/2
Né tante volte ti vedrò giamai, CVIII/2
Né v'accorgete ancor per tante prove, CXXVIII/5
Nel cominciar credia, LXXIII/2
Nel dolce tempo de la prima etade, XXIII/1
Nel qual provo dolcesse tante et tali, CXCIV/2
Nelli occhi ov'abitar solea 'l mio core, CCCXXXI/4
"Nessun mi tocchi," al bel collo d'intorno, CXC/2
Nessun visse giamai più di me lieto, CCCXXXII/7
No la bella romana che col ferro, CCLX/2
Non à tanti animale il mar fra l'onde, CCXXXVII/1
Non al sua amante più Diana piacque, LII/1
Non credo che pascesse mai per selva, XXII/4
Non d'atra et et tempestosa onda marina, CLI/1
Non da l'ispano Ibero a l'indo Idaspe, CCX/1
"Non è questo 'l terren ch'i' toccai pria?, CXXVIII/6
Non è sterpo né sasso in questi monti, CCLXXXVIII/2
Non era l'andar suo cosa mortale, XC/2
Non fu simil bellezza antica o nova, CCCL/2
Non fur giamai veduti sì begli occhi, XXX/4
Non fur ma' Giove et Cesare sì mossi, CLV/1

Non fur mai spente, a quel ch'i' veggio, LV/2
Non perch'io non m'aveggia, LXXI/2
Non perch'io sia securo ancor del fine, LXXX/5
Non po far Morte il dolce viso amaro, CCCLVIII/1
Non po più la vertù fragile et stanca, CLII/2
Non pur quell'una bella ignuda mano, CC/1
Non son al sommo ancor giunte le rime, CCCIX/2
"Non son, come a voi par, le ragion pari, LXXXIV/1
Non spero che giamai dal pigro sonno, LIII/2
Non spero del mio affanno aver mai posa, CXCV/2
Non Tesin, Po, Varo, Arno, Adige et Tebro, CXLVIII/1
"Non ti soven di quella ultima sera,", CCL/2
"Non vede un simil par d'amanti il sole,", CCXLV/2
Non veggio ove scampar mi possa omai, CVII/1
Non vide il mondo sì leggiadri rami, CLII/2
Non vidi mai dopo notturna pioggia, CXXVII/5
Nova angeletta sovra l'ale accorta, CVI/1
Novo piacer che ne gli umani ingengi, XXXVII/5
Nulla posso levar io per mi' 'ngegno, CLXXI/2


O

O aspettata in Ciel beata et bella, XXVIII/1
O bel viso, ove Amor inseme pose, CLXI/2
O bella man che mi destringi 'l core, CXCIX/1
O cameretta che già fosti un porto, CCXXXIV/1
O che dolci accoglienze et caste et pie!, CCCXLIII/2
O che lieve è inganar chi s'assecura!, CCCXI/2
O d'ardente vertute ornata et calda, CXLVI/1
O di diamante, o d'un bel marmo bianco, LI/2
O dolci sguardi, o parolette accorte, CCLIII/1
O felice quel dì che del terreno, CCCXLIX/2
O giorno, o ora, o ultimo momento, CCCXXIX/1
O Invidia nimica di vertute, CLXXII/1
O miracol gentile, o felce alma, CCXCV/2
O misera et orribil visione!, CCLI/1
O Natura, pietosa et fera madre, CCXXXI/2
O passi sparsi, o pensier vaghi et pronti, CLXI/1
O poverella mia, come se' rozza!, CXXV/7
O soave contrada, o puro fiume, CLXII/2
O tempo, O ciel volubil che fuggendo, CCCLV/1
O vaghi abitator de' verdi boschi, CCCIII/2
O voi che sospirate a miglior notti, CCCXXXII/12
Occhi miei lassi, mentre ch'io vi giro, XIV/1
Occhi miei, oscurato è 'l nostro sole, CCLXXV/1
"Occhi, piangete, accompagnate il core, LXXXIV/1
Ogni angelica vista, ogni atto umile, CXXIII/2
Ogni giorno mi par più di mill'anni, CCCLVII/1
Ogni loco m'atrista ov'io non veggio, XXXVII/3
Ogni mio ben crudel Morte m'à tolto, CCCXLIV/2
Oimè il bel viso, oimè il soave sguardo, CCLXVII/1
Oimè, lasso! e quando fia quel giorno, CXXII/2
Oimè, terra è fatto il suo bel viso, CCLXVIII/4
Omini et dei solea vincer per forza, CCXXXIX/4

Ond'i' spero che 'nfin al Ciel si doglia, CCCXXXIV/2
Ond'io consiglio: "Voi che siete in via, LXXXVIII/2
Ond'io non pote' mai formar parola, CLXX/2
Onde Amore paventoso fugge al core, CXL/2
Onde come colui che 'l colpo teme, CXLVII/2
Onde più volte sospirando indietro, LXXXIX/2
Onde qua giuso un ben pietoso core, CCCXL/2
Onde quant'io di lei parlai né scrissi, CCCXXXIX/2
Onde tal frutto et simile si colga, IX/2
Onde tolse Amor l'oro et di qual vena, CCXX/1
Or ài fatto l'estremo di tua possa, CCCXXVI/1
Or avess'io un sì pietoso stile, CCCXXXII/9
Or che 'l ciel et la terra e 'l vento tace, CLXIV/1
Or con sì chiara luce et con tai segni, CCIV/2
Or di madre, or d'amante. Or teme or arde, CCLXXXV/2
Or ecco in parte le question mie nove, CCXIV/7
Or in forma di ninfa o d'altra diva, CCLXXXI/2
Or non odio per lei, per me pietate, CCXVII/2
Or qui son, lasso, et voglio esser altrove, CXVIII/2
Or s'io lo scaccio, et e' non trova in voi, XXI/2
Or tu ch'ài posto te stesso in oblio, CCXLII/2
Or vedi, Amor, che giovenetta donna, CXXI/1
Or volge, Signor mio, l'undecimo anno, LXII/2
Orsi, lupi, leoni, aquile, et serpi, LIII/6
Orso, al vostro destrier si po ben porre, XCVIII/1
Orso, e' non furon mai fiumi né stagni, XXXVIII/1
Ov'è l'ombra gentil del viso umano, CCXCIX/2
Ov'è la fronte che con picciol cenno, CCXCIX/1
Ove ch'i' posi gli occhi lassi o giri, CLVIII/1
Ove d'altra montagna ombra non tocchi, CXXIX/5
Ove è condutto il mio amoroso stile?, CCCXXXII/3
Ove porge ombra un pino alto od un colle, CXXIX/3
Ovunque gli occhi volgo, CXXV/6


      P
Pace non trovo et non ò da far guerra, CXXXIV/1
Padre del Ciel, dopo i perduti giorni, LXII/1
Parmi d'udirla, udendo i rami et l'ore, CLXXVI/2
Parrà forse ad alcun che 'n lodar quella, CCXLVII/1
Pasco la mente d'un sì nobil cibo, CXCIII/1
Passa la nave mia colma d'oblio, CLXXXIX/1
Passato è 'l tempo omai, lasso, che tanto, CCCXIII/1
Passer mai solitario in alcun tetto, CCXXVI/1
Pentito et tristo de' miei sì spesi anni, CCCLXIV/2
Per alti monti et per selve aspre trovo, CXXIX/2
Per divina bellezza indarno mira, CLIX/2
Per fare una leggiadra sua vendetta, II/1
Per la camere tue fanciulle et vecchi, CXXXVI/2
Per mezz' i boschi inospiti et selvaggi, CLXXVI/1
Per mirar Policleto a prova fiso, LXXVII/1
Per questi estremi duo contrari et misti, CLXXIII/2
Per Rachel ò servito e non per Lia, CCVI/7
Per voi conven ch'io arda e 'n voi respiro, CCLXVII/2

Pur vivendo veniasi ove deposto, CCCXVII/2
Purpurea vesta d'un ceruleo lembo, CLXXXV/2


Q

Qual dolcezza fu quella, misera alma, CCCXIV/2
Qual donna attende a gloriosa fama, CCLXI/1
Qual foco non avrian già spento et morto, LV/3
Qual mi fec'io quando primier m'accorsi, XXIII/3
Qual mio destin, qual forza o qual inganno, CCXXI/1
Qual miracolo è quel, quando tra l'erba, CLX/2
Qual paura ò quando mi torna a mente, CCXLIX/1
Qual più diversa et nova, CXXXV/1
Qual vaghezza di lauro, qual di mirto?, VII/2
Qual ventura mi fu quando da l'uno, CCXXXIII/1
Qualor tenera neve per li colli, CXXVII/4
Quand'io mi volgo indietro a mirar gli anni, CCXCVIII/1
Quand'io son tutto volto in quella parte, XVIII/1
Quand'io veggio dal ciel scender l'Aurora, CCXCI/1
Quando 'l pianeta che distingue l'ore, IX/1
Quando 'l sol bagna in mar l'aurato carro, CCXXIII/1
Quando 'l voler, che con due sproni ardenti, CXLVII/1
Quando Amor i belli occhi a terra inchina, CLXVII/1
Quando dal proprio sito si rimove, XLI/1
Quando fra l'altre donne ad ora ad ora, XIII/1
Quando giugne per gli occhi al cor profondo, XCIV/1
Quando giunse a Simon l'alto concetto, LXXVIII/1
Quando il soave mio fido conforto, CCCLIX/1
Quando io movo i sospiri a chiamar voi, V/1
Quando io v'odo parlar sì dolcemente, CXLIII/1
Quando la sera scaccia il chiaro giorno, XXII/3
Quando mi vene inanzi il tempo e 'l loco, CLXXV/1
Quando mia speme già condutta al verde, XXXIII/2
Quando vede 'l pastor calare i raggi, L/3
Quanta dolcezza unquanco, LXXII/4
Quanta invidia a quell'anime che 'n sorte, CCC/2
Quanta invidia io ti porto, avara terra, CCC/1
Quante fiate al mio dolce ricetto, CCLXXXI/1
Quante lagrime, lasso, et quanti versi, CCXXXIX/3
Quante volte diss'io, CXXVI/5
Quanto iù sol gira, Amor più caro pegno, XXIX/9
Quanto più disiose l'ali spando, CXXXIX/1
Quanto più m'avicino al giorno estremo, XXXII/1
Que' ch'infinita providenzia et arte, IV/1
Que' che 'n Tesaglia ebbe le man sì pronte, XLIV/1
Quel antiquo mio dolce empio signore, CCCLX/1
Quel ch'i' fo veggio, et non m'inganna il vero, CCLXIV/6
Quel che d'odore et di color vincea, CCCXXXVII/1
Quel dolce pianto mi depinse Amore, CLV/2
Quel fiore antico di vertuti et d'arme, CLXXXVI/2
Quel foco ch'i' pensai che fosse spento, LV/1
Quel foco è morto e 'l copre un picciol marmo, CCCIV/2
Quel rosigniuol che sì soave piagne, CCCXI/1
Quel sempre acerbo et onorato giorno, CLVII/1

Quel sol che mi mostrava il cammin destro, CCCVI/1
Quel sol che solo agli occhi mei resplende, CLXXV/2
Quel vago impallidir, che 'l dolce riso, CXXIII/1
Quel vago, dolce, caro, onesto sguardo, CCCXXX/1
Quel vivo lauro, ove solean far nido, CCCXVIII/2
Quella fenestra ove l'un sol si vede, C/1
Quella per cui con Sorga ò cangiato Arno, CCCVIII/1
Quelle pietose rime in ch'io m'accorsi, CXX/1
Quest'arder mio di che vi cal sì poco, CCIII/2
Questa anima gentil che si diparte, XXXI/1
Questa fenice de l'aurata piume, CLXXXV/1
Questa mia donna mi menò molt'anni, CXIX/2
Questa umil fera, un cor di tigre o d'orsa, CLII/1
"Questi m'à fatto men amare Dio, CCCLX/3
Questi poser silenzio al signor mio, XLVI/2
Questi son que' begli occhi che l'imprese, LXXV/2
"Questo fu il fel, questi li sdegni et l'ire, CCCLX/8
Questo nostro caduco et fragil bene, CCCL/1
Questo un soccorso trovo fra gli assalti, CXLVIII/2
Questo un, Morte, m'à tolto la tua mano, CCLXXVI/2
Qui cantò dolcemente, et qui s'assise, CXII/2
Qui dove mezzo son, Sennuccio mio, CXIII/1
Quinci in duo volti un color morto appare, XCIV/2


      R
Rade volte adiven ch'a l'alte imprese, LIII/7
"Rado fu al mondo fra così gran turba, CXIX/4
Ragion è ben ch'alcuna volta io canti, LXX/2
Rapido fiume, che d'alpestra vena, CCVIII/1
Re degli altri, superbo altero giume, CLXXX/2
Real natura, angelico intelletto, CCXXXVIII/1
Responde: "Quanto 'l Ciel et io possiamo, CCCLIV/2
Ridon or per le piagge erbette et fiori, CCXXXIX/6
Rimansi a dietro il sestodecimo anno, CXVIII/1
Ripensando a quel ch'oggi il Cielo onora, CCCXLIII/1
Riponi entro 'l bel viso il vivo lume, CCLXX/2
Rispondo: "Io non piango altro che me stesso, CCCLIX/3
Rotta è l'alta colonna e 'l verde lauro, CCLXIX/1
Ruppesi intanto di vergogna il nodo, CXIX/6


      S
S'a voi fosse sì nota, LXXI/5
S'al principio risponde il fine e 'l mezzo, LXXIX/1
S'amor non è, che dunque è quel ch'io sento?, CXXXII/1
S'Amor novo consiglio non n'apporta, CCLXXVII/1
S'Amore o Morte non dà qualche stroppio, XL/1
S'aver altrui più caro che se stesso, CCXXIV/2
S'egli è pur mio destino, CXXVI/2
S'i' 'l dissi, Amor l'aurate sue quadrella, CCVI/2
S'i' 'l dissi, coi sospir quant'io mai fei, CCVI/4
S'i' 'l dissi mai, ch'i' vegna in odio a quella, CCVI/1
S'i' 'l dissi mai, di quel ch'i' men vorrei, CCVI/3

```
S'i' fussi stato fermo a la spelunca, CLXVI/1
S'io avesse pensato che sì care, CCXCIII/1
S'io credesse per morte essere scarco, XXXVI/1
S'io esca vivo de' dubbiosi scogli, LXXX/6
S'onesto amor po meritar mercede, CCCXXXIV/1
S'una fede amorosa, un cor non finto, CCXXIV/1
Sa 'l Valentinian ch'a simil pena, CCXXXII/2
Se 'l dolce sguardo di costei m'ancide, CLXXXIII/1
Se 'l pensier che mi strugge, CXXV/1
Se 'l sasso ond'è più chiusa questa valle, CXVII/1
Se bianche non son prima ambe le tempie, LXXXIII/1
Se col cieco desir che 'l cor distrugge, LVI/1
Se l'onorata fronde che prescrive, XXIV/1
Se la mia vita de l'aspro tormento, XII/1
Se lamentar augelli, o verdi fronde, CCLXXIX/1
Se mai candide rose con vermiglie, CXXVII/6
Se mai foco per foco non si spense, XLVIII/1
Se quell'aura soave de' sospiri, CCLXXXVI/1
Se sì alto pon gir mie stanche rime, CCCXXXII/11
Se si posasse sotto al quarto nido, XXXI/2
Se stato fusse il mio poco intelletto, CCCXXXI/5
Se tu avessi ornamenti quant'ài voglia, CXXVI/6
Se Virgilio et Omero avessin visto, CLXXXVI/1
Se voi poteste per turbati segni, LXIV/1
Seco si stringe et dice a ciascun passo, CCXLIII/2
Selve, sassi, campagne, fiumi, et poggi, CXLII/5
Sennuccio, i' vo' che sapi in qual manera, CXII/1
Sennuccio mio, benché doglioso et solo, CCLXXXVII/1
Sento i messi di Morte ove apparire, CCXXI/2
Sento l'aura mia antica, e i dolci colli, CCCXX/1
Sì breve è'l tempo e 'l penser sì veloce, CCLXXXIV/1
Sì ch'io mi credo omai che monti et piagge, XXXV/2
Sì ch'io non veggia il gran publico danno, CCXLVI/2
Sì che, s'io vissi in guerra e in tempesta, CCCLXV/2
Sì come eterna vita è veder Dio, CXCI/1
"Sì come piacque al nostro eterno padre, CXIX/7
Sì dirà ben: Quello ove questi aspira, CCXLVII/2
Sì è debile il filo a cui s'attene, XXXVII/1
Sì profondo era et di sì larga vena, CCXXX/2
Sì tosto come aven che l'arco scocchi, LXXXVII/1
Sì traviato è'l folle mi' desio, VI/1
Signor de la mia fine et de la vita, LXXX/7
Signor mio caro, ogni pensier mi tira, CCLXVI/1
Signor: mirate come 'l tempo vola, CXXVIII/7
So come i dì, come i momenti et l'ore, CI/2
So io ben ch'a voler chiuder in versi, XXIX/8
Sol di lei ragionando viva et morta, CCCXXXIII/2
Solea da la fontana di mia vita, CCCXXXI/1
Solea lontana in sonno consolarme, CCL/1
Soleano i miei penser soavemente, CCXCV/1
Soleasi nel mio cor star bella et viva, CCXCIV/1
Solo et pensoso i più deserti campi, XXXV/1
Solo ov'io era tra' boschetti e' colli, LXVII/2
Son animali al mondo de sì altera, XIX/1
```

"Son questi i capei biondi et l'aureo nodo,", CCCLIX/6
Sopra 'l monte Tarpeio, canzon, vedrai, LIII/8
Sovra dure onde al lume de la luna, CCXXXVII/7
Sperando alfin da le soavi piante, CCCXX/2
Spinse amore et dolor ove ir non debbe, CCCXLV/1
Spirito doglioso errante mi rimembra, XXIII/8
Spirito gentil che quelle membra reggi, LIII/1
Spirto felice che sì dolcemente, CCCLII/1
Standomi un giorno sola a la fenestra, CCCXXIII/1
Stiamo, Amor, a veder la gloria nostra, CXCII/1
Subito in allegrezza si converse, CXV/2
Surge nel mezzo giorno, CXXXV/4


     T
Tacer non posso, et temo non adopre, CCCXXV/1
Taciti, sfavillando oltra lor modo, CCCXXX/2
Tal che mi fece, or quand'egli arde 'l cielo, LII/3
Talor m'assale in mezzo a' tristi pianti, XV/2
Talor risponde et talor non fa motto, CCCXXXVI/2
"Talor tace la lingua e 'l cor si lagna, CL/2
Tanto mi piacque prima il dolce lume, CXLII/6
Tempo ben fora omai d'avere spinto, XXXVI/2
Tempo era omai da trovar pace o tregua, CCCXVI/1
Tempo verrà ancor forse, CXXVI/3
Temprar potess'io in sì soavi note, CCCXXXIX/2
Tengan dunque ver me l'ustato stile, CCXXIX/2
Tennemi Amor anni ventuno ardendo, CCCLXIV/1
Tolta m'è poi di que' biondi capelli, LIX/3
Tornami a mente (anzi v'è dentro quella, CCCXXXVI/1
Tornami avanti s'alcun dolce mai, CCLXXII/2
Tosto che giunto a l'amorosa reggia, CXIII/2
Tra le chiome de l'or nascose il lacci, LIX/2
Tra quantunque leggiadre donne et belle, CCXXVIII/1
Tranquillo porto avea mostrato Amore, CCCXVII/1
Trovommi Amor del tutto disarmato, III/2
Tu ch'ài per arricchir d'un bel tesauro, XXVIII/6
Tu se'armato, et ella in treccie e 'n gonna, CXXXI/2
Tu vedrai Italia et l'onorata riva, XXVIII/8
Tutta la mia fiorita et verde etade, CCCXV/1
Tutte le cose di che 'l mondo è adorno, LXX/5
Tutto 'l dì piango; et poi la notte, quando, CCXVI/1


     U
Un amico penser le mostra il vado, CLXXVIII/2
Un lauro mi difese allor dal cielo, CXLII/3
Un'altra fonte à Epiro, CXXXV/5
Una candida cerva sopra l'erba, CXC/1
Una donna più bella assai che 'l sole, CXIX/1
Una parte del mondo è che si giace, XXVIII/4
Una petra è sì ardita, CXXXV/2
Una strania fenice, ambedue l'ale, CCCXXIII/5

V
Vaghi pensier che così passo passo, LXX/3
Vago augelletto, che cantando vai, CCCLIII/1
Valle che de' lamenti miei se' piena, CCCI/1
Vedendo ardere i lumi ond'io m'accendo, CXCVIII/2
Vedrà, s'arriva a tempo, ogni vertute, CCXLVIII/2
Veggio senza occhi, et non ò lingua et grido, CXXXIV/2
Verdi panni sanguigni oscuri o persi, XXIX/1
Vergine bella, che di sol vestita, CCCLXVI/1
Vergine chiara et stabile in eterno, CCCLXVI/6
Vergine in cui ò tutta mia speranza, CCCLXVI/9
Vergine pura, d'ogni parte intera, CCCLXVI/3
Vergine, quante lagrime ò già sparte, CCCLXVI/7
Vergine saggia et del bel numero una, CCCLXVI/2
Vergine santa, d'ogni grazia piena, CCCLXVI/4
Vergine sola al mondo, senza esempio, CCCLXVI/5
Vergine, tale è terra et posta à in doglia, CCCLXVI/8
Vergine umana et nemica d'orgoglio, CCCLXVI/10
Vergognando talor ch'ancor si taccia, XX/1
Vertute, onor, bellezza, atto gentile, CCXI/2
Vincitore Alessandro l'ira vinse, CCXXXII/1
Vinse Anibàl, et non seppe usar poi, CIII/1
Vive faville uscian de' duo bei lumi, CCLVIII/1
Vivi far mille donne una già tale, CCCXXXV/1
Vivo sol di speranza, rimembrando, CCLXV/2
Voglia mi sprona, Amor mi guida et scorge, CCXI/1
Voi ch'ascoltate in rime sparse il suono, I/1
Voi con quel cor che di sì chiaro ingegno, CCXL/2
Voi cui Fortuna à posto in mano il freno, CXXVIII/2
Voi dunque, se cercate aver la mente, XCIX/2
Volgendo gli occi al mio novo colore, LXIII/1
Volo con l'ali de' pensieri al Cielo, CCCLXII/1


Z
Zefiro torna e 'l bel tempo rimena, CCCX/1

# II.
## Ludovico Ariosto
### *Orlando Furioso*

A
A Bradamente il messaggier novella, II/63
A Carlo Magno, il quale io stimo e onoro, XXXII/57
A Carlo riventi appresentarsi, XXXVIII/10
A caso si trovò che fuor di testa, XXIII/10
A caso venne il furioso conte, XXIX/40
A chi 'l petto, a chi 'l ventre, a chi la testa, XIII/38
A chi te la narrò non do credenza, XXVIII/77
A chiamar la patrona andò il famiglio, XXXXIII/124
A conforto di lui rotto avea il patto, XXXIX/16
A cui fu sopra ogn'aventura, grata, V/75
A cui là dove, de la vita in forse, XXXXVI/65
A cui non par ch'abbi a bastar lor fame, XVII/4
A domandar poi ritornò Marfisa, XXXVI/69
A duo cavalli che venuti a paro, XXIX/34
A grande uopo gli fia l'esser prudente, III/52
A lei non fu di molta maraviglia, XXIII/13
A maledir comincio l'amor d'esso, XXXIV/26
A me duro parea pur di partire, XXXXIII/31
A me par, s'a te par, ch'a dir si mandi, XXXVIII/63
A me par, se a voi par, che statuito, XX/48
A mezza spada vengono di botto, XXXVI/49
A mezzo il giorno, nel calar d'un monte, XXIII/33
A mille cavallieri alla sua vita, XIX/95
A pena avea la vigilante Aurora, XXXVIII/76
A pena ella fu in terra, che rizzosse, XXXVI/23
A pena ha Bradamate da la soglia, III/16
A pena un giorno si fermò in Irlanda, XI/78
A piedi è l'un, l'altro a cavallo: or quale, II/6
A piena vela si cacciaron lunge, XX/99
A prima giunta Astolfo raffigura, XVIII/122
A prima giunta io gli getto le braccia, V/51
A qualche legno pensa dar di piglio, XXXX/70
A qualunque io non creda esser nimico, XXXI/46
A quattro o sei dai colli i capi netti, XXV/13
A quel parpar si ritrovò presente, XXXI/98
A quella guisa che veggiàn talora, XXIX/56
A quella mensa citare, arpe e lire, VII/19
A quella vecchia che l'odiava quanto, XXXVII/108
A questa impresa un'altra spada volle, XXXXV/68
A questo annunzio, stimulato e punto, XXXVI/15
A questo capitan non pur cortese, XV/35
A questo effetto il re di Tremisenne, XII/73
A questo la mestissima Issabella, XXIV/80
A Riccardetto in cambio di saluto, XXV/74
A Ricciadetto, ancor che discortese, XXVI/62
A Ricciardetto tutta rivoltosse, XXVI/57
A sì grande uopo, come era, dovendo, XXXXI/28
A sì strano spettacolo Iocondo, XXVIII/39
A te non graverà prima aspettarme, XXI/47

A tutti par, l'incantator mirando, XIII/50
A vecchie donne e caste fe' nutrire, XXXXIII/15
A voi, Ruggier, tutto il dominio ho dato, XXXXIV/63
A' prieghi dunque di Ruggier, rifatto, VIII/17
Abbial chi aver lo vuol con lite e guerra, XXXIII/94
Accadde a questi di, che pei vicini, XXV/26
Acciò che de le due progenie illustri, XXXXIV/10
Acciò chi poi succedera, comprenda, XXXIII/12
Acciò dunque il voler del ciel si metta, III/19
Acciò il sesso viril non le soggioghi, XX/33
Acciò l'inganni, in che son tanti e tanti, XIII/52
Acciò per questi e per li primi merti, XXXVIII/25
Acciò per te non mi vedessi tolta, XXXXVI/35
Accompagnolla un pezzo Fiordispina, XXV/46
Accusato Ruggier dal proprio scudo, XXXXV/10
Ad accusar Melissa si converse, XXXXII/26
Ad ingrossare, et a figliar appresso, XX/32
Ad Issabella il re d'Algier scongiuri, XXIX/19
Ad ogni piccol moto ch'egli udiva, VII/24
Ad uno che fuggia, dietro si mise, XIX/87
Adonio intanto misero e tapino, XXXXIII/95
Adonio lungamente frutto colse, XXXXIII/116
Adornerà la sua progenie bella, III/57
Afflitto e stanco al fin cade ne l'erba, XXIII/132
Affretta il piede e ve cercando invano, XXII/15
Aggiungi che sapea ch'era Ruggiero, XXVI/94
Agliato, in man lo raccomanda, II/75
Agramante ch'intanto avea deserta, XXXX/36
Agramante dal muro una gran banda, XVI/76
Ah (dicea) valentuomini, ah compagni, XVIII/43
Ah (disse a lui Ruggier), senza più basti, XXX/61
Ah lasso! che poss'io più che mirare, II/44
Ah lasso! da quel dì con lui dimora, XXXXIII/43
Ah lasso! io non potrei (seco dicea), VI/10
Ahimè! vorrò quel che non vuol chi deve, XXXXIV/41
Al bel dominio accrescerà costui, III/39
Al brutto Saracin, che le venìa, XXIX/13
Al comparir del paladin di Francia, XVI/44
Al detto suo Martano Orrigille have, XVII/127
Al fin chiama quel servo a chi fu imposta, XXXXIII/131
Al fin de le parole urta il destriero, XVII/16
Al fin del campo il destrier tenne e volse, XIX/85
Al fin di mille colpi un gli ne colse, XV/83
Al monister, dove altre volte avea, XXVII/37
Al monte Sinaì gu peregtino, XIX/48
Al nudo sasso, all'Isola del pianto, X/93
Al padron fu commessa la risposta, XIX/70
Al pagan la proposta non dispiacque, I/21
Al pagan, che non sa come ne possa, XVIII/17
Al partir che Ruggier fe' dal castello, XXII/95
Al primo incontro credea porlo in terra, XXXVII/50
Al primo suon di quella voce torse, VI/29
Al re Agramante assai parve oportuna, XXXX/51
Al re d'Algier come cingial si scaglia, XXVI/116

Al re Gradasso e al buon re Sacripante, XXVII/14
Al re parve impossibil cosa udire, XXVIII/8
Al Saracin parea discortesia, XXIII/92
Al tempo che tornar dopo anni venti, XX/10
Al tornar de lo spirto, ella alle chiome, XXXXIII/158
Al trar degli elmi, tutti vider come, XXVI/28
Al venir quivi, era, lasciando Spagna, X/70
Al vento di maestro alzò la nave, XVIII/141
Al volgersi dei canti in varii lochi, XXXXIV/33
Alceste, il cavallier di ch'io ti parlo, XXXIV/20
Alcina, ch'avea intanto avuto aviso, VIII/12
Alcina i pesci uscir facea de l'acque, VI/38
Alcina, poi ch'a' preziosi odori, VII/26
Alcun ch'intende quivi esser Marfisa, XVIII/125
Alcun la terra e 'l mare e 'l ciel misura, XXXXIII/2
Alcun non può saper da chi sia amato, XIX/1
Alcuni cavallieri in questo mezzo, XXXVI/24
Alessandra a quel detto non rispose, XX/46
Alessandra, bramosa di vedere, XX/39
Alessandra gentil, ch'umidi avea, XX/42
All'abondante e sontuosa mensa, XV/78
All'apparir che fece all'improviso, I/29
All'atto incomparabile e stupendo, XXIX/28
All'Immortalitade il luogo è sacro, XXXV/16
All'infernal caliginosa buca, XXXIII/128
All'ultimo Ruggier la spada trasse, XXXVI/53
Alla città, che molte miglia gira, XIV/105
Alla donna d'Islanda, che non sanza, XXXII/99
Alla fera crudele il più molesto, XXVI/43
Alla più parte dei signor pagani, XXXIX/3
Alla prima città ch'egli rituova, XII/67
Alla vista de l'elmo gli appresenta, XXXXVI/137
Alle guerriere et a Ruggier, che meno, XXXVII/32
Allei però non si concede tanto, XIV/53
Allier, ch'all'ombra d'un boscetto, II/35
Allo scudier fe' dimandar come era, XIV/33
Allor sentì parlar con voce mesta, XXXIV/9
Allora la Bastia credo non v'era, XXXXIII/146
Allui venne un scudier pallido in volto, XVI/86
Almonio disse: -- Poi che piace a Dio, XXIV/20
Almen l'avesse posta in guardia buona, VIII/75
Almonio, che di ciò nulla temea, XIII/23
Alquanto la sua istoria io vo' seguire, VIII/30
Alquanto malagevole et aspretta, VII/8
Alstro destrier non è che meglio intenda, XXXXI/80
Altante riparar non sa né puote, XII/33
Altra fiata che de' questa via, XXXXIII/57
Altra là giù, senza apparir più, resta, XXXXI/21
Altra volta a battaglia erano stati, XXVI/101
Altre donne e scudier venivano anco, XXXII/51
Altri che 'l ferro e l'inimico caccia, XXXIX/84
Altri che spera in mar salvar la vita, XXXIX/85
Altri dicean: -- Come stan ben insieme, XVIII/89
Altri fiumi, altri laghi, altre campagne, XXXIV/72

Altri in amar lo perde, altri in onori, XXXIV/85
Altri per tema di spiedo o d'accetta, XXXIX/86
Altri Perduta, altri ha nomata Islanda, XXXII/52
Altrimente il Silenzio non rispose, XIV/96
Altrimente Tanacro riportarla, XXXVII/57
Altrove intanto il paladin s'avea, XVI/79
Alzi nel capo, o sia nel cor gli siede, XXVIII/88
Amando una gentil giovane e bella, XXII/39
Amava il cavallier, per sua sciagura, XV/101
Ambi d'un sangue, ambi in un nido natim XXXIII/47
Ambi gioveni siamo, e di bellezza, XXVIII/46
Ami d'oro e d'argento appresso vedee, XXXIV/77
Amor n'è causa, che nel cor m'ha impresso, XXXXV/32
Amor, pietà, sdegno, dolore et ira, XXXVII/77
Amore ha volto sottosopra spesso, XXIV/39
"Anch'io (suggiunse il re) senza alcun fallo, XXVIII/67
Ancor ch'a sue promesse e a suoi scongiuri, XXXXIII/86
Ancor che del finissimo metallo, XXXIII/104
Ancor che quivi non venne Grifone, XVII/24
Ancor che sdegno e còlera la madre, XXXXV/25
Andaro insieme ove del letto mosso, XVIII/91
Andò nel fondo, e vi traea la salma, XXX/14
Angelica a Medor la prima rosa, XIX/33
Angelica e Medor con cento nodi, XXIII/103
Angelica invisibile e soletta, XII/63
Angelica si ferma alle chiare onde, XII/57
Anna, bella, gentil, cortese e saggia, XXXXVI/9
Annibal e Iugurta di ciò foro, XXXX/41
Anselmo che non vede altro da cui, XXXXIII/136
Antiqua nimicizia avea il marito, XXI/36
Anzi Astolfo e la donna, che portata, XXXXV/66
Anzi, come egli sente che 'l signor, XXXI/90
Anzi non attendata, perché sotto, IX/3
Anzi non vo' morir; ma vo' che muoia, XXXXIV/56
Anzi pur creder vuol che da costei, VII/17
Anzi t'usurpi tu l'insegna mia!, XXVI/105
Anzi tutta l'Italia, che con lei, XXXXII/92
Anzi via più che del disir, mi deggio, XXXII/22
Aperse al primo che trovò, sì il petto, XIX/82
Apparecchiar per lo seguente giorno, XXXVIII/22
Appresso a dua mila anni il costume empio, XX/60
Appresso alle ragioni avea il sincero, XXVIII/84
Appresso ove il sol cade, per suo amore, I/46
Apron la cataratta, onde sospeso, XXXXV/45
Arde nel core, e fuor nel viso avampa, XVII/92
Ariodante, che Ginevra pianto, VI/4
Armato era d'un forte e duro usbergo, XIV/118
Arroge a tanto mal, ch'a corpo vòto, XXXIII/67
Artur, ch'impresa ancor senza consiglio, XXXIII/9
Ascoltando, Ruggier mostra nel volto, XXVI/65
Aspro concento, orribile armonia, XIV/134
Assai più larga piaga e più profonda, XIX/28
Assaltò li guardiani all'improviso, VII/80
Astolfo a gran fatica e Sansonetto, XXXXI/35
Astolfo, ch'andar giù vede il gran peso, XV/55

B

Bagna talor ne la chiara onda e fresca, VI/25
Bagnossi, come disse, e lieta porse, XXIX/25
Balugante del popul di Leone, XIV/12
Basti che nel servar fede al mio amante, XXXXV/101
Bastò di quattro l'animo e il valore, XXVI/25
Bella accoglienza i monachi e l'abbate, IV/55
Bello et ornato alloggiamento dielli, XVII/114
Ben certo è di morir; perche, se lascia, XXXXV/58
Ben che da fier dolor, tosto che questa, XXXXV/57
Ben che di Ruggier fosse ogni desire, X/72
Ben che du quella ancor brutta vendetta, XXXVI/4
Ben che io sia certa (dice), o cavalliero, XIII/3
Ben che l'avea lasciate in su la strada, XVIII/109
Ben che né gonna né faldiglia avesse, VII/28
Ben che Rinaldo con pochi danari, XXXIII/147
Ben che Ruggier sia d'animo constante, VI/17
Ben che soglia la Fraude esser bugiarda, XIV/91
Ben che sol tre fiate bisognolli, XXII/82
Ben che tua fellonia si veggia aperta, XXXXVI/106
Ben, come a Bradamante già promesse, XXXVI/81
Ben comprende all'insegne e sopravesti, XXXXIV/90
Ben furo aventurosi i cavallieri, XIII/1
Ben l'avea il re Sobrin riconosciuto, XXXXIII/198
Ben la vergogna è assai, ma più lo sdegno, XXXXIII/41
Ben lo mostrar; che gli nimici a pena, XXXIX/21
Ben mi dicea ch'uguale al mio non era, V/13
Ben mi duol che celar t'abbi voluto, XXXXVI/31
Ben mi par di veder ch'al secol nostro, XX/3
Ben mi si potria dir: -- Frate, tu vai, XXIV/3
Ben pensa quel che le parole denno, XXXVI/36
Ben se ne pent in breve; che colui, XXXXV/116
Ben son contento, per la compagnia, XXVII/74
Ben son degli altri ancor, c'hanno le chiome, XXXII/103
Ben spero, donne, in vostra cortesia, XXX/3
Ben veduto l'avea su quel cavallo, VII/40
Benedetto, il nipote, ecco là veggio, XXXXVI/11
Bestemmiò il cielo e gli elementi il crudo, XXVI/83
Bianca nieve è il bel collo, e 'l petto latte, VII/14
Bireno a pena era da noi partito, IX/25
Bisogna che proveggia il re Luigi, XIV/8
Bisogna, prima ch'io vi narri il caso, VIII/51
Bisogno non sarà, per trovar gonne, XI/74
Bradamante, che come era animosa, II/74
Bradamante conosce il suo cavallo, XXII/73
Bradamante, disposta di far tutti, XXII/34
Bradamante e Marfisa la corazza, XXXXVI/110
Bradamante la sera ad un castello, XXXIII/77
Bradamante ode, e par ch'assai le prema, XXII/42
Bradamante pregò molto Ruggiero, XXII/63
Bramavano i guerrier venire a proda, XIX/61

Bramoso di ritarlo ove fosse ella, II/22
Brandimarte, ch'Orlando amava a pare, VIII/88
Brandimarte, che 'l conte amava quanto, XXXI/64
Brandimarte sì strana e ria novella, XXXI/62
Breaco e Landriglier lascia a man manca, IX/16
Buon fu per me (dicea quell'altro ancora), XIX/100


C


C'e 'l duca de' Carnuti Ercol, figliuolo, XXXVII/13
Caccia Angelica in fretta la giumenta, XXIX/64
Cadde Sobrin del fiero colpo in terra, XXXXI/78
Cade a terra il cavallo e il cavalliero, IX/77
Cade in tanto dolor, che si dispone, V/52
Cagion del suo venir fu, che da Brava, XXX/91
Calano tosto i marinari accorti, II/29
Calcata serpe mai tanto non ebbe, XXX/56
Cambiato a tutti parve esser nel volto, XXVIII/24
Cantan fra i rami gli augelletti vaghi, XXXIV/50
Capitaro in un prato ove a diletto, XXV/4
Capitò al fin a Malega, e più danno, XXX/9
Capitò quivi un cavallier di corte, XXXVII/48
Carlo avea di Sicilia avuto avviso, XXXXIV/27
Carlo benignamente la raccolse, XXXVIII/11
Carlo, ch'aviso da Rinaldo avuto, XXXI/59
Carlo e molt'altri seco, che Leone, XXXXV/81
Carlo e tutta la corte stupefatta, XXXXVI/56
Carlo non torna più dentro alla terra, XVIII/163
Carlo si volse a quelle man robuste, XVII/14
Caro Guidone a' suoi fratelli stato, XXXI/36
Castello e ballador spezza e fraccassa, XIX/44
Cento a cavallo, e gli son tutti intorno, XIX/6
Cento messi a cercar che di lei fusse, XXXXII/30
Cerca far morir lei, che morir merta, V/54
Cercando già nel più intricato calle, XIX/3
Cercati pur fornir d'un'altra spada, XXVII/58
Cercere, poi che de la madre Idea, XII/1
Ch'a' bei sembianti et alìa ricca vesta, II/73
Ch'abbiate, Signor mio, gia inteso estimo, XII/48
Ch'abominevol peste, che Megera, V/2
Ch'agli nemici gli uomini sien crudi, V/6
Ch'Amor de' far gentile un cor villano, XXXII/93
Ch'apparecchiata era la stanza e 'l letto, XXXXIII/51
Ch'Arpalice non fu, non fu Tomiri, XXXVII/5
Ch'aver può donna al mondo più di buono, VIII/42
Ch'ella non v'era si chiarì di corto, XI/77
Ch'ella più giorni per si lunga via, XXXI/60
Ch'entrar facesse in campo la donzella, XXXXV/63
Ch'era, pugnando per la fé di Christo, XXXXIII/191
Ch'in visione alla fedel consorte, XXXXI/66
Ch'io vinca o perda, o debba nel mio regno, XXXXI/44
Ch'ogni suo stanza avea piena di velli, XXXIV/88
Ch'ordine abbian tra lor, come s'assaglia, XXXIX/65

Ch'Orlando non ci sia, ne aiuta; ch'ove, XXXVIII/54
Ch'un cavallier istrano era venuto, V/77
Che 'l cavallier ch'abbia maggior possanza, XXXII/94
Che 'l lasciar Durindana sì gran fallo, XXIV/75
Che 'l populo ha di liu quella paura, XXXVII/41
Che 'l suo fratello era uom che mosso il piede, XXVIII/9
Che come Adam, poi che gustò del pomo, XXXXIII/8
Che, come gli fu presso: -- Saulo, Saulo, XXXXI/53
Che con lei molte volte per camino, XXXIII/71
Che con un suo fratel ben giovinetto, V/17
Che d'alcune dirò belle e gran donne, XXXXIII/4
Che d'Atila dirò? che de l'iniquo, XVII/3
Che da doni grandissimi corrotta, XXXXIII/118
"Che debbo far, che mi consigli, frate, XXVIII/45
Che di Marfisa in quel discorso udito, XXX/88
Che di secreto ha commesso alla guida, V/74
Che dieci passi gli ba dietro o venti, XVII/89
Che dirò del favor, che de le tante, XXX/70
Che dolce più, che più giocondo stato, XXXI/1
Che dopo una sì trista e brutta pruova, XVII/122
Che facendol, fara quel che far deve, XXVI/96
Che ferro e fuoco e merli e tetti gravi, XXXX/19
Che fosse Orlando, nulla le soviene, XXIX/59
Che fosse Rodomonte, era più presto, XXXV/65
Che gloria, qual già Ippolita e Camilla, XXV/32
Che ha costei che t'hai fatto regina, VII/64
Che ha visto in piazza rompere steccato, XVIII/19
Che lo potria la donna facilmente, XXXXV/67
Che lo prese per mano, e seco scórse, XXXIV/62
Che mentre duo suoi figli erano vivi, XXXVII/45
Che mercanti e corsar che vanno attorno, IX/13
Che mille miglia e più, per questo solo, XXXXIV/99
Che nessum altro cavallier, ch'arriva, IX/20
Che non potrà, se non con biasmo e scorno, XXXVIII/72
Che non può far d'un cor ch'abbia suggetto, IX/1
Che, oltre che d'acciar murata sia, III/67
Che pensandovi sol, de la radice, XXVIII/13
Che per certificarne che voi séte, XXXI/33
Che piaceri amorosi e riso e gioco, XX/62
Che posta in braccio e su l'arcion davante, XII/5
Che prima il nome di Ruggiero odiassi, XXXXVI/41
Che producendo quella notte in giuoco, XXIX/21
Che prosuposto (che né ancor confesso, XXXXV/109
Che quando dianzi avea all'uscir del chiuso, XVII/59
Che, quanto può, nasconde il petto e 'l ventre, XI/59
Che quella nazion, la qual s'avea, XXXXVI/49
Che questo ingrato, perfido e crudele, V/73
Che rami e ceppi e tronchi e sassi e zolle, XXIII/131
Che rapiti gli avevano a Gismonda, XV/73
Che s'abbia a ritrovar con numer pare, XXXX/55
Che s'abbia da partire anco lo punge, XXV/83
Che sanguinoso e de la spada privo, XXXXII/8
Che se ben il trovarmi ora in procinto, XVII/51
Che se l'amante de l'amato deve, XXXVIII/4

Che se tra lor queste parole stanno, XXXXV/108
Che, senza ch'assoldiate altra persona, XXXXIV/64
Che senza più voltarsi mostrò loro, XXXIII/70
Che si può ben così nomar quel loco, VI/73
Che sia il disegno suo, ben io comprendo, VIII/34
Che spezza i rami e fa cadere i sassi, IX/74
Che tante volte ve lo fei venire, V/10
Che ti farò veder cosa che debbe, XXXXII/72
Che ti riposi insino al giorno nuovo, XIX/90
Che tornare in Selandia avea disegno, IX/87
Che tra Lurcandio e un cavallier istrano, V/79
Che tra' nemici alla ripa più interna, XV/5
Che trovar bisogna una donzella, VIII/56
Che vi fu tolta la sua donna poi, I/7
Che voi m'abbiate visto esser potria, XXV/22
Che vuole uscir di nuovo alla campagna, II/26
Chelindo e Mosco, i duo figli bastardi, XVI/60
Chi a piedi e che in arcion tutte partita, XXXXIV/21
Chi avesse il suo ramarico e 'l suo pianto, XXV/34
Chi costui fosse, altrove ho da narrarvi, XXXI/79
Chi d'una fromba e chi d'un arco armato, XI/48
Chi di qua, chi di là cade per terra, XXII/86
Chi dice: -- Sopra Limissò venuti, XIX/46
Chi fugge l'un pericolo, rimane, XXVII/27
Chi l'annello d'Angelica, o più tosto, VIII/2
Chi la donzella, chi 'l monaco sia, XXVIII/96
Chi mette il piè su l'amorosa pania, XXIV/1
Chi mi darà la voce e le parole, III/1
Chi narrerà l'angoscie, i pianti, i gridi, VIII/66
Chi parla per Ruggier, chi per Leone, XXXV/113
Chi può contar l'esercito che mosso, XIV/99
Chi questa cosa e chi quell'altra getta, XXXX/17
Chi salirà per me, madonna, in cielo, XXXV/1
Chi scese al mare, e chi poggio su al monte, XX/94
Chi senza freno in s'un destrier galoppa, VI/62
Chi sia quel vecchio, e perché al rio, XXXV/17
Chi va lontan da la sua patria, vede, VII/1
Chi vide mai dal ciel cadere il foco, IX/78
Chi vide quelli incendi e quei naufragi, XXXX/5
Chi vuol fuggir, Rinaldo fuggir lassa, XVIII/155
Chiama duo vecchi, e chiama alcune sue, XXXII/98
Chiede licenzia al figlio di Pipino, XXXXII/42
Chiedimi la metà di questo regno, XVIII/68
Chiusa ch'ebbe la lettera, chiuse anco, XXV/93
Ci ungemo i corpi di quel grasso opimo, XVII/54
Ci venne incontra con allegra faccia, VI/39
Ciascun marito, a mio giudizio, deve, XXXXII/100
Cibo soave e precioso vino, XXXXVI/46
Cillaro, so, no fu, non fu Arione, XXXXV/93
Cinque o sei mesi il singular certame, XXX/30
Ciò che di ruginoso e di brunito, XXXX/60
Ciò che si possa far per sua salute, IX/48
Cloridan, cacciator tutta sua vita, XVIII/166
Cloridan, che non sa come l'aiuti, XIX/8

Cloridan s'è ridutto ove non sente, XIX/4
Col corpo morto il vivo spirto alberga, III/11
Col cortese oste ragionando stava, XXXXII/97
Col fuoco dietro ove la canna è chiusa, IX/29
Colà mi trassi, e con la spada in mano, XXV/61
Colea dicea: "Pria che venisse a questo, V/58
Colei che di bellezze e di virtuti, XX/133
Colui ch'indosso il non suo cuoio aveva, XVII/112
Colui che fu de tutti i vizii il vaso, XVII/124
Colui, che tutto il mondo vilipende, XIV/41
Colui lascia il cavallo, e via carpone, XVI/64
Com'ella vide Astolfo e Sansonetto, XVIII/100
Come a colei che più che gli occhi sui, IV/41
Come a sé ritornar senza il suo amante, XIII/47
Come ai meridional tiepidi venti, XXXVI/40
Come aiutar ne le fortune estreme, XX/88
Come al partir del sol si far maggiore, XXXXV/36
Come al soffiar de' più benigni venti, XXXIX/14
Come Alzirdo appressar vide quel conte, XII/74
Come assalire o vasi pastorali, XIV/109
Come bambin, se ben la cara madre, XXXXIV/92
Come ben riscaldato arrido legno, XXVI/103
Come cadere il bue suole al macello, IX/42
Come Calamidor quel colpo mira, XVI/63
Come ceppo talor, che le medolle, VI/27
Come ch'in viso pallida e smarrita, XXVIII/97
Come ch'io avessi sopra il legno e vesti, XIII/19
Come che fosse il suo primier disegno, XII/35
Come che la Discordia avesse rotto, XXVII/39
Come chi assedia una città che forte, XXXXV/75
Come chi da noioso e grave sonno, XXXIX/58
Come chi visto abbia, l'aprile o il maggio, XXXXV/26
Come con questi, ovunque andar per terra, XV/30
Come d'alto venendo aquile suole, X/103
Come d'oscura valle umida ascende, XI/35
Come dal traditore io fui scernito, XXIV/21
Come di capitani bisogna ora, XIV/10
Come di lei s'accorse Orlando stolto, XXIX/61
Come di questi il cavallier s'accorse, XXVI/4
Come due belle e generose parde, XXXIX/69
Come è più presso, lo sfida a battaglia, I/61
Come è Ruggier, possibil che tu solo, XXXXV/98
Come egli de n'accese immantinente, X/12
Come egli è in terra, gli son tutti adosso, XXXIX/55
Come egli è presso al luminsoso tetto, XXXIV/53
Come ella s'orna e come il crin dispone, V/25
Come era a punto quella cosa stata, XXIV/17
Come esso a' prieghi d'Angelica bella, XXIII/119
Come fanciullo che maturo frutto, VII/71
Come Febo la condida sorella, XXXVII/17
Come fu presso alle sì ricche mura, VI/60
Come il gran fiume che di Vesulo esce, XXXVII/92
Come il mastin che con furor s'aventa, XX/139
Come il Guascon questo affermò per vero, XXXII/35

```
Come il Tartaro vede quel bel viso, XIV/52
Come il veloce can che 'l porco assalta, XXIV/62
Come il villan, se fuor per l'alte sponde, XXVI/111
Come impasto leone in stalla piena, XVIII/178
Come in palude asciutta dura poco, XIV/48
Come interviene a chi già fuor di speme, XXV/66
Come io vi dico, dal figliuol d'Otone, XXXIX/34
Come io vi dico, il cavallier venìa, XVI/7
Come io vi dico, sopraggiunta a caso, XXIV/56
Come l'inferno acceso di gran sete, XXV/43
Come l'inferno, che dirotto e stanco, XXVIII/90
Come l'uom riparar debba agl'incanti, XV/14
Come l'usanza (che non è più antiqua), XXII/49
Come la donna conosciuto ha il loco, XXIII/21
Come la donna il cominciò a vedere, VIII/46
Come la donna in tal periglio vede, XIII/76
Come la notte ogni fiammella è viva, XXXV/37
Come la terra, il cui produr di rose, III/41
Come la tigre, poi ch'ivan discende, XVIII/35
Come la voce aver potè Issabella, XXIII/69
Come levrier che la fugace fera, XXXIX/10
Come lupo o mastin ch'ultimo giugne, XIV/37
Come mastin sotto il feroce alano, XXXXVI/138
Come nave, che vento da la riva, XXXII/62
Come ne l'alto mar legno talora, XXI/53
Come nel bosco de l'umil ginepre, XII/87
Come nel mar che per tempesta freme, XXXX/29
Come ode Alceste ch'io vo a ritrovarlo, XXXIV/25
Come Orlando sentì battersi dietro, XXIX/63
Come orsa, che l'alpestre cacciatore, XIX/7
Come, partendo, afflitto tauro suole, XXVII/111
Come pensi, signor, che rimanesse, XXI/62
Come più presso il cavallier si specchia, XXI/7
"Come potrò (diceagli la fanciulla), XXVIII/61
Come può il Saracin ritrovar sesto, XXIII/85
Come purpureo fior languendo muore, XVIII/153
Come quando si dà fuoco alla mina, XXVII/24
Come quel figlio di Vulcan, che venne, XXXVII/27
Come re Norandino ode quel nome, XVIII/126
Come Rinaldo il vide ritornato, XXXII/59
Come s'allegra un bene acceso amante, XXXII/74
Come s'intese poi che la compagna, XXXVIII/9
Come se dentro a ben rinchiusa gabbia, XVIII/14
Come servo fedel, che più d'amore, XXVII/36
Come si presso è l'ippogrifo a terra, VI/23
Come si senton, s'austro o borea spira, XXXXV/112
Come si vede in un momento oscura, XXXII/100
Come si vide il successor d'Astolfo, VII/27
Come si vide Maganzese al bosco, II/69
Come soglion talor duo can mordenti, II/5
Come sparvier che nel piede grifagno, XXI/63
Come stormo d'augei ch'in ripa a un stagno, XXV/12
Come talor si getta e si periglia, XX/89
Come talvolta, ove si cava l'oro, XXXXVI/136
```

```
Come toro salvatico ch'al corno, XI/42
Come torrente che superbo faccia, XXXVII/110
Come trovasti, o scelerata e brutta, XI/26
Come trovato avesse o piume o paglia, XXXX/26
Come tu giungi (disse) in quella parte, XIII/51
Come turbar l'aria sentiano, armate, XX/28
Come venire il paladin lo vede, XV/53
Come veri cristiani Astolfo e Orlando, XXXX/11
Come vide Gradasso d'Agramante, XXXXII/10
Come vogliono alzar per l'aria i voli, XXXV/14
Comincia l'eremita a confortarla, VIII/47
Cominciar quivi una crudel battaglia, I/17
Cominciavan le schiere a ritirarse, XVIII/42
Cominciò a poco a poco indi a levarse, II/49
Cominciò il pazzo a gridar forte: -- Aspetta! --, XXX/11
Commanda al servo, ch'alla moglie Argia, XXXXIII/123
Commune il letto ebbon la notte insieme, XXV/42
Communico con loro il mio disegno, IX/38
Con accoglienza grata il cavalliero, XXXIV/60
Con briglia e sproni i cavallieri instando, XXXXVI/118
Con buono intenzione (e sallo Idio), XII/64
Con cor trafitto e con pallida faccia, V/41
Con eccellente e singulare ornato, XXXXVI/76
Con essi ragionava una donzella, XXXI/38
Con esso lui t'accaderà soggetto, III/73
Con esso un colpo il capo fesse e il collo, XXI/49
"Con facultade (disse) che ne' tuoi, XXXXIII/91
Con fresco vento ch'in favor veniva, XXXXIII/166
Con gli occhi cerca or questo lato or quello, IX/9
Con gli occhi fissi al ciel lo segue quanto, IV/48
Con gli scudieri e con la donna, dove, XVII/111
Con gran silenzio fece quella notte, XXXVII/55
Con grande ingegno, e non minor bellezza, XXXXIII/19
Con l'arme l'altre spoglie a Ruggier sono, XXX/75
Con l'una e l'altra man va ricercando, XXIX/46
Con la gente d'Esperia Soridano, XIV/22
Con la medesima asta con che avea, XXII/81
Con la qual non saria stato quel crudo, XI/3
Con la sinistra man prende la briglia, I/76
Con la vecchia Zerbin quindi partisse, XXI/70
Con larghi giri circondando prova, XXXXIII/119
Con lor Lattanzio e Claudio Tolomei, XXXXVI/12
Con maggior fretta fa movere il piede, XXXII/64
Con man fe' cenno di volere, inanti, XIX/89
Con Marifsa la giovane di Francia, XXXVII/101
Con Melicerta in collo Ino piangendo, XI/45
Con miraviglia molta e più dolore, XXXI/105
Con molta attanzion la bella donna, I/49
Con molta diligenzia il re Agramante, XXX/74
Con molto ardir vien Ricciardetto appresso, XXVI/77
Con molto dispiacer Gradasso intese, XXXX/47
Con occhi d'Argo il figlio di Pipino, XIV/107
Con patto, che qual d'essi perde, faccia, XXXVIII/64
Con patto, che se fa che son lo stuolo, XXXII/87
```

Con pompa trionfal, con festa grande, XXXXIV/32
Con prieghi il re Agramante e buon ricordi, XXVII/44
Con qual rumor la setolosa frotta, XII/77
Con quei che falsan le monete ha usanza, XIV/90
Con quel furor che 'l re de' fiumi altiero, XXXX/31
Con quel furor l'impetuosa gente, XXXX/32
Con quel rumor ch'un sacco s'arme cade, XXIII/88
Con quella estrema forza che percuote, XXXXVI/122
Con quella festa il paladin la piglia, XXIX/68
Con questa compagnia lieto e gioioso, XIV/61
Con questa intenzion prese il camino, VII/38
Con questa intenzione una mattina, XXXXIII/77
Con queste et altre et infinite addresso, XXVII/122
Con questi, che passar dovean gl'incudi, XXII/67
Con questi et altri più efficaci detti, XXXVIII/65
Con questo et altri detti accortamente, XXXVIII/48
Con ricca sopraveste e bello arnese, XXXV/67
Con ricche vesti e regalmente ornato, XXXXVI/53
Con si animosi petti che vi foro, XIV/4
Con suo gran dispiacer s'avede Carlo, VIII/87
Con tai le cerca et altre assai parole, XXXXIII/85
Con tai parole e simili altre assai, XXX/37
Con tal condizion fu stabilita, XXVI/108
Con tal parole e simili non cessa, XXXXIII/27
Con tali e simil detti il vecchio accorto, XXXX/40
Con tutte l'arme andò per mezzo l'acque, XVIII/24
Con un gran ramo d'albero rimondo, I/25
Con un sospir quest'ultime parole, XXXV/40
Con voce qual conviene al suo furore, XXXI/66
Conceti foste da Ruggier secondo, XXXVI/60
Conchiuso ch'ebbon questo, chiamar fero, XXVIII/74
Concluso ch'ebbe questo nel pensiero, VI/13
Confuso e lasso d'aggirarsi tanto, XXII/16
Conobbe i cavallier, come essi lui, XXXI/39
Conobbel, come prima alzò la fronte, XXIV/95
Conobbi tardi il suo mobil ingegno, VI/50
Conosce ben che, poi che 'l cor fellone, XXXXIII/129
Conosce ella Brunel come lo vede, III/76
Conosce il re Agramante che gli e vero, XXX/29
Conosce, tosto che lo scudo vede, XXXXIV/104
Conoscete alcun voi, che non lasciasse, XXVIII/80
Conquesto uscì invisibil de la torre, XI/5
Considerando poi, s'io lo facessi, XXXIV/42
Continuando la medesma botta, XXVI/22
Continuò per molti giorni e mesi, V/11
Contra il fratel d'ira minor non arse, VI/8
Contra la donna per giostrar si fece, XXXV/75
Contra la voluntà d'ogni nocchiero, II/28
Contra quel disleal mi fu adiutrice, XIII/30
Convien ch'ovunque sia, sempre cortese, XXXVI/1
Corcate su tapeti alessandrini, X/37
Corebo, che gentile era e cortese, XIII/25
Corebo, consentendo Almonio, sciolse, XXIV/44
Corni, bussoni, timpani moreschi, XXVII/29

Corre di nuovo in su l'estreme sabbia, X/34
Correndo viene, e '1 muso a guisa porta, XVII/31
Correno a morte que' miseri a gara, XIV/46
Corrò la fresca e matutina rosa, I/58
Corron chi qua chi là; ma poco lece, XVII/32
Cortese come bella, Doralice, XXIV/72
Cortesemente dico in apparenza, XX/105
Cortesi donne, che benigna udienza, XXXVIII/1
Cortesi donne e grate al vostro amante, XXII/1
Cortesi donne ebbe l'antiqua etade, XXVI/1
Cosa, qual vogli sia, non gli domdando, XXXXIII/111
Così a Ruggier narrava Ricciardetto, XXV/71
Così a tutta la plebe e alla piu parte, XXXXVI/112
Così all'incontro, quanto più depresso, XXXXV/2
Così ben piange, e così ben si duole, XXXXV/18
Così con voluntà de la donzella, III/60
Cosi contra i pensieri empi e maligni, XXXV/15
Così, cor mio vogliate (le diceva), XXIV/78
Cosi correndo l'uno, e seguitando, XI/21
Così de le vittorie le qual, poi, XV/36
Così dice; e una gemma allora nata, XXXXIII/112
Così dice egli; e mentre s'apparecchia, I/59
Così dice egli, e torna al suo destriero, II/62
Cosi dicea Grifon, cosi Aquilante, XXII/78
Così dicea l'imperator devoto, XIV/73
Così dicean; ma non sapean ch'Amone, XXXXIV/12
Così dicendo, all cima superna, II/70
Così dicendo, di morir disposta, XXXII/44
Così dicendo, e put tuttavia in fretta, XXXXIII/56
Così dicendo il buon Rinaldo, e intanto, XXXXIII/9
Così dicendo, intorno alla fontana, XI/9
Così dicendo, le guerriere mosse, XXXVII/86
Così dicendo, mostragli il marchese, XXXIII/33
Così dicendo, ne la torta via, XIX/5
Così dicendo, se stesso riprendes, XXXIII/36
Così dicendo, subito gli sparve, XXXXII/65
Così diceva Malagigi, e messe, XXVI/48
Cosi dipoi ch'ebbono presi i muri, XXXX/30
Così disposti, messero in quel loco, XVIII/172
Così disse Agramante; e volse gli occhi, XXXVIII/41
Cosi disse; e menò le donne dove, XXXIII/13
Cosi disse egli, e fe' portare in fretta, XIX/92
Così disse egli; e molto ben risposto, XXX/43
Cosi disse egli, e tosto il parlar tenne, XVIII/174
Così disse egli. Io che divisa e sevra, V/26
Così disse il nocchier di Logistilla, X/50
Così disse il nocchiero; e mosse a riso, XXXXIII/144
Così disse Odorico, e poi soggiunse, XXIV/33
Così fa ch'ella un poco il duol raffrena, XXXXII/28
Cosi fan questi giovani, che tanto, X/8
Cosi far mi promesse, e ne la ròcca, XXXIV/32
Cosi fra pochi di gente raccolse, XI/79
Così fu differita la tenzone, XIX/106

Così furendo il Saracin bizzaro, XVIII/36
Così già fu che Marganorre intorno, XXXVII/111
Così gli amanti suo l'avrian seguita, XXVII/4
Così Grifone et Aquilante tolse, XV/92
Così il rapace nibio furar suole, II/39
Così l'uom giusto lo battezza, et anco, XXXXIII/194
Così la donna, poi che tocca e vede, XXV/67
Così la moglie ancor de l'Orvo priega, XVII/62
Così le due magnanime guerriere, XXXIX/15
Così le fa la donna che venuta, XXXII/78
Così li duo guerrieri incominciaro, XII/47
Così lo spirto mio per le belle ombre, XXXVI/66
Cosi lor lancie van d'effetto vòte, XXXVI/38
Così mando per tutta la sua terra, VIII/25
Cosi Marsilio e così il buon Sobrino, XXXI/82
Così, mentre Ruggiero e Mandricardo, XXVI/112
Così narrava il mesto cavalliero, XXXXIII/47
Così noceva ai suoi come agli strani, XX/93
Cosi non fosse la legge più forte, XX/44
Così parlando, giunsero sul mare, III/75
Così parlava Brandimarte, et era, XXXXI/42
Così parlava la gentil donzella, XIII/32
Così per colpa de' ministri avari, XXXIII/51
Così per ogni via dal re di Frisa, IX/66
Così più volte la sfacciata donna, XXI/34
Così, poi che i protesti e i prieghi invano, IX/35
Così Ruggier con l'asta e con la spada, X/104
Così Ruggier, poi che Melisse fece, VII/72
Così scornato, de vergogna e d'ira, XXVII/64
Cosi si duole e si consuma et ange, XXV/38
Così solinghe vissero qualch'anno, XX/29
Così talora un bel purpureo nastro, XXIV/66
Così tosto come ebbe il capo chino, XXXXIII/53
Così venìa l'imitator du Cristo, XXXV/10
Così venìa Rinaldo ricordando, XXXXIII/60
Costei (dicea) stupore e riverenza, X/46
Costei sarà la saggia Leonora, XIII/69
Costui con lieta faccia al paladino, XXXIV/55
Costui dietro al cugin suo di Pescara, XXXIII/49
Costui, dopo il saluto, con bel modo, XXXXII/71
Costui face ad Ungiardo saper, come, XXXXV/7
Costui, richiesto da Zerbin, gli diede, XXIV/52
Costui sarà, col senno e con la lancia, III/55
Cotali esser doveano i duoi ladroni, V/4
Crebbe il tempo crudel tutta la notte, XVIII/144
Crebbe il timor, come venir lo vide, XIV/51
Crebbero in quantità fuor d'ogni stima, XXXIX/27
Crede ciascun, fuor che l'iniqua moglie, XXI/39
Credea il Guascon quel che dicea, non senza, XXXII/32
Credendo quivi ritrovarlo, mosse, XIV/80
Credendolo incontrar, talora armossi, XXXII/16
Crederò ben, che sian gli Arabi scesi, XXXVIII/44
Credette Pinabel questa donzella, XXIII/3
Credi che Dio questi ignoranti ha privi, XXXV/24

Credo che 'l resto di quel verno cose, XI/81
Credo che t'abbia la Natura e Dio, XXVII/119
Credo fusse un Alchino o un Farfarello, VII/50
Creduta avria che fosse statua finta, X/96
Cresce la forza e l'animo indefesso, XXXXI/50
Crescer più sempre l'appetito cieco, XXIX/12
Crudel, si che peccato a dolor t'hai, XXXII/40


# D

D'abitazioni è l'isoletta vòta, XXXX/45
D'adonio voglio dir, che 'l ricco dono, XXXXIII/71
D'Africa v'era la men trista gente, XVI/54
D'alto cader sente gran sassi e graci, XXXIX/83
D'amar quel Rabicano avea ragione, XXII/29
D'Azzi, d'Alberti, d'Obici discorso, XXXXI/67
D'inimicar con Rodomonte il figlio, XVIII/31
D'ogni fin che sortisca la contesa, XXXVIII/71
D'ogni puerrier l'usbergo era perfetto, XX/87
D'ogni suo colpo mai non cadea manco, XXV/15
D'oro e di seta i latti ornati vede, XII/10
D'un bel drappo di seta avea coperto, II/55
D'un suo scudier una grossa asta afferra, XVI/81
D'una in un'altra via si leva ratto, IX/73
D'una vecchiezza valida e robusta, XXXX/54
D'uomini morti pieno era per tutto, XXXX/33
Da Bradimarte senza farle motto, XXIV/54
Da Carlo impetrai grazia, ch'a nessuno, XXXXV/99
Da che, donna (dicea), l'annello hai teco, VII/47
Da Ercole partisi riverente, XXXXVI/87
Da indi in qua ch'ebbe la trista nuova, XV/103
Da iniqua stella e fier destin fu giunto, XXXXII/37
Da l'altra parte fuor dei gran ripari, XXXVIII/79
Da l'altra parte il cavallier estrano, XXXI/24
Da l'altra parte il figli d'Oliviero, XVIII/127
Da l'altra parte odi che fama lascia, XXXV/28
Da l'altra parte, ovunque il Saracino, XXIV/63
Da l'altro canto avea l'acerba etade, XX/69
Da la battaglia il figlio d'Ulieno, XXVI/131
Da la cittade al mar ratto io veniva, XXIV/22
Da la rabbia del vento che si fende, XXXXI/12
Da le lor donne i gioveni assai foro, XX/18
Da le mogli così furo i mariti, XXXVII/82
Da le sue terre, le quai son vicine, XXXVII/39
Da limpida fontana tutta quella, XVIII/139
Da lungi par che come fiamma lustri, II/42
Da Mandricardo fu Ruggier percosso, XXX/66
Da mezza notte tacito si parte, VIII/86
Da mezzogiorno e da la porta d'austro, XIX/78
Da poi che due e tre volte ritornati, XXIII/12
Da quattro canti era tagliato, e tale, IV/13
Da questa voglia è ben diversa quella, XXXXV/15
Da te uscir veggio le pudiche donne, XIII/57

Da tutti i canti risforzar l'assalto, XXXX/20
Da voi domando in guideron di questo, XXIX/17
Dagli altri nodi acendol sciolto prima, XV/60
Dagli anni e dal digiuna attenuato, II/13
Dal bosco alla città feci portallo, XXIV/25
Dal collo un suo monile ella si sciolse, XXVIII/15
Dal Creator accelerata forse, XVIII/162
Dal dolor vinta, or sopra il mar si lancia, XI/40
Dal duro colto de la terra il sole, XX/82
Dal mar sei miglia o sette, a poco a poco, XVIII/138
Dal nostro re siàn (disse) di Granata, XIV/40
Dal re pregato fu di dire il nome, V/92
Dal re, senza indugiar, gli fu risposto, VIII/23
Dal soldano d'Egitto, tuo vicino, XXXX/39
Dal suo principio infin a secol nostro, XXVI/41
Dal suo scudier l'elmo allacciar si fece, XXVII/88
Dato avea a peno a quel loco le spalle, XXIII/39
Dato che fu de la battaglia il segno, XIX/80
De al battaglia ha detto, ch'in favore, XXXXVI/50
De al vittoria poco rallegrosse, XXXXII/18
De cento venti (che Turpin sottrasse, XXIII/62
De l'alato destrier presto discese, XXXIV/6
De l'alta stirpe d'Aragone antica, XIII/68
De l'altre tacerò; che, come ho detto, XIII/65
De l'isola non pochi erano corsi, XI/46
De l'orizzonte il sol fatte avea rosse, XXXIII/65
De l'un, come de l'altro, fatte rosse, XXX/63
De l'un di questi il figlio Guidobaldo, XXVI/50
De la battaglia che Rinaldo avere, XXXI/107
De la giostra era il prezzo un'armatura, XVII/82
De la gran moltitudine ch'uccisa, XXXIX/72
De la gran preda il Tartaro contento, XIV/56
De la piacevolezza le sovenne, XVIII/101
De la piazza si vede in guisa torre, XVIII/21
De la puttana sua balia i conforti, XXXXIII/115
De la sentenzia Mandricardo altiero, XXX/18
De la sinistra sol lo scudo avea, IV/17
De la tua chiara stirpe uscirà quella, XIII/59
De la vittoria ch'avea avuto Orlando, XXXXIII/154
De le due corna il nocchier prese il destro, XXXXIII/54
De le fate io son una; et il fatale, XXXXIII/98
De le lor donne e de le lor donzelle, XXXI/61
De le più ricce terre di Levante, XVII/18
De le quai non più tosto entrò le porte, XIII/79
De' corpi nostri ho ancor non poca speme, XXIV/82
De' duo pagani, senza pari in terra, XXIV/100
Debbo forse ire in Frisa, ove io ptoei, X/32
Decimo ha quel Leon scritto sul dosso, XXVI/36
Degna d'eterna laude è Bradamante, XXVI/2
Deh avesse Amor così nei pensier miei, XXXXV/33
Deh che farò? farò dunque vendetta, XXXXIV/54
Deh ci fosse egli! (gli rispose Ippalca), XXIII/35
Deh, come, o prudentissima mia scorta, XIII/56
Deh, cortese signor, s'unque tu amasti, XXXI/74

Deh! (diss'ella) signor, non vi rincresca!, I/67
"Deh (disse al fine), a che l'error nascondo, XXI/22
Deh (disse Orlando al re di Circassia), XII/41
Deh, dove senza me, dolce mia vita, VIII/76
Deh ferma, Amor, costui che così sciolto, XXXII/20
Deh, non vietar che le piu nobil alme, VII/61
Deh perché, Brandimarte, ti lasciai, XXXXIII/160
Deh, perché dinanzi in prova non venni io, XXX/42
Deh! perché vo le mie piaghe toccando, VI/49
Deh perché voglio anco di me dolermi?, XXXII/23
Deh, pur che da color che vanno in corso, X/33
Deh, Ruggier mio (dicea), dove sei gito?, XXXXV/97
Deh, se non hai del viso il cor men bello, IV/33
Deh torna a me, mio sol, torna, e rimena, XXXXV/39
Deh, vita mia, non vi mettete affanno, XXX/38
Dei cavallieri e de la fanteria, XVIII/16
Dei paladini e dei guerrier più degni, XVI/89
Del a cortese offerta ti ringrazio, XIX/91
Del campo d'infedeli a prima giunta, XXXI/52
Del capo e de le scene Rodomonte, XXXXVI/135
Del caso strano di Rinaldo a pieno, XXXXII/38
Del danno c'han de te ricevut'oggi, XIX/104
Del duca di Trasfordia è quella insegna, X/86
Del generoso, illustre e chiaro sangue, XXVI/52
Del mago ogn'altra cosa era figmento, IV/20
Del mare al fondo; e seco trasse quanti, XXXXI/20
Del mio error consapevole, non chieggio, XXXIII/115
Del mio signor di Bozolo la moglie, XXXXV/7
Del palafren discende anco Issabella, XXIV/53
Del palafreno Angelica giù scese, XIX/24
Del palazzo incantato era difuso, XXII/17
Del parer del padrone i marinari, XIX/60
Del re de la Zumara non si scorda, XVIII/47
Del re de' fiumi tra l'aliere corna, XXXV/6
Del sangue d'Austria e d'Aragon io veggio, XV/25
Del suon del colpo fu tanto smarrito, XXXXI/97
Dentro a Belgrado, e fuor per tutto il monte, XXXXIV/80
Dentro a Biserta i sacerdoti santi, XXXX/13
Dentro a Parigi non sariano state, XXXXVI/75
Dentro a Valenza o dentro a Barcellona, XIX/41
Dentro e d'intorno il duca la cittade, XX/96
Dentro il palagio il villanel si caccia, XXII/14
Dentro la cella il vecchio accese il fuoco, XXXXI/59
Dentro letto vi fan tenere erbette, I/38
Dentro non vi trovò piccol né grande, XXIV/12
Dentro una ricca sala immantinente, XXXIII/119
Desideroso di condurre a fine, XXII/18
Di barche e di sottil legni era tutto, XXVII/128
Di bocca il sangue in tanta copia fonde, XI/43
Di Bradamante e di Marfisa dico, XXXVII/24
Di Bradamante, poi che conosciuta, XXXVIII/8
Di Buovo era costui figliuol bastardo, XXV/72
Di ch'altri a favorir la turba venne, XVIII/116
Di ch'apparecchio fa tanto solenne, XVIII/96

Di che contaminato anco esser parme, XVII/126
Di chi mi debbo, ohimè! (dicea) dolere, XXXXV/87
Di ciò, cor mio, nessun timor vi tocchi, XXIV/81
Di ciò si ride la Discordia pazza, XXVII/100
Di citatorie piene e di libelli, XIV/84
Di cocenti sospir l'aria accendea, XXVII/117
Di commune parer le sopraveste, XXXVII/33
Di condurla in Provenza ebbe pensiero, XXIV/92
Di contrario liquor la piage gli unge, XXVIII/26
Di cortesia, di gentilezza esempi, XXXVI/2
Di così nobili arbori non suole, X/62
Di così strano e misero accidente, XXXI/48
Di costei prima che degli altri dico, VII/34
Di cui fra tutti li signori illustri, III/1
Di cui fu per campar tanto la fretta, XXXXI/26
Di devota umiltà la donna tocca, III/8
Di dover dervar questo, Zerbin diede, XXIV/43
Di faccia, di parole e di sembiante, VII/52
Di fango brutto, e molle d'acqua vanne, XIV/120
Di ferro un cerchio grosso era suo dita, XXXXI/101
Di filisofi altrove e di poeti, XXXXVI/92
Di Fiordispina gran notizia ebb'io, XXV/49
Di forza a Rodomonte una gran parte, XXXXVI/132
Di furto ancora, oltre ogni vizio rio, XXXII/42
Di giorno ritrovata non sarebbe, XII/89
Di levar lei di qui non ho consiglio, XVII/43
Di loro in arme pochi eran migliori, XXXII/73
Di Marfisa, d'Astolfo, d'Aquilante, XIX/43
Di meco conferir non ti rincresca, XXXXVI/32
Di medolle già d'orsi e di leoni, VII/57
Di Merlin posso e di Melissa insieme, XXXII/25
Di molte cose l'ammonisce e molte, XXIII/32
Di molte fila esser bisogno parme, XIII/81
Di monte in monte e d'uno in altro bosco, IV/11
Di nodi d'oro e di gemmati ceppi, XXXIV/78
Di non tosto abbracciarla lo ritiene, XXIII/65
Di nuovo Mandricardo era risorto, XXVII/109
Di pensiero in pensiero andò vagando, XXVII/133
Di perdonargli in somma fu concluso, XX/56
Di persona era tanto ben formata, VII/11
Di pianger mai, mai di gridar non resta, XXIII/125
Di piano in monte, e di campagna in lido, XI/83
Di piatto usar potea, come di taglio, XXXX/82
Di prestezza Zerbin pare una fiamma, XXXV/61
Di pur cercar nuovo desir lo prese, XXXV/56
Di qua, di là, di su, di giù discorre, XXIV/14
Di qua di là, di su di giù smarrita, XX/90
Di qua di là gridar si sente all'arme, XXXVI/29
Di qua di là si volse, né persona, XXIII/20
Di qua di là va le noiose piume, XXXII/13
Di qua e di là sin alla nuova luce, XXXXI/37
Di qua la Francia, e di là il campo ingrosso, XXXIII/40
Di quali era però la maggior parte, III/66
Di quanti re mai d'Etiopia foro, XXXIII/107

Di quei che primi giunsero alla porta, XVIII/5
Di quei di Saragosa e de la corte, XIV/15
Di quel che disse il re, molto contento, XXVIII/52
Di quel Martanto ivi ebbe ad informarse, XVIII/76
Di quelli ch'abbatea, s'eran pagani, XXIX/39
Di questa donna valorosa e bella, XXXVI/11
Di questa speme Amore ordisce i nodi, XXV/50
Di questa terra a lei non parve torsi, XX/26
Di questi cavallieri e di Marfisa, XXVII/31
Di questi duo guerrier dissi che tratti, XXXX/62
Di questi il capitano si vedea, VI/63
Di questi l'uno, oltre che 'l proprio instinto, XXXVII/9
Di questo accordo lieto parimente, XXXVIII/66
Di questo avuto aviso il re frisone, IX/40
Di questo e d'altre cose fu diffuso, XXXIV/68
Di questo ho da contarvi più di sotto, XVII/84
Di questo Orlando avea gran doglia, e seco, VIII/73
Di qui nacque un error tra gli assaliti, XXVI/15
Di qui presso a tre leghe a quella torre, XXVII/93
Di ricche gemme un splendido monile, VII/54
Di serpentin, di porfido le dure, XXXXII/74
Di sì belle figure è adorno il loco, XXXII/96
Di sì forbito acciar luce ogni torre, II/43
Di sopra a Costantin ch'avea l'impero, XXXXVI/79
Di sopra io vi dicea ch'una figliuola, X/10
Di sopra siede alla devota cella, XXXXI/57
Di sopran vi narrai che ne la grotta, XIII/2
Di su la soglia Atlante un sasso tolle, IV/38
Di sua sciochezza indarno ora si duole, XVII/117
Di tal finezza è quella Balisarda, XXXXI/75
Di tal vittoria non troppo gioioso, XXXXII/12
Di tali n'avea più d'una decina, XXII/66
Di tanta preda il paladino allegro, XXXVIII/31
Di tanto core è il generoso Orlando, IX/4
Di terra si levò tacito e mesto, XXXV/51
Di trala, anco che morta, non rimase, XXIX/72
Di trombe, di  tambur, di suon de corni, XX/83
Di tutti gli altri beni, o che concede, XXXXIV/49
Di tutti i lochi intorno fa venire, XXIX/32
Di tutti i velli ch'erano già messi, XXXIV/91
Di Vallombrosa pensò far la strada, XXIII/19
Di vari marmi con suttil lavoro, XII/8
Di vedovelle i gridi e le querele, XXVII/34
Di versate minestre una gran massa, XXXIV/80
Di viso era costui bello e giocondo, XX/37
Di voce in voce e d'una in altro orecchia, XXIII/48
Di volervi venir prese partito, V/44
Dianzi Marullo et il Pontan per vui, XXXVII/8
Dicea: -- Fortuna, che piu a far ti resta, VIII/40
Dicea la donne al suo Ruggiero absente, XXX/84
Dicea Ruggier: -- Se pur è Amon disposto, XXXXIV/52
Dicea Sobrin: -- Che più vittoria lieta, XXXX/37
Dicendo: -- Alcun non me ne può riprendere, XXIV/59
Dicendo che lodevole non era, XX/103

Dicendole ch'a donna né bellezza, XXXXIII/84
Diceva queste et altre cose molte, XXXXIV/59
Dico che 'l corno è di sì orribil suono, XV/15
Dico che 'l mago al gatto, e gli altri al topo, IV/23
Dico che, come arrica in su la sponda, XXXV/12
Dico così, per dimostrar che quello, XXXVIII/52
Dico l'annel che Bradamante, avea, X/108
Dico, la vella istoria ripigliando, XVI/5
"Dico (rispose Fausto) che secondo, XXVIII/7
Dico Rinaldo, il qual, come sapete, XXXXII/29
Dico, salvando voi questa cittade, XVI/35
Diede ad Arganio quei di Libicana, XIV/19
Diedi alla madre sepoltura onesta, XXXVI/62
Diegli, pregando, di vedere assunto, XXXXIII/87
Dietro a me tutti in un drappel ristretti, XX/76
Dietro lampeggia a guisa di baleno, IX/75
Dietro non gli galoppa né gli correm XXXII/60
Difendendosi poi mio padre un giorno, IX/31
Digli questo, e non altro; e se quel vuole, XXXV/61
Dimandògli Aquilante, se di questo, XVIII/72
"Dimmi (le disse il re con fiero sguardo), XXVIII/69
Dinanzi agli altri un cavalliero adocchia, XXXXIV/86
Dinanzi vien Oldrado e Fieramonte, XVI/67
Dio così dissi, e fe' serena intorno, XXIX/30
Dio gli ripresse il temerario ardire, XXXIII/111
Dio vi provederà d'aiuto forse, XXIV/84
Dio vòlse che all'entrar che Rodomonte, XVI/29
Dio vuol ch'ascosa antiquamente questa, XV/24
Dirò d'Orlando in un medesmo tratto, I/2
Dirò prima la causa del partire, XXV/59
Discorreva il Silenzio, e tuttavolta, XIV/97
Disegnando levargli ella la testa, IV/27
Dismontò il duca Astolfo alla gran corte, XXXIII/103
Disse al pagan: -- Me sol creduto avrai, I/19
Disse ch'era di al poco lontanto, XXXXIII/187
Disse, che chi le avea tolto il destriero, XXVI/64
Disse d'andare; e partesi ch'ognuno, XXI/37
Disse il pastore: -- Io non so loco alcuno, XXXII/65
Disse l'imperator con viso lieto, XXXXIV/71
Disse la fata: -- Io ci porrò il pensiero, X/66
Disse Marfisa: -- E molto più sieno elle, XX/73
Disse Melissa: "Io ti darò un vasello, XXXXIII/28
Disse Rinaldo a lui: -- Se 'l destrier morto, XXXI/16
Disse Ruggier: -- Non riguardiamo a questo, XXII/57
Disse, tra più ragion che dovea farlo, XXXIX/63
Dissel tra sé, ma non che fosse inteso, XXXI/13
Dissi di lui, che di vederla sotto, XXI/4
Ditemi un poco: è di voi forse alcuno, XXVIII/79
Divenimmo ambi di color di morte, XXXXIII/40
Dolce quantunque e pien di grazia tanto, XXXXII/95
Domanda a costei l'angelo, che via, XIV/88
Domandar non ardisce che ne sia, XXXXV/27
Domandò lor perdono, che d'amore, XXVIII/70
Domiziano e l'ultimo Antonino, XVII/2

```
Donne e donzelle con pallida faccia, XXXXVI/111
Donne e donzelle e vecchi e altra gente, XIV/54
Donne, e voi che le donne avete in pregio, XXVIII/1
Donne gentil, per quel ch'a biasmo vostro, XXIX/2
Donne, io conchiudo in somma, ch'ogni etate, XXXVII/23
Dopo, accordando affettuosi gesti, XVI/10
Dopo alcun di si mostrò nuovo amante, V/12
Dopo i saluti e 'l giunger mano a mano, XXXXI/38
Dopo molt'anni alle ripe omicide, XX/36
Dopo non molto la bara funèbre, XXIII/46
Doralice che vede la sua guida, XXIII/89
Dove abbassar dovrebono la lancia, XVII/74
Dove averne piacer deve e conforto, XVII/50
Dove con loro audacia tanto fenno, XVII/63
Dove dal sole alquanto si ricuopra, XXIX/58
Dove entra in mare il gran fiume etiopo, XV/58
Dove entrar si potea, con l'arme indosso, XIV/39
Dove, ferito, alquanti giorni, inante, XVIII/70
Dove gli Scotti ritornar fuggendo, XVI/80
Dove intendo poi ch'eran salvati, XXX/92
Dove l'avea veduta domandolle, XX/142
Dove la vecchia ritrovar timore, XIX/69
Dove lascio il fratel Aldrobandino?, III/35
Dove ne' prati alla citta vicini, X/74
Dove onorato e splendido certame, XIII/60
Dove passato era il piccol drappello, XXVII/22
Dove, poi che rimase la donzella, I/10
Dove, speranza mia, dove ora sei?, VIII/77
Dove tenea le sue cose più care, V/9
Dove trovollo, e come fu conteso, XXVII/116
Dove una squadra per stanchezza è mossa, XVI/58
Dove vede appair lungo la sabbia, XVII/38
Dovea cantarne, et altro incominciai, XXXII/2
Dovea in memoria avere il signor mio, XXXXIII/70
Doveano allora aver gli eccessi loro, XVII/6
Dovunque drizza Michel angel l'ale, XIV/78
Dovunque il viso drizza il paladino, XVIII/148
Dovunque intorno il gran muro circonda, XIV/106
Dovunque io vo, sì gran vestigio resta, XXIII/37
Drizzati che gli ha tutti al lor camino, XVI/41
Dubitò che per fraude di colei, XVIII/79
Duca di Bocchingamia è quel dinante, X/83
Duca era di Selandia, e se ne giva, IX/23
Dudon con gran vigor dietro l'abbraccia, XXXIX/52
Dudone, Astolfo, Brandimarte, essendo, XXXIX/38
Dudone ode il rumor, la strage vede, XXXX/75
Due belle donne onestamente ornate, XV/72
Due spade altre non so per prova elette, XXXIII/80
Due squadre, una di Mulga, una d'Arzilla, XIV/23
Dunque baciar sì belle e dolce labbia, XXXVI/32
Dunque fia ver (dicea) che mi convegna, XXXII/18
Dunque (rispose sorridendo il conte), XII/43
Dunque un uom solo in vostra terra preso, XVII/8
Duo Erculi, duo Ippoliti da Este, XXVI/51
```

Duo Mori ivi fra gli altri si trovaro, XVIII/165
Durindana cercò per la foresta, XXIV/50
Duro l'assalto un'ora e più che 'l mezzo, XXXI/22


E

E 'l padre suo da un altro, o padre o fosse, XXXIII/26
E 'l stare in dubbio era con gran periglio, XIX/56
E al punizion che qui, secondo, XXXVII/73
E Balisarda al suo ritorno trasse, XXX/58
E Balisarda poi si messe al fianco, VII/76
E ben che possan gir di preda carchi, XVIII/182
E ben di questo e dogni male indegna, X/98
E ben lor disse il ver, ch'ella era inferma, XXX/95
E ben si fece far subito piazza, XI/50
E ben si ritrovò salito a tempo, XVI/83
E Bradimarte, e il fratel d'Aldabella, XXXIX/59
E capita in questi pochi giorni, XX/141
E cavalcando poi meglio la guata, IV/72
E ch'a difender la sua causa era atto, XXXXVI/108
E ch'al suo cavallier volea provallo, XX/114
E ch'esso era in speranza, pel valore, V/34
E ch'in bellezza et in valor cresciuto, XXXXI/64
E che 'l consiglio che mi dài, proceda, XXXXI/43
E che come Ruggier si faccia sano, XXXII/31
E che con esso lei s'era partito, XXX/77
E che con tante e con sì chiare note, X/2
E che facesse udir tanti metalli, XXXI/87
E che fatt'abbia ancor qualche disegno, XXXXV/29
E che guinta la sera ad un castello, XXXV/32
E che l'eletta ella de l'arme dona, XXXXV/24
E che la patria e 'l padre e duo fratelli, XXXVI/74
E che la porti per suo amore al collo, XXVIII/16
E che manco mal era meretrici, XX/24
E che meglio sarà di chieder pace, XI/47
E che n'andranno a piè pur tuttavia, XXXIII/76
E che non denno dubitare, andando, XXXXIII/188
E che non pur non l'abondoni mai, X/3
E che non si voleva indi partire, XXXXIII/79
E che nuotando un cavallier era ito, XI/60
E che per se medesime potuto, XXXVII/2
E che quel tradimento andrà sì occulto, XXXXI/62
E che quindici mila suoi vasalli, XV/64
E che Ravenna saccheggiata resta, XXXIII/41
E che sarebbe tal per studio e cura, XXXXIII/59
E che sia da se stesso senza caccia, XXXXV/9
E che spinto del regno, in duolo e in lutto, XXVII/126
E che traean con lor sopra un cavallo, XXXVII/88
E che venuta era la nuova certa, XXXXVI/51
E chi n'avea notizia, il riputava, VI/9
E chi saria quel cavallier, che questa, XX/122
E chi? -- Ferraù disse. Ella rispose:, XXXV/76
E chiama intenzione erronea e lieve, XXVIII/100

```
E circa il vespro, poi che rifrescossi, XI/11
E col mio quel del mio marito insieme, XXI/40
E colli e casse e ciò che v'è di grave, XIX/49
E come accade nel parlar sovente, XXXXIII/197
E come cavallier d'animo saldo, XXXXII/55
E come di splendore e di beltade, XXXV/5
E come egli aspettò, così gli avvenne, XXXXIII/121
E come il nuovo amor lo punge e scalda, XXIX/4
E come il padre mio parente e servo, Ss/17
E come la via nostra e il duro e fello, VI/35
E come menò seco una donzella, XXXVI/73
E come mi fu tolta lor narrai,/47
E come ne' begli occhi gli affisse, X/97
E come piu dormendo un ripa all'acque, XXV/48
E come qua su i corvi e gli avoltori, XXXV/20
E come quei che non sapean se l'una, I/23
E come quel ch'avea il paese noto, XXI/25
E come quel ch'avea il pensier ben fermo, XI/36
E come raccordògli il suo maestro, XXXVIII/30
E come sono inique e scelerate, VI/44
E come sotto il monte di Carena, XXXXI/27
E come uom d'alto e di sublime core, XXXXIV/91
E come vi compar quella guerriera, XXXV/41
E cominciò: -- Signor, io conducea, II/37
E cominciò: -- Signor, Lidia sono io, XXXIV/11
E commandò ch'a porta San Marcello, XVIII/39
E con chiari anitrir giù per quei calli, XXXVIII/34
E con gran gente, chi in arcion, chi a piede, XXXXIV/82
E con gran risa, aviluppati in quella, XV/45
E con gran tema fin dentro alle porte, XVIII/161
E con gran voce e con minaccie chiede, IX/71
E con la faccia in giù stesa sul letto, X/27
E con lui se ne vien verso le porte, XVI/15
E con mano e con piè quivi s'attacca, XXXX/24
E con migliore auspizio ecco ritorna, XXXIII/43
E con quel miglior modo ch'usar puote, XXXIV/33
E con quella ne vien nuotando in fretta, XI/41
E con tant'ira e tanto sdegno espresse, XXXXVI/58
E con una catena ne correa, IV/26
E conosciutol per Ruggier, non solo, XXXXVI/39
E coperto con man s'avrebbe il volto, X/99
E Corineo di Mulga, e Prusione, XV/7
E corre al mar, graffiandosi le gote, X/22
E corse senza indugio ad abbracciarlo, XXXXVI/60
E cosi cominciò la dura sorte, VIII/57
E così di disporre a poco a poco, XXIX/10
E così fu publicamente detto, XXXX/10
E così il fior de li begli anni suoi, VII/41
E così in una loggia s'apparecchia, XXXIII/125
E così la stracina, e la conforta, XXIX/71
E così, poi che fuor de la marea, IX/90
E così, poi che le astinenzie i voti, XXXX/12
E così quando al re, quando alla donna, XXVII/127
E così Ricciardetto; ma Aldigiero, XXVI/137
```

E così sia, -- Zerbin rispose; e volse, XX/126
E così tutte l'altre avean scritto anco, XXXIV/84
E così una galea fu apparechiata, XV/11
E crederò che Dio, perché vendetta, XI/28
E crescer abbia di sì piccol borgo, XXXXIII/61
E da lo sdegno e da la furia spinti, XXXIII/75
E da lui, da Vivian, da Malagigi, XXVI/136
E da parte il pregò d'una donzella, IX/19
E de la moglie sua, che così spesso, XXVIII/36
E de la regal casa, alata e sublime, XVII/10
E de le sue ferite ancora inferno, XXI/20
E dei lavoratori alla capanne, XXXXIII/107
E di ben modi e tanto graziosi, XXXXIII/73
E di due azze ha il duca Namo l'una, XXXVIII/80
E di fedeli e caste e sagge e forti, XXXVII/6
E di lor una s'accostò al cavallo, X/39
E di marmore un tempio ti prometto, XXXIII/116
E di mia man le fia più grato il dono, XXXV/43
E di panni di razza, e di cortine, XXXXIII/133
E di pregare ogni signore amante, XXIII/109
E di quel giovenile abito vòlse, XX/116
E di tua fama invidiosa, come, XXXVIII/16
E dice ch'egli vuol ch'un suo germano, IX/88
E dice che sicura ivi si stia, V/80
E dice: -- Con ciò sia ch'esser non possa, XXXXV/114
E dice: -- Se quel dì, Ruggier, ch'offeso, XXXXVI/40
E dicea ch'imitato avea il castore, XXVII/57
E dicea il ver; ch'era viltade espressa, XXV/31
E didioso di saper se fusse, XXXXI/25
E diede d'urto a chi venìa secondo, XIX/83
E dimandògli se per forza o patto, XXVII/56
E dimostrogli un luogo a dirimpetto, V/43
E Dio per questo fa ch'egli va folle, XXXIV/65
E dir di più vi voglio ancora, ch'esso, XXXVII/85
E dirgli: -- Orlando, fa che ti raccordi, XXXXII/14
E dirò prima di Ricciarda, degno, XIII/67
E dispregiando e nominando folle, VI/6
E disse a quella mesta: -- Io ti conforto, XXII/43
E disse e fece col villano in guisa, XXXXIII/80
E disse: -- O generosa Bradamante, III/9
E disse per lo giusto e per dritto, V/33
E dopo alquanti giorni in Natalia, XXII/6
E Doralice in mezzo il prato vede, XIV/50
E dove aspetta il suo Baiardo, passo, II/19
E dove col nocchier tenne via incerta, XXXXI/24
E dove non potea la debil voce, X/25
E due e tre volte ne l'orribil fronte, XXXXVI/140
E durò quella festa così poco, XVII/105
E fa, all'incontro, a lui Bologna torre, XXXIII/39
E fa gridarlo al suon degli oricalchi, XVII/113
E far esperienza se l'effetto, XVIII/134
E fatto sopra il Rodano tagliare, XXXIX/71
E fattosegli appresso, domandollo, XXIII/56
E fe' che 'l suo amator ratto soccorse, XXXI/75

```
E fece iscusa tal, che quel messaggio, II/66
E finita la mostra che faceano, X/76
E fra l'altre (che tante me ne disse, XXVII/139
E fu sempre il mio intento, et è, che m'ami, XXXXIV/55
E fuor di quel cespuglio oscuro e cieco, I/52
E furo altri infiniti in quello instante, XIV/74
E getta l'arco, e tutto pien di rabbia, XIX/15
E già, tratta la spada ch'avea cinta, VII/7
E gitto il carco, perché si pensava, XVIII/190
E giunse, traversando una foresta, XXII/11
E giunto poi di qua dal giogo, in parte, XXXVIII/32
E gli diè forza, che poté salire, XIX/25
E gli fa la medesima richiesta, XXXXIII/139
E gli menò Brunello, e gli ne fece, XXXII/7
E gli minaccia poi, se non consente, XXI/51
E gli mostrò quei sette re ch'io dissi, XXXXI/7
E gli narra del ponte periglioso, XXXI/63
E gli narrar che di Ruggier di Risa, XXXXIV/30
E gli narrò ch'Alzirdo e Manilardo, XIV/29
E gli offerisce, se la vuol vedere, XXXXIII/137
E gli vietò che con la propria mano, V/53
E in nome de le eterne tre Persone, XXXXIII/192
E inanzi agli altri, a lei provar lo vuole, XXXXV/104
E inanzi al re, quando era più di gente, V/63
E insanguinargli per tuttavia il fianco, XXXXVI/129
E la Bontà ineffabile, ch'invano, XIV/75
E la difficultà saria maggiore, XXVIII/10
E la donzella di nuovo consiglia, XIII/75
E la gente di Francia malaccorta, XXXIII/22
E la matina s'appresenta avante, XXXXIII/42
E la notte medesima mi trassi, V/71
E la roppe alla penna de lo scudo, XII/83
E lacrimando al ciel leva le mani, XXIII/50
E le dico che poco è questo dono, XXXXIII/37
E le diede la lettera che scrisse, XXVI/90
E le donzelle ch'avesson con loro, XXII/54
E le parve ch'andria con più possanza, XVIII/27
E le promette andar seco in Olanda, XI/73
E lei, che dato orecchie abbia, riprende, XXXXV/30
E li dispone in oportuni lochi, XIV/103
E lieta de l'insolita aventura, III/14
E lo facea; se non, tosto ch'al Sole, XXX/44
E lo lasciò con Alessandra bella, XX/58
E lo trovò ne la spelonca cava, XXXIII/93
E mai più non pigliar spada né lancia, XXXXI/49
E mandata glie l'ha fin a Constanza, XXXVII/91
E me, che tanto espressamente ha offeso, VI/12
E me so come, e te salvar non meno, XXXVII/67
E mentre a dietro il caccia o tiene a bada, XXXXII/57
E mentre or quinci or quindi invano il passo, XI/11
E mi vendero in Persia per ischiava, XXXVIII/15
E molte volte ripetendo seco, V/62
E molto più gli duol che sia in podesta, XXIII/66
E Moro e Sforza e Viscontei colubri, XIII/63
```

E movea sempre al mio fratello assalti, XXI/30
E narrò lor come il re Norandino, XVII/23
E ne la face de' begli occhi accende, XI/66
E nel fuoco gli accese di Vulcano, XII/2
E nel parer di Ferrau concorse, XII/55
E nel volto e nel petto e ne la coscia, XXXXI/84
E non avendo gioie o miglior pegni, III/36
E non lo bramo tanto per diletto, V/24
È ordine tra lor, che chi per sorte, XXII/55
E par che le suggiunga: -- Io son venuto, XXXIII/61
E parea dir: --- Pur hammi il signor mio, XXXXIII/156
E parimente fece ad Orrigille, XVIII/86
E per far questo avea gente infinita, XII/71
E per la fretta ch'ella n'ebbe, avenne, XVIII/111
E per mezzo gli fende la visiera, XXX/62
E per mostrar che veri i detti foro, XXXXIII/110
E, per narrarti il ver, sola mi mosse, XXXVIII/13
E per non fare in ciò lunga dimora, XXXXV/19
E per parer Leon, le sopraveste, XXXXV/69
E per potere entrare ogni sentiero, VIII/85
E per sua inclinazion (ch'assai l'amava), VI/15
E per un che ti sia fatto ribelle, XIV/71
E per venire a fin di questo amore, XXXXIII/75
E per vietar che simil la figliuola, XXXXIII/14
E perch'abbian più facile successo, XV/27
E perché dal re d'Africa battaglia, II/25
E perché del tornar la via sia tronca, XXXIV/46
E perché detto m'hai che con l'aiuto, XXXX/48
E perché dira Carlo in latino: -- Este, XXXXI/65
E perché era cortese, e n'evea forse, I/16
E perché essi non vadano pel mondo, VI/51
E perché gli facean poco mestiero, XXXXI/29
E perché i prieghi non v'avriano loco, XXXVII/49
E perché il luogo ben sapea (che v'era, XXVI/56
E perché molto dilungata s'era, VIII/32
E perché non andian (disse Ruggiero), XXII/47
E perché sa nuotar come una lontra, XXX/5
E perché so che ne l'antiquo nodo, XXXXIII/104
E perché tratto avean quell'arme a terra, XVIII/123
E perché vieta la diversa fede, XIII/10
E perdé amici a un tempo e vita e stato, VI/3
E perfido Ruggier di nuovo chiama, XXXVI/45
E però ne la guerra che gli mosse, XXXX/42
E più degli altri il frate di Viviano, XXXI/108
E più di tutti i bei ragionamenti, XIII/55
E poi ch'a salutar la nuova luce, XXV/94
E poi ch'al fin le parve esserne chiara, II/60
E poi ch'al trar de l'elmo conosciuto, V/91
E poi ch'avicinar questo drappello, XVIII/62
E poi ch'ella aspettato quasi un mese, VIII/90
E poi ch'invano il monaco interroppe, XXVIII/102
E poi che 'l nuovo sol lucido e chiaro, XVIII/104
E poi che 'ntese che commesso questo, XXIII/57
E poi che dal Cadi fu benedetto, XXXX/14

```
E poi che di confetti e di buon vini, VII/23
E poi che dilungati dal palagio, XII/34
E poi che esercitata si fu alquanto, IV/21
E poi che fin la lite lor non ebbe, XXXVI/27
E poi che'l tristo puzzo aver le parve, XVII/46
E poi che nota l'impietà vi fia, X/5
E poi che per stracciarlo e farne scempio, XXXVII/79
E poi che più lor fur fatti vicini, XXVI/10
E poi che venne il di chiaro e lucente, IX/5
E poi chiamar fece il figliuol di Buovo, XXXI/102
E poi ne fa due parti, e manda l'una, VIII/13
E portò nel cor fisso il suo compagno, XXI/56
E presso a Grillo, un Greco et un Tedesco, XVIII/177
E presso a un tempio ben murato e forte, XVIII/61
E presso ai paladini alcun perfetto, XXXIX/18
E presti o di morire, o di vendetta, XXXIII/68
E prima che più espresso io le lo chieggia, XXXXIV/69
E prima fa che 'l re con suoi baroni, XXXIII/124
E proponendo in mezzo i lor pareri, XX/23
E qual sagace can, nel monte usato, VIII/33
E quando a Clodion dormire incresca, XXXII/90
E quando anco mio padre a lui ritroso, XXXIV/28
E quando ancor fosse l'usanza tale, XXXII/105
E quando ritrovò la mia sirocchia, XXV/28
E quando sol, quando con poca gente, XXXIV/38
E quante volte uscirà giorno o notte, III/53
E quanto più aver obligo si possa, III/48
E quantunque miglio ne l'incantata, XXXXIV/17
E quei che furo a' nostri dì, o sono ora, XXXIII/2
E quel ch'a Chiariello e al re Mambrino, XX/6
E quel che già per messi ha ricercato, XXI/42
E quel che non avea potuto prima, IX/80
E quel s'armava, e se gli venìa a opporre, XXIX/36
E quella ai fiori, ai pomi e alla verzura, XXXIV/51
E quella notte in tenebrosa parte, XXIII/51
E questa opera fu del vecchio Atlante, IV/45
E questa più nocea che 'l ferro quasi, XIV/112
E queste et altre assai cose stupende, XXIX/57
E questo, Brandimarte, è questo il regno, XXXXIII/163
E questo con lo scudo e con la spada, XI/17
E questo hanno causato due fontane, I/78
E questo il primo fu di quei compagni, XXII/70
E questo, perch'essendo d'anni acerbo, XXXIII/109
È questo, quel che l'osservate stelle, VII/58
E qui si leva, e di nuovo l'abbraccia, XXXVIII/20
E quindi errando per tutto il paese, XXIV/13
E quindi per solingo e strano calle, XX/14
E quindi scenderà nel ricco piano, XXVI/45
E quindi van per mezzo la cittade, XIX/71
E quivi Adonio a comandare al cane, XXXXIII/108
E quivi appresso ove surgea una fonte, VI/24
E quivi s'incomincia una battaglia, XXXI/20
E quivi una caracca ritrovaro, XVIII/135
E replican con nuovi giuramenti, XXXIX/9
```

E riconobbe non men l'altre due, XXXVII/29
E ricordossi che passando avea, XIX/22
E ricordossi insieme de la prova, XXXXIII/65
E riferille le parole a pieno, XXX/78
E ripetendo i pianti e le querele, XXXXII/25
E riputato quel di ch'avea insegna, XVII/121
E ritrovar del lungo tratto il fine, XV/22
E riusciro in un burrone ascoso, III/65
E rivocando alla memoria l'arte, XIX/21
E Rodomonte e Mandricardo e insieme, XXVII/40
E s'a crudel, s'ad inumano effetto, XXXXII/2
E s'Alceste è mutato alle parole, XXXIV/34
E s'allor colentier fatto l'avrei, XXXXVI/42
E s'avranno in quel tempo, e se saranno, XXXVII/117
E s'ella lui Marte stimato avea, XXVI/24
E s'era altro ch'Orlando, l'avria fatto, XXXXI/96
E s'in altro potea gratificargli, XXI/69
E s'io avrò da narrarti di ciascuna, XIII/58
E s'ora o mai potrò questo dispetto, VI/31
E sanza aver rispetto ch'ella fusse, XXIII/120
E sanza più indugiar la spada stringe, XXV/11
E sapendosi già ch'era cristiano, XXXXIII/199
E sarà degno a cui Cesare Otone, III/27
E sarà in vostro arbitrio il restar anco, XIX/68
E saria sceso indi all testa, dove, XXXVI/57
E sarò pronto se tu vuoi ch'io guiri, V/32
E sarò sempremai, fin ch'io finisca, XXXVIII/51
E scapigliata e con la faccia rossa, XXI/21
E se 'l cognato non venìa ad aitarlo, XXXXII/17
E se 'l fratel di Ferraù, Isoliero, XIV/20
E se 'n ciò manco, subito s'accenda, XXXVIII/84
E se accarezza l'altra (che non puote, X/14
E se ben da principio il padre mio, XXXIV/27
E se ben era a lui venuta, mossa, XXXIV/29
E se ben per adietro io fossi stata, XX/43
E se bene all ingiuria et a quell'onta, XVIII/67
E se, come Rinaldo e come Orlando, XXVII/33
E se compiacer meglio mi volete, XXX/21
E se del tuo valor cerchi far prova, IV/57
E se di gloriò l'antiqua Creta, XXXIII/29
E se disposto sei volermel torre, IV/34
E se forse ti pensi che ti vaglia, III/68
E se fosse costei stata a Crotone, XI/71
E se gli avvien che 'l di gli uomini uccida, XX/59
E se gli è tuo voler ch'egli patisca, XIV/70
E se guadagni e perdite non sono, XXXII/106
E se l'arreca in spalla, e via la porta, XI/20
E se la prima pruova gli vien fatta, XIX/59
E se mai per adietro un nime chiaro, XXV/88
E se ne sdegno in guisa e se ne dolse, XIX/14
E se non che fu scarso il colpo alquanto, XXIV/65
E se non che la lancia non sostenne, XXXXVI/117
E se non era l'elmo più che buono, XXXIX/51
E se non fosse che senza dimora, XXV/65

E se non v'increscesse l'ascoltarmi, XXV/25
E se pur pascer voi fiere et augelli, XIX/12
E se questo mi nieghi, io dirò dunque, XXI/44
E se Rinaldo ben non era molto, XXXI/57
E se spirto a bastanza avrò nel petto, XXI/13
E se vorrà lodarne, avrà maggiore, XXVIII/78
E se vuoi che di te porti novella, XXXIV/10
E seco alquanti cavallieri avea, XVIII/189
E seguendo narrò di punto in punto, XXXXVI/63
E seguitando il suo parlar più inante, XXXXIV/11
E seguitando, del modo narrolle, VII/48
E seguitò con si efficaci prieghi, XXXXVI/33
E seguitò il santissimo eremita, XXXXI/54
E seguitò la donna fraudolente, XVI/13
E seguitò narrandogli in che guisa, XXXXIII/105
E seguitò narrandogli l'amore, VII/69
E seguitò, come egli avea veduto, V/65
E seguitò, narrandole de quello, XIII/49
E seguito, piu cose altro dicendo, XXXXV/48
E seguitò, voler cristiana farsi, XXXVIII/18
E senza disarmsi, sopra il letto, XXXII/36
E senza indugio e senza altro rispetto, XXIII/68
E senza più dimora, come pria, XXIV/113
E seppe che pel furto onde era degno, XXVII/87
E sequito con l'alma quella ch'era, XXI/66
E serbi da Gradasso anco nel fianco, XXXXI/93
E servo meglio questo giuramento, I/31
E sevaralle fin che vegga fatto, XXIX/18
E si come già a bocca le avea detto, XXV/89
E si come vezzosa era e mal usa, XX/113
E si crebbe la furia, che nel collo, XXIX/6
E si deliberò di non lasciarlo, IV/49
E si dispose al fina, da l'ira vinto, XXXXIII/122
E si lo rode la superbia e l'ira, XVIII/25
E si mostrò sì costumato allora, XXIX/9
E sì spesso dipinto di Zerbino, XX/136
E sì tre volte e più l'ira il sospinse, XVIII/23
E sia la pace e sia l'accordo fatto, XXXXIII/143
E similmente con parlar non basso, XXXVIII/86
E son chiamati cortigian gentili, XXXV/21
E sopra Luna ultimamente sorse, XX/101
E sopra ogn'altro error via più pentita, XIX/19
E sopra tutti gli altri incliti pregi, XIII/71
E sopra tutti gli altri io feci acquisito, XXXV/29
E sospirando: -- Ohimè, Fortuna fella, XX/132
E spesso vanno alle città murate, VIII/55
E stanco dimostrandosi e svogliato, XXXXV/85
E statuì nel publico conspetto, XVIII/95
E su la lancia nel partir si stringe, XVI/45
E sul lito del mar s'era condutto, XXXI/92
E svelse dopo il primo altri parecchi, XXIII/135
E talor anco che le torna a mente, XXXXV/31
E tanto gli occupò la fantasia, II/68
E tanto men prestar gli debbo fede, XXXVIII/43

E tanto più, ch'allor Rinaldo avrebbe, XXXXII/32
E tanto più, ch'era gran spazio in mezzo, V/50
E tanto stimulò, che lo dispose, XXXIV/21
E tenendo quel capo per lo naso, XV/87
E torna ad Olivier per dargli spaccio, XXXXI/89
E torno all'altra, che si raccomanda, XIII/43
E tosto l'avria giunto, se non era, XXVII/114
E tra Ginevra e l'amator suo pensa, V/22
E tra quei che vi son detti più forti, XIV/77
E tratto de la còlera, aventosse, XXVII/63
E trovar versi non tanto lugùbri, VIII/67
E trovò che la donna messaggiera, XXXIII/66
E tuttavia la còlera durando, XXXVII/81
E tutto a un tempo Balisarda stringe, XXVI/106
E una ricchezza appresso, et uno stato, IV/62
E vede l'oste e tutta la famiglia, IV/4
E vedendo le lacrime indefesse, XXXXIII/183
E venendo a guardargli più a minuto, XXVII/71
E venne con Grifon, con Aquilante, XXXI/51
E verso la città di Santo Andrea, V/76
E vi dovria pur ramentar che, solo, XXX/39
E vide Ibernia fabulosa, dove, X/92
E voglia la maggior gomona meco, XI/31
E volendo vedere una sirena, VI/40
E volendone a pien dicer gli onori, III/3
E volto a lei con più piacevol faccia, XX/140
Ebbe il destrier, che non trovò contesa, XXXXI/82
Ebbe lungo spettacolo il fedele, XXXX/2
Ebbe un ostro silocco allor possente, XVIII/74
Ebbile a pena mia domando esposta, XXV/64
Ebbon vittorie così sanguinose, XIV/2
Eccetto l'oste, fer tutti risposta, XXVII/135
Ecco Alessandro, il mio signor, Farnese, XXXXVI/13
Ecco altri duo Alessandri in quel drappello, XXXXVI/14
Ecco apparir lo smisurato mostro, X/100
Ecco (dicea) si pente Ludovico, XXXIII/31
Ecco il dotto, il fedele, il diligente, XXXXVI/18
Ecco in Italia Childiberto quanta, XXXIII/15
Ecco l'armata imperial se scioglie, XXXIII/57
Ecco la bella, ma più saggia e onesta, XXXXVI/5
Ecco levar ne la città si sente, IX/81
Ecco Luigi Borgognon, che scende, XXXIII/18
Ecco, mal grado de la lega, prenda, XXXIII/44
Ecco non lungi un bel cespuglio vede, I/37
Ecco pel bosco un cavallier venire, I/60
Ecco Rinaldo con la spada adosso, II/10
Ecco sono agli oltraggi, al grido, all'ire, XXIV/99
Ecco stridendo l'orribil procella, XXXXI/13
Ecco torna il Francese: eccolo rotto, XXXIII/42
Ecco un altro Azzo, et è quel che Verona, III/31
Ecco un altro Francesco ch'assimiglia, XXXIII/45
Ecco, volgendo il sol verso la sera, XXI/72
Eccovi fuor de la prima spelonca, III/22
Ed eran veramente, e sarian stati, XXXVII/47

Egli avea un'altra assai buona armatura, XXXXVI/120
Egli, ch'allato avea una tasca, aprilla, VIII/48
Egli che molto è offeso, piu che puote, XXV/18
Egli da la sua gente è sì temuto, XXXVII/80
Egli ha fatto offerire a Rodomonte, XXXII/5
Egli l'abbraccia et a piacer la tocca, VIII/49
Egli questi conforta, e quei riprende, XIV/128
Egli sul Pireneo tiene un castello, IV/7
Elbanio disse a lei: "Se di pietade, XX/40
Elena nominata era colei, XXXXVI/83
Elissabetta l'una, e Leonora, XXXXII/86
Ella avea ancora indossa la gonnella, XXIII/93
Ella avea fatto nel palazzo inanti, XX/81
Ella ch'auito cerca, e non conforto, XXV/39
Ella che di Zerbin sa l'odio a pieno, XXI/71
Ella, come si stima, e come in vero, XXXII/53
Ella d'esser odiata impaziente, XXXXIII/46
Ella dal di che Ferraù li prese, XXV/75
Ella disse a Guidon: -- Vientene insieme, XX/70
Ella è gagliarda, et è più bella molto, I/70
Ella era bella e costumata tanto, XXXXIII/18
Ella gli fece dar tante repulse, XXXXIII/34
Ella gli rende conto pienamente, I/55
Ella ha ben fama d'esser forte a pare, XXXVI/14
Ella non ebbe sdegno, da che nacque, X/49
Ella non gli era facile, e talmente, VII/43
Ella non sa, se non invan dolersi, XXIV/77
Ella, prima ch'avere altro consorte, XXXXV/96
Ella riman d'ogni vigor sì vòta, XXXXVI/66
Ella sapea d'incanti e di malie, XXXXIII/21
Ella si mostra tutta leita, e finge, XXXVII/61
Ella si volta, e contra l'abbattuto, XXXV/50
Ella t'insegnerà studii più grati, X/47
Ella venìa cercando un cavalliero, XXXV/34
Ella volgea i begli occhi a terra invano, VIII/37
Elle era tale; e come imposto fummi, XXII/2
Elle fur d'odio, elle fur d'ira tanta, XXXVII/93
Entra nel folto bosco, ove più spesse, XXXXV/92
Entrar nel portao remorchiando, e a forza, XIX/63
Entrato il gregge, l'Orco a noi descende, XVII/49
Entrato ne la ròcca, trova quella, XXXII/88
Entrò la bella donna in Montalbano, XXIII/24
Entrò Marfisa s'un destrier leardo, XIX/77
Entrò ne la battaglia il re Agramante, XVI/75
Era a parar, più ch'a ferire, intento, XXXVIII/90
Era a periglio di morire Orlando, XXIV/11
Era a quel tempo ivi una selva antica, XVIII/192
Era ancor sul fiorir di primavera, XXVIII/53
Era come un liquor suttile e molle, XXXIV/83
Era con lui quella fanciulla, quella, XXIII/54
Era constui quel paladin gagliardo, I/12
Era Corebo di Bilboa nomato, XIII/24
Era cortese il re di Sericana, XXXI/101
Era così incantato quello albergo, XII/32

Era costei la bella Fiordiligi, XXXI/47
Era Dudon sopra la spiaggia uscito, XXXX/72
Era, fuor che la testa, tutto armato, I/26
Era giovane Alzirdo, et arrogante, XII/75
Era il bel viso suo, quale esser suole, XI/65
Era in quel clima già sparito il giorno, XV/74
Era in quel tempo in Tracia un cavalliero, XXXIV/16
Era l'un sano e pien di nuovo sdegno, XXI/26
Era la notte, e non si vedea lume, XXXX/6
Era la sopraveste del colore, XXXII/47
Era la volontà de la donzella, XXXXV/70
Era ne l'ora, che traea i cavalli, XII/68
Era presso alla grotta in ch'egli stava, XVII/34
Era quel vecchio sì espedito e snello, XXXIV/92
Era questa una donna che fu molto, VIII/89
Era questo guerrier quel Mandricardo, XXIII/71
Era Rinaldo molto ben veduto, VIII/22
Era Ruggier dal dì che giunse a nuoto, XXXXIII/195
Era scritto in arabico, che 'l conte, XXIII/110
Era sì baldanzoso il creder mio, XXVI/59
Era ugualmente il principe d'Anglante, XII/49
Era una de le fonti di Merlino, XXVI/30
Era venuto pochi giorni avante, XIV/30
Eragli meglio andar senz'arme e nudo, XVII/118
Eramo a caso sopra Capobasso, V/59
Eran con la regina di Castiglia, XXVII/51
Eran degli anni appresso che duo milia, XXXXVI/80
Eran degli anni ormai presso a quaranta, XXXXI/58
Eran giovani tutti e belli affatto, XX/16
Eran tre cavallier che valean tanto, XXXII/72
Erane amante, e perché le sue voglie, V/64
Erano pastorali alloggiamenti, XIV/62
Erano questi duo sopra i ripari, XVIII/167
Erano sette in una schiera, e tutte, XXXIII/120
Erasi consigliato il re africano, XXXIX/77
Ercole or vien, ch'al suo vicin rinfaccia, III/46
Ermonide d'Olanda segnò basso, XXI/10
Errando giunse ad una ombrosa fonte, XXV/27
Escluso Clodione e malcontento, XXXII/91
Essendo Astolfo paladin, comprende, XXXIX/24
Essendo la battaglia in questo stato, XVIII/41
Essendo la battaglia in tale istato, XXXXI/86
"Esser di ciò argumento ti poss'io, XVII/41
Esser per certo déi pazzo solenne, XIV/42
Essi che di guadagno e di rapine, XX/21
Essi, vedendo il re che di veneno, XVIII/117
Estimasi il fratel, che dolor abbia, XXVIII/25
Et a Gabrina dice che l'aspetee, XXIII/41
Et ad un altro suo diede negozio, XXVII/15
Et al figlio d'Amon, che già rivolto, XXXI/15
Et all'incontro vuol che 'l re prometta, IX/63
Et alla donna, a cui dagli occhi cade, XXII/44
Et alla mensa, ove la Copia fuse, XXV/80
Et altri cavallieri e de la nuova, IV/53

Et altri, ch'a cadere  andò nel mare, XXIX/7
Et alzando la man nuda e senz'arme, XVIII/66
Et avea ne lo scudo e sul cimiero, VII/5
Et avendosi piene ambe le palme, XXXIX/26
Et Azzo, il fuo fratel, lascierà erede, III/37
Et è ben degno che sì ricca donna, XXXVII/11
Et ecco de la porta con gran fretta, XXII/59
Et egli tra baroni e paladini, XIV/69
Et ella, alzando i begli umidi rai, XXII/38
Et ella ch'ogni dì gli venìa al letto, XXXVI/82
Et ella, conosciuto che Bardino, XXXIX/41
Et eran poi venuti ove il destriero, XXVII/70
Et hanno appresso quel secondo Marte, XXXVIII/55
Et ho possanzo far cose stupende, XXV/62
Et impetra per me dal Signor nostro, XXXVII/74
Et in desperazion continua il messe, XXXIII/112
Et io con veste candida, e fregiata, V/47
"Et io (rispose Ariodante a lui), V/29
Et ode come avendo già di quella, XXXXII/36
Et oltra a questi et altri ch'oggi avete, XXXVII/14
Et oltre al mio destino, io ci fui spinta, XXXII/24
Et or gli ha messo il cauto Saracino, XVIII/175
Et or, perch'abbia il Magno Carlo aiuto, XXXI/58
Et un Marco Cavallo, che tal fonte, XXXXII/91
Et un per cui la terra, ove l'Isauro, XXXXII/89
Ezellino, immanissimo tiranno, III/33


F

Fa che sia tua la prima, e che si tolga, XXVII/60
Fa, giunto ne la patria, il primo volo, XXXXIII/117
Fa lunghi i passi, e sempre in quel di dietro, XXVIII/63
Fa ne l'animo suo proponimente, XXIX/11
Fa questi voti a Dio, debiti a lui, XXXIII/118
Fa Vittor Fausto, fa il Tancredi festa, XXXXVI/19
Faccio o nol faccio? Al fin mi par che buono, XXV/51
Facea Oliviero, Orlando e Bradimarte, XXXX/21
Facea parer questa medesma causa, XXVI/19
Facemmo, come sai, triegua con patto, XXVI/85
Fai ch'a Rinaldo Angelica par bella, II/2
Fan legare il gigante alla verdura, XV/77
Fanno le statue in mezzo un luogo tondo, XXXXII/96
Fanno or con lunghi, ora con finti e scarsi, II/9
Fannosi i dolci miei disegni amari, XXVIII/58
Fansi le nozze splendide e reali, XXXXVI/73
Farà de' suoi ribelli uscire a vòto, III/43
Farà Ruggiero il debito a tornare, XXXVIII/6
Farà strage crudel, né sarà loco, XXVI/42
Farei (disse Aldigier) teco, o volessi, XXVI/5
Farò che gli altri Nubi che da loro, XXXX/50
Fatta da mastro diligente e dotto, XXXXII/79
Fatto avea farsi alla sua fata intanto, XXXXIII/132
Fatto avea intanto il re Agramante sciorre, XXXIX/73

Fatto disegno l'ippogrifo torsi, XXII/28
Fatto è 'l porto a sembianza d'una luna, XIX/64
Fatto il pensier: "Dalinda mia, mi dice, V/23
Fatto in quel tempo con Ariodante, V/27
Fatto l'avea ne la gran sala porre, XXXII/95
Fattosi appresso al nudo scoglio, quanto, XI/33
Fe' la mattina la donzella altiera, XXXXV/103
Fe' quattro brevi porre: un Mandricardo, XXVII/45
Fece Aquilante lor scudieri e some, XVIII/87
Fece disegno Brandimarte, il giorno, XXXXI/31
Fece la donna di sua man le sopra, XXXXI/32
Fece morir diece persone e diece, XXIV/10
Fece Rinaldo per maggior spavento, XXXI/53
Fece Ruggiero il debito a seguire, XXXVIII/5
Feci col core e con l'effetto tutto, V/16
Feci la pruova ancor de le donzelle, XX/8
Federico, ch'ancor non ha la guancia, XXXIII/46
Ferì negli occhi l'incantato lume, X/110
Ferì quel di Selucia all visera, XVII/102
Ferirsi alla visiera al primo tratto, XXX/50
Ferirsi alla visiera, ch'era doppia, XXX/51
Fermasi a riguardar che fine avere, XXIX/45
Fermava il piè ciascun di questi segni, XXXXII/81
Fermossi alquanto Cloridano, e disse, XVIII/173
Fero ad Ullania et alle damigelle, XXXVII/37
Fersi le nozze sotto all'umil tetto, XIX/34
Festi, barbar crudel, del capo scemo, XXXVI/9
Figlia d'Amone e di Beatrice sono, XXXXIV/44
Fin a quell'ora avean quel di vedute, XXXIX/11
Fin ch'ella un giorno ai neghitosi figli, XXXIV/3
Fin che quel non avea, che 'l paladino, XII/31
Fin che venimmo a questa isola bella, VI/43
Fin sul collo al destrier Ruggier s'inchina, XXVI/117
Finge ella teco, né t'ama né prezza, V/37
Finì il parlare insieme con al vita, XXXVII/75
Finir quel giuoco tosto, e molto inanzi, VII/22
Finita, ch'ella fu (che saria forse, XXXII/110
Finita che d'accordo è poi la guerra, XX/17
Finita la battaglia di quel giorno, XXXXIV/96
Finito ch'ebbe Almonio il suo sermone, XXIV/29
Finito ch'ebbe la lodevol opra, XXIV/58
Fiordiligi cercando pure invano, XXIV/74
Fiordiligi, che mal vede difesa, XXIV/73
Fiordiligi lei mira, e veder parte, XXXV/35
Fisse locondo alla partitia il giorno, XXVIII/12
Fisso nel tronco lo transporta in terra, V/89
Fora de la corazza il lato manco, XXX/64
Fornito a punto era l'ottavo mese, XXII/72
Fornito questo, il vecchio s'era messo, XXI/64
Forse era ver, ma non però credibile, I/56
Forse era vero augel, ma non so dove, XXXIII/85
Forse fu da Dio vindice permesso, XXXXII/5
Fortuna mi tirò fuor del camino, XXV/60
Fortuna sempremai la via lor tolse, XVIII/58

Forza è a Marfisa ch'a quel colpo vada, XXXVI/20
Forza è ch'al fin nell'acqua il cavallo entre, XXX/12
Fra cento alme città ch'erano in Creta, XX/15
Fra duo guerrieri in terra et uno in cielo, II/54
Fra duo montagne entrò in un stretto calle, XXII/4
Fra gli altri che giacean vede la donna, XXII/89
Fra il suon d'argute trompe e di canore, XXXXIV/34
Fra l'Adice e la Brenta a piè de' colli, XXXXI/63
Fra l'una e l'altra gamba di Fiammetta, XXVIII/64
Fra mille colpi il Tartaro una volta, XXIV/102
Fra molti ch'al servizio erano stati, IX/37
Fra piacer tanti, ovunque un arbor dritto, XIX/36
Fra quanti amor, fra quante fede al mondo, X/1
Fra sé discorre, e vede che supplire, XXXXV/54
Fra tanti e innumerabili capelli, XV/86
Francesco, il terzo; Alfonsi gli altri dui, III/59
Frettoloso, or da questo or da quel canto, X/115
Frontino or per via dritta or per via torta, XXXXV/86
Fu 'l re di Feza ad esquir ben presto, XVI/77
Fu allora per uscir del sentimento, XXIII/112
Fu Bucifar de l'algazera morto, XXXX/35
Fu conclusa la triegua fra costoro, XXIV/115
Fu d'Artemia crudel questo il parere, XX/54
Fu da l'autorità d'un uom si degno, V/85
Fu da molti pensier ridutto in forse, XXV/6
Fu grande il salto, non però di sorte, XXVI/130
Fu grave e mala aggiunta all'altro danno, XI/14
Fu Grifon tratto a gran vergogna in piazza, XVII/131
Fu il colpo di Ruggier di sì gran forza, XXVI/123
Fu il vincer sempremai laudabil cosa, XV/1
Fu la notte seguente a prova messo, XX/57
Fu morta da Troian (non so se 'l sai), XXX/83
Fu ne la donna ogni allegrezza spenta, XXXI/76
Fu ne la terra il paladin condutto, IX/21
Fu posto in chiesa; e poi che da le donne, XXXXIII/181
Fu quasi il re Agramante abbandonato, XXXIX/66
Fu quel che piacque, un falso sogno; e questo, SS/62
Fu quel da Montalbano il primo a dire, XXXI/26
Fu questo colpo del pagan maggiore, XXIV/67
Fu repulso dal re, ch'in grande stato, XXXIV/19
Fu Ruggier primo e Gianbaron di questi, XXXVI/72
Fu tal risposta un venenato telo, XXXXIII/39
Fu voluntà di Dio che non venisse, XI/30
Fugge Agramante, et ha con lui Sobrino, XXXX/9
Fugge Baiardo all vicina selva, XXXIII/88
Fugge il populo in rotta, che non scorge, IX/82
Fugge tra selve spaventose e scure, I/33
Fuggendo, posso con dinor salvarmi, XV/47
Fuggesi Alcina, e sua misera gente, X/55
Fuggì il guardian coi suo' prigioni; e dopo, XXII/22
Fuggita me ne son per non vedere, XXII/41
Fummo gittati a salvamento al lito, XIII/18
Fuor che queste tre volte, tutto 'l resto, XXII/83
Fuor de la grotta il vecchio Proteo, quando, XI/44

Fur benedetti dal vecchio devoto, XXXXIV/18
Fur molti che temer che 'l fier Grifone, XVIII/7
Fur tutti gli altri che nel mar si diero, XXXXI/51
Furo al segnar degli aspri colpi, pari, XVI/46
Furo tutti i ripar, fu la cittade, XVIII/13
Furon di quei ch'eaver poteano in fretta, XXXIX/20


G

Gente infinita poi di minor conto, XV/9
Getta da' merli Andropono e Moschino, XIV/124
Getta il pagan lo scudo, e a duo man prende, XIV/122
Già con mia moglie avendo simulato, XXXXIII/35
Già dietro rimarsi erano e perduti, X/16
Già in mai presenza e d'altre più persone, XXI/60
Già in ogni parte gli animanti lassi, VIII/79
Gia l'un da l'altro è dipartito lunge, XXIII/82
Già la lancia avea tolta su la coscia, XVII/93
Già mi vivea di mia sorte felice, XIII/5
Già mosso prima era Dudon; ma quando, XXXX/77
Gia non fero i cavalli un correr torto, I/63
Già non poté fuggir quindi il nocchiero, XXXIX/33
Già non vòlse Marfisa imitar l'atto, XXXII/6
Già non vuol che lo vegga il re improviso, XXVIII/29
Gia potreste sentir coe rimbombe, XXIV/8
Gia, quando prima s'erano alla vista, XIX/62
Già s'inchinava il sol molto alla sera, XXXXII/70
Gia scale innumerabili per questo, XIV/67
Già sendo in atto di partir, s'udiro, XXXVII/87
Già son cresciute e fatte lunghe in modo, XXXII/81
Già son le lor querele differite, XXVI/68
Giace in Arabia una valletta amena, XIV/92
Giace tra l'altro fiume e la palude, XV/49
Giacea non lungi da Parigi un loco, XXVII/47
Giaceva Pinabello in terra spento, XXIII/40
Giodon, ch'altrove avria fatto gran festa, XX/67
Giovane e bella ella si fa con arte, VII/74
Gira una piazza al sommo de la terra, XIX/76
Gittaro i tronchi, e si tornaro adosso, XVII/101
Gittò Leone al cavallier le braccia, XXXXV/83
Giunge Orlando a Dordreche, e quivi truova, IX/61
Giunge più inanzi, e ne ritrova molti, XXVII/21
Giungean da l'una pate i Maganzesi, XXVI/12
Giunse a punto Ruggier, che si facea, X/75
Giunse ch'a punto il principe d'Anglante, XXXXIII/151
Giunse il giorno seguente a Basilea, XXXXII/68
Giunseno in somma onde vedeano al basso, XXXVII/98
Giunsero al loco il dì che si dovea, XXV/96
Giunsero il dì medesmo, come accade, XXII/52
Giunsero in piazza, e trassonsi in disparte, XVII/72
Giunsero taciturni ad una fonte, XXIII/67
Giunte al timore, al dubbio ch'avea prima, XXXXIII/89
Giunte son quattro donne in su la spiaggia, X/52

Giunti che fur, correndo, ove i sentieri, XII/38
Giunto Carlo all'altar che statuito, XXXVIII/82
Giunto, lo fa alloggiat nel suo palagio, XXVIII/31
Giunto Sobrin de le sue piaghe a tanto, XXXXIII/193
Giurar lo fe' che né per cosa detta, XXVIII/41
Gl'insidiosi ferri eran vicini, XVIII/181
Gli agricultori, accorti agli altrui' esempli, XXIV/7
Gli altri ch'erano intorno, e che vantarsi, XXVII/86
Gli altri tre cavallier de la fortezza, XXII/76
Gli amorosi tormenti che sostenne, XXX/76
Gli archi di sopra escono fuor del segno, XXXXII/76
Gli avea riconosciuti egli non manco, XXXI/40
Gli diede a prima giunta ella di piglio, XXVII/89
Gli duol che gli altri cavallieri ancora, XX/68
Gli è di morir disporto; ma che sorte, XXXXV/59
Gli è meglio una trvarne che di faccia, XXVIII/50
Gli è questo creder mio, come io l'avessi, XXXXIII/66
Gli è teco cortesia l'esser villano, XXVII/77
Gli è tempo ch'io ritorni ove lasciai, XV/10
Gli è ver (dicea) che s'uom si ritrovasse, XIX/67
Gli è ver (risipose il re) che mi fur date, XVIII/129
Gli è ver che 'l negromante venuto era, XV/68
Gli è ver che si smarriro in faccia alquanto, XII/93
Gli è ver ti bisogna altro viaggio, XXXIV/67
Gli fu nel primier odio ritornata, XXXXII/67
Gli imbasciatori bulgari che in corte, XXXXVI/69
Gli mostra come egli abbia a far, se vuole, X/67
Gli orro che dianzi avean col mondo impresa, XVII/104
Gli par ch'avendo in mano il cavalliero, IX/64
Gli parve il luogo a fornir ciò disposto, XIII/11
Gli ritornano a mente le promesse, XXXXI/48
Gli sdegni, le repulse, e finalmente, XXXI/4
Gli sopravenne a caso una donzella, XIX/17
Gli sparve, come io dico, ella davante, XII/59
Gli sprona contra in questo dir, ma prima, XXXVI/35
Gli uomini d'arme e gli arcieri a cavallo, X/82
Gli va gli occhi alle man spesso voltando, III/77
Gradasso disperato, che si vede, XXXXI/95
Gradasso ha mezzo Orlando disarmato, XXXXI/94
Gran cose e molte in brevi detti accolgo, XIII/61
Gran maraviglia di sì strano caso, XXXXII/31
Gran maraviglia, et indi gran desire, XXXXIII/109
Grande è l'ardir del Tartaro, che vado, XIV/44
Grande ombra d'ogn'intorno il ciel involve, XVI/57
Grandi eran l'ale e di color diverso, IV/5
Grandine sembran le spesse saette, XVI/19
Grandonio di Volterna furibondo, XXXV/69
Grata ebbe la venuto di Iocondo, XXVIII/30
Grato era al re, più grato era alla figlia, V/18
Gravi pene in amor si provan molte, XVI/1
Grida Aquilante, e fulminar non resta, XVIII/81
Grida che si ritiri ognun da canto, XXXX/76
Grida la voce orribile: -- Non sia, XXXVI/59
Grifon che poco a cor avea quell'arme, XVIII/131

Grifon, che 'l vede in sella, e cho non basta, XVII/95
Grifon gagliardo duo ne piglia in quella, XVIII/6
Grifon, vedendo il re fatto benigno, XVIII/69
Grifone, appresso a questi, in terra getta, XVII/99
Grifone intanto avea fatto ritorno, XVII/106
Grifone, o ch'egli o che 'l cavallo fosse, XVII/108
Guardatevi da questi che sul fiore, X/7
Guardati, Carlo, che 'l ti viene adosso, XXVII/7
Guicciardo pone incontinente in resta, XXXI/11
Guido, Ranier, Ricardo, Salamone, XVIII/10
Guidon, che questo esser Rinaldo udio, XXXI/30
Guidon la notte con Aleria parla, XX/80
Guidon lo segue, e non fa men di lui, XXXI/55
Guidon qui fine alle parole pose, XX/65
Guidone e gli altri cavallier gagliardi, XX/86


H

Ha ben di darlo al conte intenzione, XII/53
Ha fatto il re bandir, per liberala, V/68
Ha sempre in mente, e mai non se ne parte, XXXXII/45
Hagli commesso il santo evangelista, XXXXIV/25
Hai sentito, signor, con quanti effetti, V/72
Ho notizia d'un'erba, e l'ho veduta, XXIX/15
Ho sacramento di non ciger spada, XXIII/78


I

I Bulgari sin qui fatto avean testa, XXXXIV/84
I camarier discreti et aveduti, XXV/86
I capitani e il cavallier robusti, III/18
I cariaggi e gli altri impedimenti, XVI/31
I cavallier, di giostra ambi maestri, XXXI/69
I cavallier di pregio e di gran pruova, XVIII/119
I cavallier domandano a Giodone, XX/9
I cavallieri di nazion diverse, XVIII/115
I cavallieri e insieme quei ch'a piede, XXII/87
I cavallieri stavano e Marfisa, XXVI/37
I conforti d'Ippalca, e la speranza, XXX/85
I Cretesi in quel tempo, che cacciato, XX/14
I descendenti suoi di qua dal Faro, XXXVI/71
I duo campion che vedeno turbarsi, XXXIX/8
I duo cavalli andar con tutto 'l pondo, XXXI/71
I duo ch'in mezzo avean preso Odorico, XXIV/18
I duo che mostran disiosi affetti, XXXXII/85
I duo di Chiaramonte e il buon Ruggiro, XXVI/9
I giuramenti e le promesse vanno, X/6
I Greci son quattro contr'uno et hanno, XXXXIV/81
I mezzi, o che non abbiano potuto, IX/49
I Mori fur quel giorno in gran periglio, XVIII/156
I naviganti a dimostrare effetto, XVIII/143
I Nubi d'ogni indugio impazienti, XXXX/18

I pastor che sentito hanno il fracasso, XXIII/136
I patroni a veder strade a palazzi, XXVIII/55
I quattro primi si trocaro insieme, XXVII/17
I rilevati fianchi e le belle anche, XI/69
I simulacri inferiori in mano, XXXXII/82
I tre guerrieri arditi si fermaro, XXV/97
I tronchi fin al ciel ne sono ascesi, XXX/49
I vincitori uscir de le funeste, XXXX/34
Il batter de le mani, il grido intorno, XVII/91
Il buon Rinaldo, il quale a porre in terra, XVI/84
Il buon Turpin, che sa che dice il vero, XXVI/23
Il buono ostier, che fu dei diligenti, XXVII/132
Il capo, il re de' Bulgari Vatrano, XXXXIV/83
Il castellan, senza ch'alcun de' sui, XXXXV/44
Il cavallier buon conto ne rendette, XXXII/29
Il cavallier che con Rinaldo viene, XXXXII/62
Il cavallier d'Anglante, ove più spesse, IX/68
Il cavallier di Spagne, che venuto, XII/58
Il cavallier, perché da lei beffato, XXII/50
Il cavallier, poi ch'alla scura buca, XXXXII/58
Il cavallier su ben guernita sella, XX/110
Il cavallo del Tartaro, ch'aborre, XXIV/105
Il chiaro lume lor, ch'imita il sole, X/60
Il conforto ch'io prendo, è che di quanti, XXXXIII/44
Il conte d'Arindelia è quel c'ha messo, X/80
Il conte si risente, e gli occhi gira, XXXXI/102
Il conte tuttavia dal capo al piede, XXIII/77
Il cortese Leon che Ruggiero ama, XXXXV/42
Il creder d'aver seco il re d'Algieri, XXXIX/7
Il dì seguente, alla medesima ora, XXVIII/37
Il desiderio che conduce Ippalca, XXVI/67
Il destrier, ch'avea andar trito e soave, XIX/81
Il destrier di Marfisa in un voltarsi, XXVI/125
Il destrier la magnanima guerriera, XXXV/72
Il destrier punto, ponta i piè all'arena, X/112
Il dì seguente la sua armata spinse, XXXIX/64
Il disleal con le ginocchia in terra, XXIV/30
Il dolce sonno mi promise pace, XXXIII/63
Il don ch'io bramo da l'Altezza vosta, XXXXIV/70
Il duca Astolfo e la compagnia bella, XXXIX/36
Il duca, come al fin trasse l'impresa, XV/91
Il falcon che sul nido i vanni inchina, X/81
Il falso amante che i pensati inganni, X/19
Il fante domandò dove ella gisse, XXVIII/57
Il gentil cavallier, non men giocondo, XXXIX/43
Il giovanetto con piedi e con braccia, XXXXI/47
Il giovine che 'l pazzo seguir vede, XXIX/62
Il giovinetto si rivolse a' prieghi, XIX/11
Il giudice, sì come io vi dicea, XXXXIII/134
Il giusto Dio, quando i peccati nostri, XVII/1
Il grande amor di questa bella coppia, III/51
Il grave odor che la palude esala, XVIII/137
Il guerrier peregrin conobbe quello, XXXI/28
Il legno sciolse, e fe' scioglier la vela, XXXXI/8

```
Il magno imperator, fuor che la testa, XXVII/20
Il manigoldo, in loco inculto et ermo, XXXII/9
Il medesmo desir Marfisa avea, XXXIX/68
Il merigge facea grato l'orezzo, XXIII/101
Il mesto conte a piè quivi discese, XXIII/107
Il miglior cavallier, che spada a lato, XXXXVI/24
Il minacciare e il por mano alla spada, XXII/74
Il mio buon padre, al qual sol piacea quanto, IX/27
Il mio voler cercare oltre alla meta, XXXXIII/45
Il monaco, ch'a questo avea l'orecchia, XXVIII/101
Il mordace parlare, acre et acerbo, XXXV/71
Il mostro al petto il serpe ora gli appicca, XXXXII/50
Il mutar spesso de le piante ha vista, XXXIV/45
Il negro fumo de la scura pece, XXXIV/47
Il nocchier cominciò: -- Già fu di questa, XXXXIII/72
Il nocchier suggiungea: -- Ben gli dicesti, XXXXIII/69
Il nome mio fu Astolfo; e paladino, VI/33
Il non aver saputo che s'asconda, VI/30
Il padron narrò lui che quella riva, XIX/57
Il pagan ferì lui dal lato manco, XXVI/76
Il paladin col suono orribil venne, XXXIV/4
Il palafren ch'avea il demonio al fianco, XXVII/5
Il palafren, ch'udito di lontano, XXIV/36
Il pianto e 'l grido insino al ciel saliva, XX/91
Il più cortese cavallier che mai, XXXXVI/81
Il popul la donzella nel paterno, IX/86
Il popul tutto al vil Martano infesto, XVIII/88
Il pozzo è cavo, e pieno al sommo d'acque, XXII/93
Il primo d'essi, uom di spietato viso, XIII/33
Il primo fu Ruggier, ch'andò per terra, XXX/67
Il primo giorno e l'ultimo, che pugno, XXVI/93
Il principe ch'io dico, ch'era, in vece, VIII/28
Il qual con gran fatica, ancor ch'aiuto, XXXXVI/47
Il qual mandato, l'un a l'altro appresso, XXXXVI/22
Il qual poi che far pruove in campo vidi, XIII/7
Il qual, poi che mutato ebbe d'Almonte, VIII/91
Il qual, se sarà ver, come tu parli, XXIII/36
Il quarto giorno un cavallier trovaro, XX/117
Il re african, ch'era con gran famiglia, XXXV/68
Il re Agramante al parer lor s'attenne, XXXI/84
Il re Agramante all'oriente avea, XXXX/43
Il re Agramante andò per porre accordo, XXVII/103
Il re Agramante d'Africa uno annello, III/69
Il re Agramante in questo mezzo in sella, XVIII/40
Il re Agramante volentier s'attenne, XXVII/99
Il re, ch'intanto cerca di sapere, V/70
Il re, ch'ogn'altra cosa, se non questa, XXVIII/42
Il re chiede al Circasso, che ragione, XXVII/84
Il re circasso il suo destrier non vuole, XXVII/83
Il re d'Algier che si risente in questo, XXVI/127
Il re d'Ibernia, ancor che fosse Orlando, XI/61
Il re de Svezia, che primier si mosse, XXXII/76
Il re di Sarza, che gran tempo prima, XXVII/105
Il re disse al compagno mottegiando, XXVIII/66
```

```
Il  re, dolente per Ginevra bella, IV/60
Il  re e Iocondo si guardaro in viso, XXVIII/71
Il  re gagliardo si difende a piede, XXXIII/53
Il  re Gradasso, che lasciar non volle, XXXI/103
Il  re Luigi, suocero del figlio, XXXXV/3
Il  re Marsilio che sta in gran paura, XXXIX/74
Il  re pagan, ch'avea più l'asta dura, XXVI/74
Il  re s'Algier, perché gli sopravenne, XXVII/130
Il  re volta le spalle, e signor lassa, IX/72
Il  resto dì quel di, che da l'accordo, XXX/26
Il  rimembrare Almonte così accese, XVIII/52
Il  rumor scorse di costui per tutto, V/61
Il  santo vecchiarel ne la sua stanza, XXXXIV/4
Il  Saracin non avea manco sdegno, XXVII/125
Il  Saracino ogni poter vi mette, XXIII/87
Il  seguente matin, senza far motto, V/56
Il  servo del Signor del paradiso, XXXXIII/190
Il  servo in pugno avea un augel grifagno, VIII/4
Il  signor de la casa allora alquanto, XXXXII/99
Il  signor de la ròcca, che venìa, XXXIII/25
Il  signor di Seleucia ancor restava, XVII/100
Il  signor di Seleucia, di quell'uno, XVII/87
Il  signor nostro intanto ritornato, XVII/36
Il  Sole a pena avea il dorato crine, XVII/129
Il  sommo Creator gli occhi rivolse, VIII/70
Il  suo camin (di lei chiedendo spesso), XII/86
Il  suo destrier ch'avea continuo uso, XXXI/68
Il  termine ch'Orlando aspettar disse, XXIV/48
Il  termine passò d'uno, di dui, XXXII/17
Il  terzo giorno con maggior dispetto, XIX/47
Il  timor del supplicio infame e brutto, XXI/55
Il  traditore intanto dar parole, IX/65
Il  travaglio del mare e la paura, X/18
Il  tuo comapgno ha l'onor mio distrutto, XXI/24
Il  valor di ciasun meglio si puote, XXXX/22
Il  vantator Spagnuol disse: -- Gia molte, XII/44
Il  vedermi lograr dei miglior anni, XX/63
Il  vedersi coprir del brutto scoglio, XXXXIII/99
Il  vedervi cader causò il dolore, XXXXII/4
Il  venerabile uom, ch'alta bontade, XXIV/88
Il  vostro Orlando, a cui nascendo diede, XXXIV/63
Imagini ch'Orlando fosse tale, XXXIX/53
Imita quasi la superba mole, XXIX/33
In abito succinta era Marfisa, XXVII/52
In altra parte i liberali spassi, XXXXVI/91
In altra parte ucciso avea Rinaldo, XVIII/45
In campo non aveano altri a venire, XIV/28
In capo d'otto o di piu giorni in corte, V/57
In capo de la sale, ove e piu scuro, XXVIII/33
In che stato, in che termine si trove, Ss/35
In così poca, in così debol speme, XXIII/115
In dieci giorni e in manco fu perfetta, XXIX/35
In dua squadre incontrossi: e Manilardo, XII/69
In giuochi onesti e parlament lieti, XXVI/54
```

In Lidia venne; e d'un laccio più forte, XXXIV/17
In luogo di trionfo, al suo ritorno, XXXIV/37
In mezzo la spelonca, appresso a un fuoco, XII/91
In mura, in tetti, in pavimenti sparte, XXXIII/105
In odio gli la pose, ancor che tanto, VII/70
In poco spazio ne gittò per terra, XXXVI/39
In preda del dolor tenace e forte, XXXXVI/21
In premio promettendola a quel d'essi, I/9
In quel boscetto era di bianchi marmi, XXXVI/42
In quel duro aspettare ella talvolta, XXXII/11
In questa è di Marsilio il gran bastardo, XIV/16
In questa parte il giovene si vede, XXXXVI/94
In questa prima parte era dipinta, XXXXVI/93
In questa terra un mese, in quella dui, XXVIII/49
In questo caso è il giovene Grifone, XVI/4
In questo loco fu la lizza fatta, XXVII/48
In questo mezzo de la ròcca usciti, XXII/65
In questo mezzo un cavallier villano, XIX/13
In questo tempo alla mia patria accade, XXXXIII/82
In questo tempo, alzando gli occhi al mare, XXXXII/23
In questo tempo i nostri, da chi tese, XIV/131
In questo tempo Orlando e Brandimarte, XXXXI/68
In questo tempo una gentil donzella, XXIX/43
In Rodi, in Cipro, e per città e castella, XVII/66
In simil parole si diffuse, XXV/92
In supplimento de le turbe uccise, XIII/83
In tanta rabbia, in tal furor sommersa, XXIV/87
In tanta rabbia, in tanto furor venne, XXIII/134
In tanto aspro travaglio gli soccorre, XXIII/123
In terra, in aria, in mar, sola son io, XXV/36
Inanzi a Carlo, inanzi al re Agramante, XVI/18
Inanzi albracca glie l'avea Brunello, XXVII/72
Incontra se le fece, e col più molle, XXVIII/99
Indi d'uno in un altro luogo errando, XIV/64
Indi giunse ad un'altra Tremisenne, XXXIII/101
Indi i pagani tanto a spaventarsi, XVI/70
Indi il messo soggiunse il gran periglio, XXIV/112
Indi le roppe un manico di croce, XXVII/38
Indi pei campi accelerando i passi, VIII/15
Indi roppe il silenzio, e con sembianti, XXVII/134
Indi s'offerse di voler provare, V/86
Indi van mansueto alla donzella, I/75
Indi verso i duo giovani s'aventa, XXIX/54
Indosso la corazzo, l'elmo in testa, I/11
Ingiustissimo Amor, perché sì raro, II/1
Ingrata damigella, è questo quello, XI/8
Intanto Bradamante iva accusando, XXXII/10
Intanto il re Agramante mossa avea, XV/6
Intanto il re di Circassia, stimando, XII/51
Intanto il re di Sarza avea cacciato, XIV/113
Intanto l'infelice (e non sa come), VII/82
Intenderete ancor, che come l'ebbe, XVIII/110
Intese prima, che per gran dolore, VI/7
Inteso avea che su quel monte alpestre, XXXIII/110

Invitto Alfonso, simile ira accese, XXXXII/3
Io 'l so, e tu 'l sai che Ruggier nostro è tale, XXXVIII/62
Io ch'a difender questa causa toglio, XXXII/102
Io ch'all'amante mio di quella fede, IX/26
Io, ch'era tutta a satisfargli intenta, V/15
Io che l'uso sapea del mio palagio, XXXXIII/36
Io che sforzar cosi mi veggio, voglio, IX/36
Io chiedea un colpo o dui con voi scontrarme, XXVI/7
Io confortai l'amator mio sovente, V/20
Io credo che qualche agnol s'interpose, XXX/54
Io da lei altretanto era o più amato, VI/48
Io dico e disse, e dirò fin ch'io viva, XVI/2
Io dico forse, non ch'io ve l'accerti, XXX/72
Io dico, se tre volte se n'immolla, XXIX/16
Io dietro alle cortine avea nascoso, IX/41
Io dubito che poi ch'm'avrà in gabbia, IX/52
Io fo ben voto a Dio (ch'adorar voglio, XXXVI/78
Io fui già ne l'error che siete voi, XXVII/137
Io gli ho al mio regno in Africa mandati, XXXV/45
Io lo lasciai ne la città crudele, XXII/5
Io m'offerisco (disse Bradamante), XXXV/59
Io me ne vo la notte (Amore è duce), XXV/52
Io mi godea le delicate membra, VI/47
Io non credo che mai Bireno, nudo, XI/72
Io non credo, signor, che ti sia nuova, V/67
Io non mi leverò da questi piedi, XXXXV/16
Io non parlo di questo né di tanti, XXXVI/5
Io non ti potre' esprimere il gran danno, XXXIV/22
Io non vi so ben dir come si fosse, XXXVI/58
Io non voglio altra gente, altri sussidi, XXV/78
Io parlo di quella inclita donzella, II/31
Io per l'odio non sì, che grave porto, IX/33
Io piglierò per amor tuo l'impresa, XXXX/49
Io solea più di questi dui narrarti, VII/63
Io son ben certo che comprendi e sai, V/28
Io son di tal valor, son di tal nerbo, XXXV/47
Io son Leone, acciò tu intenda, figlio, XXXXV/47
Io sono a dir tante altre cose intento, XXX/17
Io sto in sospetto, e già di veder parmi, X/29
Io te la mostrero di qui, se vuoi, XXX/6
Io te n'ho dato volentieri aviso, VI/53
Io ti dico d'Orlando e di Rinaldo, XXVII/8
Io v'ho da dir de la Discordia altiera, XVIII/26
Io v'ho da ringraziar ch'una maniera, XI/57
Io v'ho già detto che con tanta forza, XXII/68
Io vi dicea ch'alquanto pensar volle, XXXXIII/6
Io vi lasciai, come assaltato avea, XVI/17
Io voglio a far il saggio esser la prima, XXIX/24
Io voglio andar, perché non stia insepulto, XVIII/169
Io voglio che sappiate che figliuola, IX/22
Io voglio il tuo cavallo: olà, non odi?, ss/7
Io voglio questo ladro tuo vasallo, XXVII/91
Iocondo ancor duo miglia ito non era, XXVIII/18
Ippalca la donzella era nomata, XXIII/30

Ippolito diceva una scrittura, XXXXVI/86
Isabella sono io, che figlia fui, XIII/4
Istima alcun che Malagigi parte, XXXI/86
Italia e Francia e tutte l'altre bande, XI/24
Iulia Gonzaga, che dovunqu il piede, XXXXVI/8


L

L'abito giovenil mosse la figlia, XXIII/94
L'acciaio allora la Discordia prese, XVIII/34
L'acqua gli fece distaccare in fretta, XXIX/48
L'adornamento che s'aggira sopra, VI/71
L'affanno di Ruggier ben veramente, XXXIX/1
L'African che mancarsi il destrier sente, XXIV/107
L'almo liquor che si meditori suoi, XXXXI/2
L'alte colonne e i capitelli d'oro, XXXXII/77
L'alto parlare e la fiera sembianza, XXII/45
L'alto rumor de le sonore trombe, XVI/56
L'altra che segue in ordine, è Diana, XXXXII/90
L'altro, ch'ebbe l'artefice men dotto, XXII/69
L'altro comincia, poi che tocca a lui, XX/5
L'altro con più ragion sua spada inchina, XXXIII/82
L'altro fratel fu prima del cugino, XXVI/75
L'altro non l'ascoltava, se non quanto, XXV/79
L'altro non sa se s'abbia dritto o torto, V/84
L'altro s'attacca ad un scheggion ch'usciva, XXIX/55
L'amar che dunque alla facea colui, V/19
L'animose guerriere a lato un tempio, XXXVII/119
L'anno primier del fortunato regno, XXVI/44
L'antiquo sangue che venne da Troia, III/17
L'ardita Bradamante in questo mezzo, XXII/97
L'ardito Astolfo e il forte Sansonetto, XVIII/114
L'ardito Brandimarte in su Frontino, XXXXI/79
L'armata che i pagan roppe ne l'onde, XXXXIV/20
L'arme che del suo male erano state, XVII/133
L'arme che fur già del troiano Ettorre, XXXXIV/77
L'arme che ne la giostra fatta dianzi, XVIII/107
L'aspra legge di Scozia, empia e severa, IV/59
L'aspra percossa agghiacciò il cor nel petto, XXX/53
L'assedio d'Agramante ch'avea il giorno, XXV/81
L'astrologo tenea le labra chiuse, XXXXIII/88
L'avea mandato all'isola d'Alcina, VII/44
L'aver Elbanio di bellezza il vanto, XX/55
L'aver Ruggiero ella apsettato, e invece, XXX/79
L'elmo, che dianzi con travaglio tanto, XXXVIII/78
L'elmo e lo scudo anche a portae gli diede, XV/61
L'eloqueszia del Greco assai potea, XXXXV/56
L'esercito cristian che con sì fida, XVI/42
L'esercito cristian mosso a tumulto, XXVII/19
L'esercito cristian sopra le mura, XIV/110
L'esercito d'Alzerbe avea il primiero, XVIII/46
L'esser venuta a' Mori ella in aita, XXXII/33
L'ha cercata per Francia: or s'apparecchia, XII/4

La cortina levò senza far motto, XXVIII/21
La cosa fu gravissima e molesta, VIII/53
La cosa stava tacita fra noi, XXV/70
La crudel meretrice ch'avea fatto, XXII/77
La crudeltà ch'usa l'iniqua vecchia, XXXXV/41
La damigella non passava ancora, X/11
La diè senza contrasto in poter loro, XXXVII/112
La Discordia ch'udì questo pensiero, XVIII/37
La Discordia, credendo non potere, XXVI/122
La donna al fraticel chiede la via, II/14
La donna amata fu da un cavalliero, II/32
La donna, ancor che Rabican ben trotte, XXXII/69
La donna, cominciando a disarmarsi, XXXII/79
La donna del castel da un lato preme, XXII/80
La donna disse lui: -- Tua villania, XXXV/70
La donna il palafreno a dietro volta, I/13
La donna il tutto ascolta, e le ne giova, IV/8
La donna in questo mezzo la caldaia, XXIX/23
La donna in suo discarco, et in vergogna, XXXXIII/141
La donna incominciò: -- Tu intenderai, V/5
La donna, poi che fu partito il duca, XXIII/17
La donna Ruggier guida, e non soggiorna, XXVI/66
La donna sua, che gli ritorna a mente, VIII/72
La donna va per prenderlo nel freno, IV/43
La donna vecchia, amica a' malandrini, XIII/42
La dura nuova a Ricciardetto spiace, XXV/77
La fanziulla negli omeri si stringe, XXVIII/59
La fata, poi che vide acconcio il tutto, XV/13
La fede unqua non debbe esser corrotta, XXI/2
La femina crudel lo fece porre, XXXXV/20
La femina nel maschio fe' disegno, XXV/37
La fiera gente inospitale e cruda, X/95
La fiera pugna un pezzo andò di pare, XVI/68
La figliuola d'Amon, che vuol morire, XXXVI/47
La figliuola d'Amon, mossa a pietade, XXXII/107
La figliuola d'Amon quanti ne tocca, XXXVII/102
La fonte discorrea per mezzo un prato, II/34
La forma, il sito, il ricco e bel lavoro, XXXXIII/138
La forza del terribil Rodomonte, XXVII/30
La forza di Ruggier non era quale, XXV/14
La fraude insegnò a noi, che contra il naso, XVII/53
La Gelosia quel nano avea trovato, XVIII/30
La gente qui, là perdi a un tempo il regno, XXXVIII/60
La giovane riman presso che morta, VII/46
La giustizia del re, che il loco franco, XXIV/26
La gran beltà che fu da Sacripante, VIII/63
La gran Colonna del nome romano, XIV/5
La incontinenza è quanto mal si puote, XXVIII/83
La lancia del pagan, che venne a corre, XXXXVI/116
La lucente armatura il Maganzese, XXIII/59
La Luna a quel pregar la nube aperse, XVIII/185
La lunga absenzia, il veder vari luoghi, XXVIII/47
La machina infernal, di più di cento, XI/23
La madre, ch'aver crede alle sue voglie, XXXXIV/38

La magnanima donna, a cui fu grato, XXXV/38
La man gli prese, quando a punto dava, XXI/61
La messaggiera e le sue giovani anco, XXXVII/109
La mia sorella avea ben conosciuto, XXV/30
La moglie Argia che stava appresso ascosa, XXXXIII/140
La notte a pena di seguir rimane, II/24
La notte ch'andò inanzi a quella aurora, XXVIII/17
La notte ch'andò inanzi al terminato, XXXXV/64
La notte che precesse a questo giorno, XXXXIII/155
La notte inanzi il dì che a suo camino, XXXVIII/29
La notte Orlando alle noiose piume, VIII/71
La parte che ti pensi, non n'avrai, XXVI/109
La partita d'Angelica non molto, XXXXII/40
La pésta seguitai, che mi condusse, XXIV/23
La pietà del figliuol, l'odio ch'avea, IX/45
La pietosa fanciulla rispondendo, XXVIII/60
La più capace e piena ampolla, ov'era, XXXIV/87
La più gioven de l'altre e la piu bella, XX/25
La prega che non faccia, se non sente, XXXXIII/92
La priega poi che le piaccia non solo, XXVI/86
La prima, appresso il gonfalon reale, X/78
La prina inscrizion ch'agli occhi occorre, XXXXII/83
La prima schiera era già messa in rotta, XVI/51
"La principal cagion ch'a far disegno, XX/50
La proferta a Rinaldo accettar piacque, XXXXIII/52
La qual mi spiacque sì, che restò poco, XVII/125
La regina Orontea fece raccorre, XX/47
La sala queste et altre istorie molte, XXXIII/58
La scaramuccia fiera e sanguinosa, XXXVI/30
La sciocca turba disiosa attende, XXX/27
La sera, quando alla spelonca mena, XVII/60
La somma fu del lor ragionamento, XXXXIII/68
La spada sola manca alle buone arme, XXIII/79
"La speme (disse il re) mi fa venire, XVII/52
La speme, la credenza, la certezza, XXXXIII/23
La spessa turba aspetta disiando, XXVII/53
La stanza, quadra e spaziosa, pare, III/7
La sua piaga più s'apre e più incrudisce, XIX/29
La sua porta ha per sé ciascuna loggia, XXXXII/75
La sua spada avea tolta ella di terra, XXXVI/54
La sua statura, acciò tu la conosca, III/72
La terza giostra il figlio di Lanfusa, XXXV/74
La turba dietro a Rodomonte presta, XIV/126
La valarosa giovane, con questa, XIII/54
La valorosa donna, che non meno, XXXXIV/74
La vecchia che conobbe il cavalliero, XXI/5
La vecchia, dando alle parole udienza, XX/137
"La vedovella che marito prende, XXXVII/63
La vergine a fatica gli rispose, XII/94
La vergine Marfisa si nomava, XVIII/99
La verginella è simile alla rosa, I/42
La vostra, Signor mio, fu degna loda, XV/2
Lance, saette e spade ebbe l'usbergo, XII/78
Lancia non tolse; non perché temesse, XXXXV/65

Languido smonta, e lascia Brigliadoro, XXIII/116
Lascia all'arcion lo scudo, che già posto, IV/25
Lascia la cura a me (dicea Gradasso), XXVII/66
Lascia quel morto, e Balisarda stringe, XXXXIV/87
Lascialo pur andar (dicea Marfisa, XXXVI/83
Lasciamo il paladin ch'errando vada, XXX/16
Lasciamolo andar pur -- ne ci rincresca, XX/98
Lasciàn costui, che mentre all'altrui vita, III/6
Lasciando il porto e l'onde più tranquille, XV/16
Lasciate questo canto, che senza esso, XXVIII/2
Lasciati avea i Cadurci e la cittade, XXXII/50
Lasciò la lingua all'ultimo in riposo, XX/143
Lasciollo andar con sua licenzia Carlo, XXXXII/43
Lassa! (dicea) che ritrovar poss'io, XXX/32
Le belle braccia al collo indi mi getta, XXV/54
Le belle donne e gli altri quivi stati, XXXIII/59
Le bellezze d'Olimpia eran di quelle, XI/67
Le campane si sentono a martello, XIV/100
Le case lor trovaro i Greci piene, XX/11
Le da l'annello e se le raccomanda, VII/49
Le donne a riposate i cavallieri, XV/76
Le donne antique hanno mirabil cose, XX/1
Le donne, che gran pezzo mirato hanno, XIX/98
Le donne, che si videro tradite, XX/22
Le donne e i cavallier che questa via, XXXVII/46
Le donne e i cavallier mirano fisi, XXXXVI/98
Le donne, i cavallier, l'arme, gli amori, I/1
Le donne molte grazie riferiro, VI/81
Le donne son venute in eccellenza, XX/2
Le Ferrarese mie qui sono, e quelle, XXXXVI/10
Le fraudi che e mogli e che l'amiche, XXVII/138
Le guerre ch'i Franceschi da far hanno, XXXIII/7
Le lacrime e i sospiri degli amanti, XXXIV/75
Le lance infin al calce si fiaccaro, XXVI/82
Le lancie ambe di secco e suttil salce, XIX/94
Le navi de' pagani, ch'avanzaro, XXXX/71
Le nozze belle e sontuose fanno, IX/94
Le porte de le carcere gittate, IX/84
Le preme il cor questo pensier; ma molto, XXXII/61
Le pruove gli narrò, che tante volte, XI/64
Le redine il destrier, ch'era possente, XXXIII/87
Le sopravenne Ferraù et Orlando, XII/29
Le stanze sue, che sono appresso al tetto, XXVIII/32
Le vaghe donne gettano dai palchi, XVII/81
Le vettovaglie in carra et in iumenti, XXVII/129
Legar lo fanno, e non tra' fiori e l'erba, XVIII/93
Legato de la sua propria catena, IV/37
Leon che, quando seco il cavalliero, XXXXV/115
Leon con le più dolci e più soavi, XXXXVI/30
Leon Ruggier con gran pietade abbraccia, XXXXV/46
Leone, acciò che la sua gente affatto, XXXXIV/94
Leone Augusto s'un poggio eminente, XXXXIV/89
Leone ha nel fuggir tanto vantaggio, XXXXIV/100
Leone, il qual sapea molto ben dire, XXXXVI/61

Lesse la carta quattro volte e sei, XXX/80
Leva al fin gli occhi, e vede il sol che 'l tergo, XXXII/6
Levan la bara, et a portala foro, XXXXIII/176
Levando intanto queste prime rudi, III/4
Levasi un grido subito et orrendo, XII/76
Levato il servo del camino s'era, XXXXIII/125
Levò il drappo vermiglio in che coperto, VIII/11
Levossi, al ritornar del paladino, XXXXIII/169
Levossi in su le staffe, et all'elmetto, XXX/57
Li pregò poi, che quando il Saracino, XXIII/98
Li quali parimente arser di grande, XXXXIV/72
Li rimandò Melissa in lor paesi, VIII/16
Libera corte fa bandire intorno, XXXXVI/74
Liete piante, verdi erbe, limpide acque, XXIII/108
Lo 'nvito di Gradasso e d'Agramante, XXXX/56
Lo conoscea, perch'era stato infante, XI/62
Lo dà ad Angelica ora, perché teme, X/109
Lo fa con diaboliche sue larve, XXII/19
Lo fa lavar Astolfo sette volte, XXXIX/56
Lo fe' al meglio che seppe; e domandolli, VI/55
Lo fece tor, che tutto era sanguigno, XXXXII/19
Lo levar quindi, e lo mostrar per tutto, XVII/134
Lo partì, dico, per dritta misura, XIX/86
Lo piglia con molto impeto a traverso, XXIII/86
Lo prese sotto a Monaco in riviera, XXXIX/23
Lo riconobbe, tosto che mirollo, XII/60
Lo riconosce all'aquila d'argento, XXXVI/31
Lo ritrovar che senza cibo stato, XXXXVI/26
Lo scritto d'oro esser costei dichiara, XXXXII/88
Lo scudo roppe solo, e su l'elmetto, XXXIX/49
Lo smemorato Oblio sta su la porta, XIV/94
Lo spettacolo enorme e disonesto, XXXVII/28
Lo statuito giorno al tempio venne, XXXVII/68
Lo stizzone ambe le palpèbre colse, XIII/36
Lo strano corso che tenne il cavallo, XXIII/100
Lo va di qua di là tanto cercando, XXXI/94
Logistilla mostrò molto aver grato, X/64
Lontan si vide una muraglia lunga, VI/59
Lor mostra appresso un govene Pipino, XXXIII/17
Lor mostra poi (ma vi parea intervallo, XXXIII/21
Lucina, o fosse perch'ella non volle, XVII/56
Lungo a dir fora, quanto il giovinetto, XXXVIII/21
Lungo e d'intorno quel fiume volando, XXXV/13
Lungo il fiume le belle e pellegrine, XXXV/62
Lungo il fiume Traiano egli cavalca, XV/40
Lungo sarà che d'Alda di Sansogna, XIII/73
Lungo sarà s'io vi vo' dire in versi, XXXXIII/180
Lungo sarebbe, se i diversi casi, XXXX/1
Lungo saria se gl'infelici spirti, XXXIV/13
Lurcanio in questo mezzo dubitando, V/48

M

Ma Alfonsin Trotto il qual si trovò in fatto, XXXX/4
Ma ben mi duol che questo per cagione, XXI/12
Ma ben ti priego che prima che sia, XXXI/100
Ma ben vi giuro per gli eterni dei, XVII/123
Ma bisogno anco, prima ch'io ne parli, XXXII/3
Ma ch'abbia in questo mezzo il sacerdote, XXXVII/64
Ma ch'egli alla promessa sua mancasse, XXX/86
Ma che direte del già tanto fiero, XX/92
Ma che mi possi nuocere non veggio, VIII/41
Ma che non pensi già che seguir possa, VI/56
Ma che parlò come ignorante e sciocco, XXIX/3
Ma che t'incresca che m'abbai ad uccidere, XIX/105
"Ma che ti sia fedel, tu non puoi dire, XXXXIII/25
Ma chi pensato avria, fuor che Dio solo, XXXVIII/39
Ma (come aviene a un disperato spesso, VI/5
Ma come ben composto e valido arco, XXIV/103
Ma come i cigni che cantando lieti, XXXV/22
Ma come l'aviso Melissa, stette, VII/75
Ma come l'orso suol, che per le fiere, XI/49
Ma come poi l'imperiale augello, XXXIX/32
Ma come poi soggiunse, una donzella, XXXII/30
Ma, come quel che men curato avrei, II/40
Ma con gli altri esser vòlse ella sortita, XIX/74
Ma con tutto 'l valor che di sé mostra, XVIII/48
Ma Consalvo Ferrante ove ho lasciato, XXVI/53
Ma costei, più volubile che foglia, XXI/15
Ma d'un parlar ne l'altro, ove sono ito, XVII/80
Ma degno di sé colpo ancor non fanno, XXX/52
Ma di che debbo lamentarmi, ahi lassa, XXXII/21
Ma di saperlo far non si dia vanto, XXXIII/4
Ma differendo questa pugna alquanto, XXXIX/19
Ma Dio, che spesso gl'innocenti aiuta, XXIII/53
Ma due cose ha da far: l'una, disporre, XXXXV/55
Ma, Fiordiligi, almen resti un conforto, XXXXIII/174
Ma Ferraù, che prima v'ebbe gli occhi, XII/54
Ma Ferraù, che sin qui mai non s'era, XVI/71
Ma Ferraù, ma Serpentino arditi, XXVII/80
Ma Fortuna che voi, ben che non nati, XXXVI/61
Ma Fortuna di me con doppio dono, XVI/12
Ma già lo stuolo svendo fatto unire, XXXI/49
Ma gli propone una crudele e dura, IX/47
Ma i venti che portavano le vele, X/26
Ma il Circasso depor, quando le piaccia, XII/28
Ma il re Sobrino, il quale era presente, XXVII/96
Ma il suo fiero destin che non risponde, XXXIX/78
Ma il volgo, nel cui arbitrio son gli onori, XXXXIV/50
Ma in casa di sua Altezza avea veduto, XXVIII/43
Ma inanzi a morte, qui dove previdi, XXXVI/65
Ma l'antiquo aversario, il qual fece Eva, XXVII/13
Ma l'escuso io pur troppo, e mi rallegro, IX/2
Ma la Fortuna, che dei pazzi ha cura, XXX/15
Ma la più prate de la gente rotta, XVIII/159
Ma la spada ne fu tosto levata, XXXI/44
Ma la sua gente ch'a difesa resta, XXXIII/32

```
Ma la virtù, ch'ai suoi spesso socorre, XVIII/64
Ma lacrimosa e addolorata quanto, IV/70
Ma lasciamo, per Dio, Signore, ormai, XVII/17
Ma lasciàn Bradamante, e non v'incresca, XIII/80
Ma lasciànla doler fin ch'io ritorno, X/35
Ma le par atto vile a insanguinarsi, IV/14
Ma lo soccorse a tempo un cavalliero, XXXXII/53
Ma mi bisogna, s'io vo' dirvi il resto, XXII/31
Ma né questi ella, né alcun altro vuole, XXXII/56
Ma né sì bella seta o sì fin'ora, XI/75
Ma nel voltar degli occhi, il re Agramante, XXXXI/98
Ma non apparirà il lume sì tosto, XXXXV/35
Ma non dirò d'Angelica or più inante, XII/66
Ma non ebbe e non ha mano né lingua, XXXVII/4
Ma non però disegna l'affanno, I/51
Ma non però quest'odio cosi ammorza, XXXVII/59
Ma non più quercia antica, o grosso muro, XXXXV/73
Ma non potei finire il mio viaggio, XX/7
Ma non sa ritrovar priego che vaglia, XXXXVI/115
Ma non sì tosto dal materno stelo, I/43
Ma non sommessa voce e a pena udita, XVIII/187
Ma non vi giunser prima, ch'un uom pazzo, XIX/42
Ma, per Dio, fa ch'io vegga tosto in fronte, XXII/62
Ma per dirvi la cosa pienamente, XVII/26
Ma per la compagnia che, come hai detto, XXVII/76
Ma per narrar di me più che d'altrui, XXXIV/15
Ma perch'assai minor del paladino, XXXIV/66
Ma perch'avea dinanzi agli occhi il tema, XXXVII/54
Ma perch'io vo' concludere, vi dico, XXXXII/6
Ma perché il tuo Ruggiero a te sol abbia, III/71
Ma perché in mente ogniora avea di meno, XXXX/80
Ma perché se mi serban, come io sono, XIII/31
Ma perché si potria forse imputarme, XXVII/92
Ma perché vede esser di lui sorella, XXXVIII/69
Ma più d'Amon la moglie Beatrice, XXXXIV/37
Ma piu d'ogni altro duol che le sia detto, XXXXIV/60
Ma più degli altri fuggon quei d'Alzerbe, XVIII/49
Ma più del re, ma più d'ognun ch'invano, XXX/31
Ma più ve l'ebbe Amor: che se non era, XXV/2
Ma pocco il cenno, e 'l gridar poco vale, XXXXI/11
Ma poco ci giovò: che 'l nimico empio, XI/22
Ma poi ch'a spese lor si furo accorti, XIV/47
Ma poi ch'a tradimento ebbe la morte, XXXXVI/82
Ma poi ch'appare a manifesti segni, XXX/68
Ma poi ch'un giorno ella ferita fu, XXV/24
Ma poi che 'l giorno aperta fu la sbarra, XVII/64
Ma poi che 'l mio destino iniquo e duro, XXIV/79
Ma poi che ben m'avrai veduto in faccia, XXIII/76
Ma poi che fumma tratti a piene vele, XVII/27
Ma poi che gu levato di sul colle, XX/112
Ma poi che l'usato ira cacciò quella, XXVII/108
Ma poi che senza lor questo non lece, XX/51
Ma poté sì, per esser tanto bella, VIII/65
Ma presupongo ancor ch'or ora arrivi, X/30
```

Ma prima liberar la donna è onesto, XXXVII/94
Ma prima quei baroni e capitani, XVI/32
Ma pur col core indomito, e constante, XXXXI/52
Ma quando ancor nessuno onor, nessuno, XVI/38
Ma quanto a Malagigi le domande, XXXXII/33
Ma quanto avea più fretta il paladino, XI/29
Ma quanto va più inanzi, più s'ingrossa, XXXIV/7
Ma quei gli dànno volentier l'impresa, XV/81
Ma quel con un lancion gli fa ripsota, XVII/98
Ma quella che di noi fa come il vento, XXXIII/50
Ma quella, che no vuol che si prometta, XXXXV/6
Ma quella gentil maga, che piu cura, VII/42
Ma quella usata ne le cose avverse, XXXVIII/73
Ma quello è a pena in terra che si rizza, XXXXII/56
Ma questo a pochi il brando rio conciede, XVI/22
Ma quivi era perpetua la verdura, X/63
Ma ridur si può in Arli o sia in Narbona, XXXI/83
Ma ritorniamo a Marfisa che s'era, XXXVI/43
Ma s'a te tocca star di sotto, come, XXXV/46
Ma s'io t'abbatto, come io credo e spero, XXXV/44
Ma scusimi apo voi d'un error tanto, XXXI/32
Ma se desir pur hai d'un elmo fino, I/28
Ma se fa senza indugio, come ha detto, XXXXIV/53
Ma se fra un mese alcun per lei non viene, IV/61
Ma se gli è stato inanzi che cristiano, XXXXV/110
Ma se gli e ver che 'l vostro amor sia quello, XXX/34
Ma se la fiera madre a quel si lancia, XVIII/15
Ma se Leon Ruggiero ammira et ama, XXXXIV/93
Ma se si de' soccorrere Agramante, XXVI/114
Ma se spazio a pensarvi avesse avuto, XXVII/3
Ma se tu mandi ancor che poche navi, XXXVIII/46
Ma sempre più raccende e più rinuova, XXIII/105
Ma sì come audacissima e scaltrita, XVI/9
Ma sia per questa volta detto assai, XVIII/59
Ma simile son fatto ad uno infermo, XXX/2
Ma stiano gli altri in dubbio, in tema, in doglia, XXXI/109
Ma tarda è la sua giunta; che si trova, XXXVI/48
Ma tornando a Ruggier, ch'io lasciai quando, XI/17
Ma torniamo ad Angelica, che seco, XII/23
Ma tosto che si pon quel corno a bocca, XXII/21
Ma tutto è indarno; che fermata e certa, XIII/27
Ma viene a Doralice, et a lei narra, XXIV/110
Ma vo' seguir la bellicosa donna, XX/106
Ma voglio a un'altra volta differire, XVIII/8
Ma volgendosi gli anni, io veggio uscire, XV/21
Magnanimo Signore, ogni vostro atto, XVIII/1
Malagigi, che sa d'ogni malia, XXVI/128
Malagigi e Vivian, che l'arme aveano, XXVI/72
Malindo uccise e Ardalico il fratello, XVIII/180
Mancati quei filosofi e quei santi, XIV/89
Manda Lotrecco il re con nuove squadre, XXXIII/56
Mandata da colei, che d'amor piena, VII/67
Mandato avea sei mila fanti arcieri, XVI/30
Mandricardo e Ruggier fu nel secondo, XXVII/46

```
Marfisa a' prieghi de' compagni avea, XXVI/69
Marfisa, alzando con un viso altiero, XXVI/79
Marfisa cacciò l'asta per lo petto, XXXIX/12
Marfisa, che fu sempre disiosa, XXVI/87
Marfisa che tra gli altri al grido venne, XXVII/85
Marfisa, che volea porgli d'accordo, XXVI/113
Marfisa cominciò con grata voce, XXXVIII/12
Marfisa con Ruggiero a questo segno, XXVI/14
Marfisa del suo caso anco favella, XXVII/41
Marfisa e 'l bon Guidone e i duo fratelli, XX/95
Marfisa incontra una gran lancia afferra, XX/115
Marfisa intanto si levò si di terra, XXVI/132
Marfisa, la qual prima avea composta, XXXVII/100
Marfisa Marganorre avea legato, XXXVII/103
Marfisa, o 'l vero o 'l falso che dicesse, XXXXV/105
Marfisa si ristringe ne le spalle, XXXXII/27
Marfisa tuttavolta combattendo, XXVI/20
Marganor che cader vede il figliuolo, XXXVII/76
Marganor il fellon (così si chiama, XXXVII/43
Marsilio a Mandricardo avea donato, XIV/34
Marsilio anco è fuggito ne la terra, XXXIX/17
Marsilio prima, e poi fece Agramente, XIV/11
Martano disegnò torre il destriero, XVII/110
Matina e sera l'infelice amante, XVII/61
Me che sua intenzione avesse effetto, XVIII/108
Me né il re, né Sobrin, né duca alcuno, XVIII/160
Me né sì dalso all'impeto marino, XXI/16
Meglio mi par che 'l viver tuo prolunghi, XIX/102
Melissa di consenso di Leone, XXXXVI/78
Melissa in questo tempo, ch'era fonte, XXXIX/4
Mena all testa a quel che gli è più presso, XVIII/12
Mena la spada, e più ferir non mira, XXXVI/22
Menava Ariodante il brando in giro, XVI/65
Menava in una squadra più di mezzo, XVI/78
Menava un suo baston di legno in volta, XXXIX/37
Mentre apparecchio si facea solenne, XXIII/47
Mentre aspettamo, in gran piacer sedendo, XVII/29
Mentre avea il paladin da questa banda, XI/52
Mentre avean quivi l'animo divoto, XV/100
Mentre ch'Orlando, poi che lo disciolse, XXIII/63
Mentre che cosi pensa, ode la voce, XIII/78
Mentre circonda la casa silvestra, XII/14
Mentre così pensando seco giva, XXII/91
Mentre costei conforta il Saracino, I/68
Mentre costui cosi s'affligge e duole, I/48
Mentre di fuor con sì crudel battaglia, XVI/85
Mentre egli quivi si giacea, convenne, XXI/18
Mentre Fortuna in mar questi travaglia, XVIII/146
Mentre io tardava quivi, ecco venire, II/45
Mentre la sete, e de l'andar fatica, X/36
Mentre lo stuol de' barbari si cala, XIV/129
Mentre quivi col ferro il maledetto, XVI/28
Mentre Rinaldo cosi parla, fende, XXXXIII/63
Mentre Rinaldo in tal fretta venia, XIV/98
```

Mentre Ruggier di quella gente bella, X/90
Mentre Ruggiero all'African domanda, XXVI/98
Mentre stava così Zerbino in forse, XXIV/35
Mentre studia placarli il re Agramante, XXVII/69
Mercurio al fabbro poi la rete invola, XV/57
Merlin gli disse, e replicògli spesso, XXXIII/30
Merlin gli fe' veder che quasi tutti, XXXIII/10
Messe in abito lui di peregrino, XXXXIII/106
Messo il puntello, e fattosi sicuro, XI/39
Metto all'incontro la morte d'un solo, XV/48
Mi duol di non vedere in questa morte, XXXVII/72
Mi partorì Costanza ne le estreme, XXXI/31
Mi persuade, se per opra mia, V/14
Mi traea dietro (disse) per la briglia, XXVI/58
Mie sono l'arme, e 'n mezzo de la via, XVIII/128
Mill'occhi in capo avea senza palpebre, XXXXII/47
Minaccia sempre, maledice e incarca, X/43
Mio padre e' miei fratelli mi son stati, IX/50
Mio patre fe' in Baiona alcune giostre, XIII/6
Mirabilmente il bel vello gli piacque, XXXV/4
Miracol fu veder le fronde sparte, XXXIX/28
Mirammo (al trar de l'elmo) al mozzo crine, XXV/47
Mirava quelle orribili percosse, XXVI/21
Miser chi mal oprando si confida, VI/1
Misera! a chi mai più creder debb'io?, XXXII/37
Misera Olimpia! a cui dopo lo scorno, XI/55
Molta incontrò de la paurosa gente, XIV/35
Molte bandiere inanzi e molte dietro, XXXXIII/178
Molti a chi fur le mogli o le sorelle, XXXVII/107
Molti che dal furor di Rodomonte, XXVII/26
Molti consigli de le donne sono, XXVII/1
Molti fra pochi dì vi capitaro, XXIX/38
Molti in potrer de' Bulgari restaro, XXXXIV/95
Molti per fretta s'affogaro in Senna, XXVII/32
Molti ringraziamenti e molte offerte, XXIII/70
Moltiplicavan l'ire e le parole, XXVI/110
Molto affrettando i suoi compagni, andava, XX/85
Molto aggirando vommi, e per quel giorno, XXIV/24
Molto è meglio morir qui, ch'ai supplìci, XVIII/51
Molto fu il gaudio e molta fu la gioia, XXXVIII/27
Molto la notte e molto il giorno pensa, XXXXV/52
Molto più a te, ch'a me, costei conviensi, XXXXVI/43
Monta a cavallo, e se stesso rampogna, XX/131
Montar la fece s'un ronzino, e in mano, XXIII/31
Morir non puote alcuna fata mai, X/56
Morte avea in casa, e d'ogni tempo appese, XVII/45
Morto cadea questo Aramone a valle, XVIII/53
Morto ch'ella ebbe il falso cavallier, XXIII/5
Morto i fratelli e il padre, e rimasa io, IX/32
Morto il suocero mio dopo cinque anni, XXXXIII/20
Mostra Pipino, e mostra Carlo appresso, XXXIII/16
Mostran le braccia sua misura giusta, VII/15
Mostrando ch'essendo egli nuovo sposo, XXXXVI/109
Mostrò turbarse l'inclita donzella, XX/121

Muove crudele e spaventoso assalto, XXXXI/15
Muta ivi legno, e verso l'isoletta, XXXXIII/150
Mutò d'andare in Africa pensiero, XXVIII/94
Mutossi da la poppa ne le sponde, XXXXI/9


# N

Narran l'antique istorie, o vere o false, VIII/52
Narrato v'ho come il fatto successe, VI/14
Narrò Bardino intanto a Brandimarte, XXXIX/62
Nascono casi, e non saprei dir quanti, XIII/39
Nata pochi di inanzi era una gara, I/8
Naviga il gorno e la notte seguente, XXVIII/89
Naviga in su la poppa uno eremita, XV/42
Né cessan raccordargli il grave danno, XXX/28
Né che tal din quella battaglia avesse, XV/89
Né ci terrebbe ormai spanna di terra, VI/45
Né da partir di Francia s'avra in fretta, XXXXVI/72
Né da te voglio un minimo vantaggio, XII/46
Ne di Buovo il figliuol né quel d'Amone, XXVI/13
Né di tal volontà gli uomini soli, XXX/71
Né fin che nol tornasse in sanitade, XIX/26
Né fino a questo dì truovo chi toglia, IX/55
Né fra vermigli fiori, azzurri e gialli, XVIII/112
Né fune intorto crederò che stringa, XXI/1
Ne l'albergo un garzon stava per fante, XXVIII/56
Ne l'animo a Leon subito cade, XXXXVI/25
Ne l'arrivar che i gran navili fenno, XXXIX/81
Ne l'arrivar di Fiordiligi al ponte, XXIX/44
Ne la bandiera, ch'e tutta vermiglia, XIV/114
Ne la città con pace e con amore, XVIII/132
Ne la città di Constantin lasciata, XV/102
Ne la città medesma un cavallerio, XXXXIII/74
Ne la donna perciò si riconforta, XXVIII/14
Ne la forma d'Atlante se gli affaccia, VII/56
Ne la guancia de l'elmo, e ne la spalla, XXXXVI/130
Ne la lizza era entrato Salinterno, XVII/97
Ne la man destra il corno d'Amaltea, XXXXII/80
Ne la nostra cittade era un uom saggio, XXXXIII/13
Né la più forte ancor né la più bella, X/58
Ne la spelonca una gran mensa siede, XIII/37
Ne la sua prima forma in uno instante, VII/66
Né le sa dir che de lo scudo sia, XXXVII/31
Né lo lasciò questo ribaldo Amore, XXVIII/23
Ne lo stendardo il primo ha un pino ardente, X/88
Né lunga servitù, né grand'amore, XXVII/118
Né mai per lontananza, né strettezza, XXXXIII/81
Né men che bella, onesta e valorosa, XXXVII/52
Né molto andò, che se trovò all'uscita, XXIII/9
Né negar, né mostrarsene contenta, XXXXIV/40
Né per lacrime, gemiti o lamenti, IV/15
Né per maligna intenzione, ahi lasso!, IV/29
Né per questo interrompe il suo lamento, XXXXVI/28

Né per tutto quel giorno si favella, XXII/96
Né picciolo è il sospetto che la preme, XXX/89
Né Pietà, né Quiete, né Umilitade, XIV/81
Né più però né manco si contese, XXXVII/51
Né potea stare in alto, né fuggire, XIX/55
Né potendo in persona far l'effetto, XIII/12
Né potendo venire al primo intento, XXXIV/40
Né primo né secondo né ben quarto, XXV/23
Né può né creder vuol che morto sia, VII/36
Ne può sola salvar, se ne succede, XX/74
Né qualunque altra parte ove s'adori, XVI/37
Né questa sola, ma fosser pur state, XXIX/74
Né qui s'indugia; e il brando intorno ruota, XVI/74
Né quindi si partir, che de l'immondo, XXXVII/118
Né s'anco stesse a te di torre e darli, IV/35
Ne sappiendo ella ove potersi altrove, XXIII/6
Né scala in Inghelterra né in Irlanda, IX/93
Né sì leggiadra né sì bella veste, XXXV/8
Né sospetto darà, se non lo tolle, VII/79
Ne tal rispetto ancor gli parria degno, VIII/24
Né tempo avendo a pensar altra scusa, I/30
Né uno ancora alleverian, se senza, XX/34
Ne veggio ricompensa che mai questa, XXXV/84
Né verisimil tien che ne l'alpestre, XXXII/21
Ne vesta pieno di cotone, o tele, XII/80
Negli ripari entrò de' Saracini, XXVII/28
Negli utri, dico, il vento die lor chiuso, XXXXIV/22
Nei medesmi confini anco saprallo, III/54
Nei molti assalti e nei crudel conflitti, XIV/1
Nel biancheggiar de la nuova alba armati, XXXXI/46
Nel campo azzur l'aquila bianca avea, XXVI/99
Nel campo saracin li troveranno, XXVI/134
Nel fondo avea una porta ampla e capace, II/71
Nel golfo di Laiazzo inver Soria, XIX/54
Nel lito armato il paladino varca, IX/60
Nel lucente vestibulo di quella, XXXIV/54
Nel mansueto ubino che sul dosso, XXVI/129
Nel medesimo albergo in su la sera, XXXXIV/103
Nel padiglion ch'è più verso ponente, XXVII/49
Nel più tristo sentier, nel peggior calle, XXXXII/52
Nel primo sonno dentro al padiglione, XXXI/80
Nel ritornar s'incontra in un pastore, XIX/23
Nel tempo che regnava Fieramonte, XXXII/83
Nel trapassar ritrovò a pena loco, XXXV/49
Nel viso s'arrossì l'angel beato, XXVII/35
Nel volersi levar con quella fretta, XXXI/70
Nessun degli altri fu di quel pensiero, XX/104
Nessun ripar fan gl'isolani, o poco, XI/53
Nessuno truova: a sé la man ritira, X/21
Nimico è sì costui del nostro nome, XXXVII/40
"No, no (disse Filandro) aver mai spene, XXI/32
Noi troveren tra via tosto una lama, VI/78
Nol vide io già, ch'era sei giorno inanti, XXXX/3
Non altrimente ne l'estreme arena, IX/69

Non avea il campo d'Africa piu forte, XIV/26
Non avea messo ancor le labra in molle, XXII/12
Non avete a temer ch'in forma nuova, XXXXIV/65
Non aveva ragion io di scusarme?, VIII/74
Non basta a molti di prestarsi l'opra, XXXVII/3
Non bisogna allegar, per farmi fede, XVIII/130
Non bisogna più aver ne l'arme fede, XXXXI/85
Non bisognò a Rinaldo pregar molto, XXXI/27
Non cavalcaro molto, ch'alle mura, V/78
Non cessa ancor la maraviglia loro, XXX/41
Non cessa e non si placa, e più furore, XVIII/145
Non cessò pria la sanguinosa spada, XII/85
Non ch'a piegarti a questo tante e tante, VII/62
Non che di lei, ma restar privo voglio, XXXXVI/44
Non che il fulgor del lucido metallo, IV/24
Non che l'apprezzi o che gli porti amore, XXVII/95
Non che lasciar del suo signor voglia unque, XXIV/90
Non che per questo gli dia alcuno aiuto, XI/18
Non come vòlse Pinabello avenne, II/76
Non così fin salnitro e zolfo puro, X/40
Non così freme in su lo scoglio alpino, XVIII/11
Non così Ricciardetto e il suo cugino, XXVI/18
Non così strettamente edera preme, VII/29
Non crediate, Signor, che fra campagna, XVI/66
Non crediate, Signor, che però stia, X/73
Non credo ch'un si grande Apulia n'abbia, VII/4
Non credo che quest'ultime parole, XXIV/85
Non di questo ch'Ippalca e che 'l fratello, XXXI/7
Non dico ch'ella fosse, ma parea, XII/6
Non dirò l'accoglienze che gli fero, XXXI/35
Non dovevi assalir con sì fiere armi, XXXXIII/49
Non dubitate già ch'ella non s'abbia, XXIX/67
Non è da domandarmi, se dolere, XVIII/56
Non è dal pozzo ancor lontano un miglio, XXV/5
Non è diletto alcun che di fuor reste, VII/31
Non è finto il destrier, ma naturale, IV/18
Non è meglio ch'al campo tu ne vada, XXXII/45
Non è senza cagion s'io me ne doglio, XXXXIII/5
Non è sì odiato altro animale in terra, XXXXIII/100
Non è sua intenzion ch'ella in man vada, IX/48
Non è, visti quei colpi, chi gli faccia, XXXXIV/88
Non ebbe così tosto il capo basso, XVII/109
Non era agli ripari anco arrivato, XXVII/23
Non era grande il Cairo così allora, XV/63
Non era la possanza e la fierezza, XXVII/79
Non era però ver che questa usanza, XXXVII/62
Non era Rodomonte usato al vino, XXIX/22
Non fe' lungo camin, che venne dove, XIV/36
Non ferro solamente vi s'adopra, XIV/111
Non fini il tutto, e in mezzo la parola, V/90
Non fu da Euristeo mai, non fu mai tanto, XXXIV/39
Non fu da indi in qua rider mai visto, XXI/57
Non fu già d'ottener questo fatica, XXXVII/104
Non fu in terra sì tosto, che risorse, XXXXVI/125

Non fu Nireo sì bel, non si eccellente, XXXIII/28
Non fu Pompeio a par di costui degno, XV/31
Non fu quivi sì tosto il legno sorto, XIX/65
Non fu sì ardito tra il popul pagano, XXXI/54
Non fu sì santo né benigno Augusto, XXXV/26
Non fu veduta mai più strana torma, VI/61
Non fui, come lo seppi, a seguir lento, XXIII/74
Non furo iti duo miglia, che sonare, I/72
Non giova calar vele, e l'arbor sopra, XIII/16
Non gli parea crudele e duro manco, XXXXIII/83
Non gli può comparir quanto sia lungo, XVII/30
Non ha avuto Agramante ancora spia, XXXIX/79
Non ha minor cagion di rallegrarsi, XXXXV/14
Non ha poter d'una risposta sola, XXXII/41
Non hai tu, Spagna, l'Africa vicina, XVII/76
Non l'ho voluto uccider né lasciarlo, XXIV/27
Non lascia alcuno a guardia del palagio, VIII/14
Non le domando a questa offerta unire, XXV/63
Non le seppe negar la mia sorella, XXV/40
Non lo ritien lo scudo, che non entre, XVI/48
Non mai con tanto gaudio o stupor tanto, I/53
Non men da l'altra parte sferza e sprona, XXXX/67
Non men de la vittoria si godea, XV/80
Non men di me tormi costei disia, XX/75
Non men di questa il giovene Tanacro, XXXVII/53
Non men giocondo statua né men bella, XXXXII/84
Non men la gigantessa ardita e presta, VII/6
Non men, se donne càpita o donzella, XXXII/68
Non men sicura a lui fia Sericana, XXXIII/95
Non men son fuor di me, che fosse Orlando, XXX/4
Non men vuol Rodomonte il primo campo, XXVII/42
Non meno Orlando di veder contento, XI/63
Non mette piede inanzi ivi persona, XXVI/49
Non molto dopo, instrutto a schiera a schiera, XXXVIII/77
Non molto va Rinaldo, che si vede, I/32
Non morì quel meschin senza vendetta, XXX/65
Non ne trova un che veder possa in fronte, XVI/24
Non niega similmente il re Gradasso, XXX/40
Non par, quantunque il fuoco ogni cosa arda, XVI/27
Non passa mese, che tre, quattro e sei, V/38
Non pensa altro Tanacro, altro non brama, XXXVII/58
Non pensando però che sia donzella, XXXIII/69
Non per amor del paladino, quanto, XIX/39
Non, per andar, di ragionar lasciando, XXXI/34
Non per nel sangue uman l'ira si stende, XVI/26
Non perché dagli artigli de l'audace, III/49
Non perché fosse assai gentile e bella, XXXXIII/22
Non però ch'altra cosa avesse manco, XXI/29
Non però di costei voglio dir tanto, XXXIII/78
Non però si fermar; ma ne la frotta, XXXIX/70
Non però son di seguitar si intento, XVI/16
Non piaccia a Dio che mi conduca a tale, XXI/27
Non più (disse Ruggier), non più; ch'io sono, XXII/61
Non più a Iason di maraviglia denno, XXXVII/36

```
Non più tenne la via, come propose, X/113
Non porta spada né baston; che quando, XIV/43
Non poté, ancor che Zerbino fosse irato, XX/119
Non poté aver più pazienzia Orlando, XII/45
Non poté udire Astolfo senza risa, XIX/59
Non potea Astolfo ritrovar persona, XXIII/11
Non potendo ella andar, face pensiero, XXIII/25
Non potrebbe esser stato piu gioconde, XXII/26
Non potria fare altri il bisogno mio, XXVIII/20
Non pregar ch'io t'uccida, ch'i tuoi preghi, IV/36
Non può schiavare al fine un gran fendente, XXIV/64
Non puote in nave aver piu pazienza, XXVIII/91
Non pur costui, ma tutti gli altri ancora, XII/22
Non pur di regni o di ricchezze parlo, XXXIV/74
Non pur di sua perfidia non riprende, XVI/14
Non pur la donna e l'arme vi lasciaro, XXXVII/96
Non pur sazio di lei, ma fastidito, X/13
Non quelle sol che di virtude amiche, XXXXIII/16
Non resta quel fellon, né gli risponde, XII/7
Non restate però, donne, a cui giova, XXXVII/7
Non risponde ella, e non sa che si faccia, I/81
Non rumor di tamburi o suon di tromba, XXV/68
Non sa che far; che né l'oltraggio grace, XXXXIII/128
Non sa stimar chi sia per lei migliore, XII/27
Non sai che non compar, se non v'è quella, XXXII/39
Non sapea il Saracin però, che questo, XXIII/72
Non sappiendo io di questo cosa alcuna, V/49
Non sasso, merlo, trave, arco o balestra, XVII/12
"Non si convien (disse Filandro) tale, XXI/45
Non si lassi seguir questa battaglia, XXXIX/6
Non sì pietoso Enea, né forte Achille, XXXV/25
Non si ponno saziar di riguardarla, XXVI/29
Non si potea, ben contemplando fiso, XXXXII/94
Non si può (gli rispose Orlando) dire, XXIII/75
Non si scordò il re d'Africa Ruggiero, XXXI/88
Non si tosto all'asciutto è Rodomonte, XIV/121
Non si trovò lo scoglio del serpente, XXXXVI/119
Non si vanno i leoni o i tori in salto, I/62
Non siate però tumide e fastose, XXVII/121
Non so se 'l re di Frisa piu dolente, IX/44
Non so se fosse caso, o li miei gridi, XIII/29
Non so se sai chi sia Guidon Selvaggio, XXXVIII/58
Non so se vi ricorda che la briglia, XXII/25
Non so se vi sia a mente, io dico quello, XXXV/11
Non so, Signor, se più vi ricodiate, XVI/20
Non son, non sono io quel che paio in viso, XXIII/128
Non stanno l'aste a quattro colpi salde, XXIII/84
Non stette il duca a ricercare il tutto, XXXIV/73
Non stette molto a uscir fuor de la porta, IV/16
Non stimava egli tanto per l'altezza, XXVIII/5
Non tanto il bel palazzo era escellente, VII/10
Non temer (disse) di Ruggier, donzella, XIII/48
Non ti mancherà guida (le rispose, IV/9
"Non ti vo' creder questo (gli rispose, V/39
```

Non tolerò Aquilante che 'l frattello, XVIII/73
Non vede il sol tra questo e il polo austrino, IV/30
Non vede Orlando più poppe né spode, XXX/13
Non vi vieto per questo (ch'avrei torto), X/9
Non vide né 'l più bel né 'l più giocondo, VI/20
Non vo' gia dir ch'ella non l'abbia fatto, IV/65
Non voglio ch'in silenzio anco Renata, XIII/72
Non volean senza medico levarsi, XXXXIII/186
Non vòlse Bradmarte a quell'altiero, XXXI/67
Non vòlse entrar Leon ne la cittate, XXXXV/62
Non vòlse il cauto vecchio ridur seco, XXIV/91
Non vuo' mai più che forestier si lagni, XIX/75
Non vuol dargli, o non puote, altra risposta, XXXVI/41
Non vuol parere il can d'esser più tardo, VIII/7
Norandino ubidisce; et alla buca, XVII/47
Nostra salute, nostra vita in questa, XIV/7
Nuda avea in man quella fulminea spada, XII/79
Nuovi trofei pon su la riva d'Oglio, XXXVII/12


O

O bene o mal che la Fama ci apporti, XXXVIII/42
O bona prole, o degna d'Ercol buono, III/62
O che m'avesse in mar bramata ancora, XIII/21
O che natura sia s'alcuni marmi, III/15
O città bene aventurosa (disse), XXXXIII/55
O conte Orlando, o re di Circassia, XIX/31
O degli uomini inferma e instabil mente!, XXIX/1
O esecrabile Avarizia, o ingorda, XXXXIII/1
O felice animai ch'un sonno forte, XXXIII/64
O forse esser potrei stata sì presta, XXXXIII/161
O forte, o caro, o mio fedel compagno, XXXXIII/170
O fosse caso, o fosse pur ricordo, XXXVIII/75
O fosse la paura, o che pigliasse, XXIX/65
O fosse pur per guadagnarsi il premio, XXIII/49
O maladetto, o abominoso ordigno, IX/91
O misera donzella, se costui, XXXXV/80
O misera Ravenna, t'era meglio, XIV/9
O per dir meglio, esser colei che crede, XXXVI/19
O pur che Dio da l'alta ierarchia, XXXII/66
O santa dea, che dagli antiqui nostri, XVIII/184
O si o no che 'l giovin gli credesse, XVII/107
O sia la fretta, o sia la troppa voglia, IX/76
O sia per sua superbia, dinotanto, XXXVI/18
O vera o falsa che fosse la cosa, VIII/58
Obizzo vedi e Folco, altri Azzi, altri Ughi, III/32
Ode Amone il figliuol con qualche sdegno, XXXXIV/36
Ode da tutto 'l mondo, che la parte, XXXX/65
Odi tu (gli disse ella), tu che sei, XX/138
Odorico, che mastro era di guerra, XIII/26
Ogni dì ne domanda a più di cento, VII/35
Ogni donna che trovin ne la valle, XXXVII/83
Ogni sua donna tosto, ogni donzella, XXIII/28

Ogni suo studio il Sericano, ogni opra, XXX/25
Ognun dunque si sforza di salire, XIV/117
Ognun potea veder quanto di sotto, XVII/103
Ognun s'allegra con Ruggiero, e sente, XXX/69
Ognun sapea ciò ch'egli avea gia fatto, XXVII/106
Oh come a quel parlar leva la faccia, XXXVI/79
Oh come ella sospira! oh come teme, XXXXV/28
Oh di che belle e saggie donne veggio, XXXXVI/3
Oh di quante battaglie il fin successe, X/54
Oh Dio, che disse e fece, poi che sola, V/60
"Oh (disse il duca a lui), grande è cotesto, V/31
Oh fallace degli uomini credenza!, XXXXI/23
Oh familice, inique e fiere arpie, XXXIV/1
Oh gran bontà de' cavallieri antiqui!, I/22
Oh gran contrasto in giovenil pensiero, XXV/1
Oh incurabil piaga che nel petto, XXXI/6
Oh infelice! oh misero! che voglio, VIII/78
Oh misera donzelle che trasporte, VIII/59
Oh quante sono incantatrici, oh quanti, VIII/1
Oh quanto volentier sopra sé tolta, XXXXVI/114
Oh quante volte da invidiar le diero, XXXII/12
Oh quanto ha il re, quanto ha il suo popul caro, V/87
Oh quanto si torrà per la tua morte, XXXXIII/173
Oh! se d'Amon la valorosa e bella, XXXXV/21
Oh se l'avesse il suo Orlando saputo, VIII/68
Oh se potessi ritornar mai vivo, XIX/32
Oh sommo Dio, come i giudicii umani, X/15
Oh troppo cara, oh troppo escelsa preda, VIII/62
Ohimè! ch'invano i' me n'andava altiera, XXX/33
Ohimè! con lunga et ostinata prova, XXXXIV /45
Ohimè! Ruggiero, ohimè! che arìa creduto, XXX/82
Olimpia Oberto si pigliò per moglie, XI/80
Oltemodo dolente si rispose, XI/15
Oltr'a quel del figliuol di Monodante, XXXV/53
Oltr'a queste e molt'altre ingiuriose, X/42
Oltra che i nostri facciano difesa, XIV/127
Oltre ch'a Fausto incresca del fratello, XXVIII/28
Oltre che di ragion, per lo tenore, XXXXVI/55
Oltre che già Rinaldo e Orlando ucciso, XXXXVI/68
Oltre che messi e lettere le mande, XXXXIII/184
Oltre che sempre si turbi il camino, VI/79
Oltre che sia robusto, e sì possente, IX/28
Oltre che tu farai quel che conviensi, XXXV/37
Oltre una buona quantità d'argento, XXVI/27
Omero Agamennón vittorioso, XXXV/27
Onde Agramante che per l'aer scuro, XXXX/7
Onde causato così strano e rio, XXXI/43
Onde con mesto e flebil voce uscio, VI/28
Onde par ch'esca il grido, va veloce, VIII/83
Or a poppa, or all'orza hann'il crudele, II/30
Or Brandimarte che vide per terra, XXXXI/72
Or c'ha inteso il partir del mio consorte, XXI/41
Or cader gli fa il pugno con la mazza, XV/82
Or cavalcando per quelle cantrade, XVIII/98

Or che con gran stupor vede la gente, XXXIII/113
Or che dovete (diceva ella), quando, XXXIII/72
Or che Gradasso esser Rinaldo intende, XXXI/93
Or che quivi la vede, e sa ben ch'ella, IV/42
Or che sel vede, come ho detto, in mano, XI/6
Or, come avviene a un cavallier ardito, XXI/17
Or cominciando i trepidi ruscelli, XII/72
Or corre a destra, or a sinistra mano, XXII/10
Or da fronte, or da tergo il vento spira, XXXXI/10
Or di Frontin quel animoso smonta, IV/46
Or Dio consente che noi siàn puniti, XVII/5
Or fatta la battaglia onde portonne, XXVII/10
Or fin a' denti il capo gli divide, XV/70
Or inanzi col calce, or col martello, XXXVIII/89
Or l'alta fantasia, ch'un sentier solo, XIV/65
Or l'uno e l'altro cavallier pagano, XXV/3
Or l'uno or l'altro ando molto cercando, XII/25
Or la cagion che conferir con voi, IX/53
Or né l'uno né l'altro è sì indovino, XVIII/71
Or per far quanti potea far ripari, XXXXIII/90
Or per l'ombrose valli e lieti colli, VII/32
Or piglia il tempo che, per esser senza, XXXVIII/47
Or pur tornando a lei, questa donzella, XX/4
Or qua Rinaldo, or là mutando il passo, XXXIII/81
Or quando fuor d'ogni ragion qui sono, XX/41
Or quella turba d'ira e d'odio pregna, XXXVII/106
Or questa meretrice, che si pensa, XXI/58
Or questo or quel pregando va, che porto, XXXXIII/159
Or quivi ritrovandosi Marfisa, XXXVI/16
Or Rinaldo lontan dal padre, quella, XXXXIV/14
Or Rodomonte che notar si vede, XXVII/110
Or, s'in voi la virtù non è diforme, IX/56
Or, se mi mostra la mia carta il vero, XXXXVI/1
Or si ferma, or volteggia, or si ritira, XXXXV/77
Or sopra ciò vostro consiglio chieggio, XXXVIII/40
Or su Gradasso, or su Ruggier percote, II/53
Or ti puoi ritornar; che se migliore, XXXXI/45
Or tornando a colei, ch'era presaga, VII/45
Or tu che sei per non usata via, VI/52
Or vedi quel ch'a Pinabello avviene, XXIII/2
Or volta all'una, or volta all'altra banda, IX/59
Or Zerbin, ch'era il capitano loro, XIX/10
Ora al demonio che mostrò a Rinaldo, II/23
Ora essendo voi qui per ascoltarmi, XXXVII/22
Ora io son qui per renderti mercede, XXXXIII/103
Orlando a tradimento gli diè morte, XXIII/80
Orlando, ancor che far dovea allegrzza, XXXXII/15
Orlando, che Gradasso in atto vede, XXXXI/73
Orlando, che gran tempo inamorato, I/5
Orlando, che l'ingegno avea sommerso, XXIX/47
Orlando che si vide fare il cerchio, XXXIX/48
Orlando, col cognato che non poco, XXXXIII/165
Orlando, come gli appertenga nulla, XI/54
Orlando (come il suo furor lo caccia), XXIX/41

Orlando (come io v'ho detto più volte), XXXX/59
Orlando di Sicilia non si parte, XXXXIII/182
Orlando domandò ch'iniqua sorte, XI/56
Orlando l'elmo gli levò dal viso, XXXXII/13
Orlando lo ferì nel destro fianco, XXXXII/11
Orlando non risponde altro a quel detto, XXIX/53
Orlando, poi che quattro volte e sei, XII/13
Orlando prega uno di lor, che vada, IX/62
Orlando se l'avea fatta compagna, XXIII/55
Orlando un suo mandò sul legno, e trarne, XXXXIII/196
Orlando volentieri o Sacripante, XII/24
Orlando volse a pena udire il tutto, IX/14
Orontea vivera ancora; e già mancate, XX/38
Ottanta mila cento e dua in un giorno, XXXVIII/35
Otto scontri di lance, che da forza, XVIII/9
Ove in Adrianapoli servato, XXXXVI/70
Ove la Sava nel Danubio scende, XXXXIV/79
Ove navilo e buona compagnia, XXXV/58
Ove posaro il resto di quel giorno, XXXXVI/48
Ove Rinaldo seco abbia il cavallo, XXXI/104
Ove sono a noi tolti questi aiuti, XXXVIII/57


P

Padre del ciel, dà fra gli eletti tuoi, XXXXI/100
Pallido e sbigottito il miser sprona, XXII/75
Pallido, crespo e macilente avea, VII/73
Panfilia e Caria e il regno de' Cilici, XXXIV/18
Par che dinanzi a questa bestia orrenda, XXVI/33
Par che gli occhi se ascondin ne la testa, XXVIII/27
Parea ad Orlando, s'una verde riva, VIII/80
Pargli angelica udir, che supplicando, XII/15
Parigi intanto avea l'assedio intorno, VIII/69
Parlando tuttavolta la donzella, XXXV/78
Parlo così, perché abbiàn qui un prigione, XX/49
Parlò in secreto a chi tenea la chiave, XXXXV/43
Parmi ch'ingiuria il mio destin mi faccia, XX/64
Parmi non sol gran mal, me che l'uom faccia, V/3
Parmi veder ch'alcun saper desia, XXVI/8
Parte la guardia, e prta l'imbasciata, XXXII/71
Parti fra gli altri un giuovinetto, figlio, XX/13
Partisse, e in pochi giorni ritrovosse, XXVIII/11
Partissi; e nulla poi più se n'intese, XXXV/52
Partita volentier la pugna avria, XXXVI/28
Parve, e non fu però buono il consiglio, XXVII/2
Parve più freddo ogni pagan che ghiaiccio, XVI/53
Passa il nocchiero, al suo viaggio intento, XX/100
Passando il paladin per quelle biche, XXXIV/76
Passando un giorno, come avea costume, IX/8
Passando una lor fusta a terra a terra, VIII/61
Passato de tre lance il destrier morto, XVI/61
Passi, chi vuol, tre carte o quattro, senza, XXVIII/3
Passò il resto del verno così cheto, XI/82
Passò in Navarra, et indi in Aragona, XXXIII/97

Passò per più d'un campo e più d'un bosco, XV/38
Pazzia sarà, se le pazzie d'Orlando, XXIX/50
Pel bosco erro tutta la notte il conte, XXIII/129
Pel dì de la battaglia ogni guerriero, XXXXI/30
Pel suo valor costei debitamente, XX/130
Pensa ella alquanto, e poi dice che vegna, XXVIII/62
Pensa la scusa, e poi gli cade in mente, XXVIII/19
Pensai per questo che l'incantatore, II/57
Pensate voi se gli tremava il core, XVII/48
Pensier (dicea) che 'l cor m'aggiacci et ardi, I/41
Pensò al fin di tornare alla spelonca, VII/37
Pensò Aquilante al primo comparire, XVIII/78
Pensò che dentro Anglante o dentro a Brava, XXVII/11
Pensò di rimontar sul suo cavallo, VI/58
Pensò Rinaldo alquanto, e poi rispose, IV/63
Pensoso più d'un'ora a capo basso, I/40
Per allegrezza de la buono nuova, XVII/67
Per altro modo punirò il tuo fallo, XXI/28
Per battezzarsi dunque, indi per sposa, XXII/36
Per ben saperne il certo, accortamente, XXV/21
Per ciò non perde il cavallier l'ardire, XXXX/25
Per cittadi mandò, ville e castella, XXXXV/117
Per compagno s'elegge alla battaglia, XXXX/58
Per cortesia (disse), un di voi mi mostre, II/16
Per debolezza più non potea gire, XXIV/76
Per Dio (dice), signore, pace facciamo, XXXXI/6
Per dunque provedergli di donzella, XXVI/71
Per far al re Marsilio e al re Agramante, I/6
Per gli ampli tetti andava il paladino, XXXV/3
Per guerrier valoroso e di gran nome, XVIII/97
Per imparar come soccorrer déi, XXXIV/56
Per l'avvenir vo' che ciasuna ch'aggia, XXIX/29
Per la città duo fiumi cristallini, XVII/19
Per la selva d'Ardenna in Aquisgrana, XXII/7
Per le cime dei pini e degli allori, VI/75
Per lei buono era vivo Madricardo, XXX/73
Per lungo e per traverso a fender teste, XXVII/25
Per medesimo messo fe' disegno, XXIII/26
Per mezzo il bosco appar sol una strada, XII/37
Per molti chiari gesti era famoso, XIV/31
Per ogni altra cagion ch'allontanto, XXXVIII/2
Per onorar costor ch'eran sostegno, XXXXIV/28
Per opra si costui sarà deserto, III/25
Per più intricarla il Tartaro viene anche, XXVII/43
Per più rispetti il paladino molto, XI/76
Per quel ch'io veglio, giovane amorosa, XXXV/39
Per quella via dove lo guida il nano, XXIII/38
Per questi merti la Bonta suprema, XV/26
Per questo dal nostro indico levante, XV/20
Per questo il re di Tartaria Agricane, VIII/43
Per questo mai di punta non gli trasse, XXXX/81
Per questo non le par men bello il viso, XXV/33
Per riavar l'ingegno mio m'è aviso, XXXV/2
Per riavere il buon destrier si mosse, XXVII/112

Per rinfacciargli che volea di Francia, XXXVIII/50
Per scender dal palazzo al mare e al porto, XX/84
Per te son giti et anderan sotterra, XI/27
Per titar briglia, non gli puo dar volta, VIII/36
Per tor lor duo de' nostri che prigioni, XXVI/6
Per troppo ardir si sarà forse messa, XXV/10
Per trovare i compagni il duca viene, XX/97
Per tutto 'l campo alto rumor si spande, XXXX/27
Per tutto 'l regno fa scriver Marsilio, XXXII/4
Per tutto avea genti ferite e morte, XXVI/32
"Per un mal ch'io patisco, ne vo' cento, IX/34
Per un piacer di sì poco momento, XXIX/14
Per una che biasmar cantando ardisco, XXII/3
Per una gamba il grave tronco prese, XXIV/6
Per veder se può far rompere il filo, XV/66
Per vendicar lei dunque debbo e voglio, XXXXV/89
Per voi saran dui principi salvati, XVI/33
Perch'era conosciuta da la gente, XXV/8
Perch'oltre i cavallieri, oltre i pedoni, XIII/82
Perché dal dì che fur tolti di sella, XXXVII/113
Perché debbo vedere in voi fortezza, XVII/15
Perché di lei nimico e di sua gente, XXI/6
Perché di vizii è questa coppia rea, VI/46
Perché egli mostrò amarmi più che molto, V/8
Perché fanciullo io sia, non creder farme, XVIII/150
Perché fatto non ha l'alma Natura, XXVII/120
Perché gli disse, e lo fe' chiaro e certo, XXXII/92
Perché gli è ancor lontana, e perché china, XI/34
Perché ha promesso contra Badamante, XXXXV/60
Perche le donne più facili e prone, XXXIV/14
Perché Marfisa una percossa orrenda, XXXVI/56
Perché non déi tu, mano, essere ardita, XXXVI/34
Perché non hai tu dunque a me il rispetto, V/30
Perché non sa dove si por, camina, XXXXIV/101
Perché non ti conobbi già dieci anni, XXXXIII/10
Perché quell'empio in tal furor venisse, XXXVII/44
Perche quei giorni che per terra il petto, XXXXIII/102
Perché, Ruggier, come di te non vive, XXXII/38
Perché sempre v'ho amato et amo molto, XXXXI/39
Perché, sì come è sola la fenice, XXVII/136
Perché stata saria, com'eran tutte, XXXVII/114
Perché vuoi tu, bestial, che gli innocenti, XXXV/42
Percosse egli il destrier di minor forza, XXXXI/70
Percuote il sole ardente il vicin colle, VIII/20
Però ch'avendo tutto quel rispetto, XXVIII/86
Però ch'in ripa al Nilo in su la foce, XV/65
Però ch'ogni altro amaro che si pone, XXXI/2
Però che Badamante, che'eseguire, XXXXIV/68
Però che conoscendo che nessuno, XXV/41
Però che dato fine alla gran festa, XIII/9
Però che l'un de l'altro non si fida, XXXVII/105
Però che lui sotto la vista offese, XXXI/10
Però che, fatta la prima battaglia, IX/39
Pero fece pensier, senza parlarne, XV/105

Piacciavi, generosa Erculea prole, I/3
Piace a Rinaldo, e piace a quel d'Anglante, XXXXV/107
Piacer, fra tanta crudeltà, si prende, XV/44
Piangeano quei signor per la più parte, XXXIX/47
Pianger de' quel che già sia fatto servo, XVI/3
Piantare i padiglioni, e le cortine, XVII/28
Pien de letizia va con l'altra schiera, XVII/65
Pien di paura e di dolor rimase, XXI/52
Piena d'un foco eterno e quella mazza, XXXXII/54
Pieno di dolce e d'amoroso affetto, I/54
Piglia una lancia, e va per far vendetta, XVIII/55
Pigliano la Fanciulla, e piacer n'hanno, XXVIII/54
Pigliar di tanta ingiuria alta vendetta, XXIV/34
Pinabel con sembiante assai cortese, XXII/53
Pinabello, un de' conti maganzesi, XX/111
Più ch'altre fosser mai, le tue famiglie, XIII/66
Più corto che quel salto era dua dita, XXIX/66
Più del terzo n'ha morto, e 'l resto caccia, XXIII/61
Più e più giorni gran spazio di terra, XXIV/93
Piu giorni ch'in questo cimiterio, III/12
Più inanzi, e poi più inanzi i passi muta, XXXXVI/29
Piu non starai tu meco; e questo sia, XXII/92
Più tosto vuol che volteggiando rada, XV/12
Piuaccia a te ancora, se privo di lei, XXXXVI/37
Placare o in parte satisfar pensosse, XXIX/31
Poca o molta ch'io ci abbia, non bisogno, VII/2
Poco dopo arrivò Zerbin, ch'avea, XXIII/43
Poco era men di trenta piedi, o tanto, XIV/130
Poco gli giova usar fraude a se stesso, XXIII/118
Poco guadagno, e perdita uscir molta, XXX/35
Poco l'onore, e molto era il periglio, XXVII/97
Poi cardinale appar, ma giovinetto, XXXXVI/90
Poi ch'a natura il duca aventuroso, XXXIV/61
Poi ch'al partir del Saracin si estinse, XVIII/38
Poi ch'alla più che mai sia stata o sia, XXXXV/94
Poi ch'allacciato s'ha il buon elmo in testa, XII/61
Poi ch'allargare il freno al dolor puote, XXIII/122
Poi ch'altro cavallier non si dimostra, XXVI/78
Poi ch'ebbe il vero Ariodante esposto, V/36
Poi ch'ebbon tanto riso, che dolere, XXVIII/72
Poi ch'in più parti quant'era a bastanza, XXIX/20
Poi ch'io lo trobo tale, io fo disegno, XXXIV/31
Poi che 'l dì venne e che lasciaro il letto, XXV/45
Poi che 'l fratello al fin le venne a dire, XXXVI/76
Poi che 'l suo annello Angelica riebbe, XIX/18
Poi che ben certi i cavallieri fece, XXXIII/74
Poi che con lunghe et iterate preci, XXXII/86
Poi che dagli altri allontanato alquanto, XXVI/63
Poi che de l'arme la seconda eletta, XXXVIII/81
Poi che de la vittoria Astolfo intese, XXXIV/19
Poi che di voce in voce si fe' questa, XXII/94
Poi che donne e donzelle ormai levate, XXV/58
Poi che Febo nel mar tutt'e nascoso, XXXXV/82
Poi che fu a Carlo et a Ruggiero a fronte, XXXXVI/105

```
Poi che fu all'esser primo ritornato, XXXIX/61
Poi che fu armata, la spada si cinse, XXVI/81
Poi che fu dentro a molte miglia andato, XXXXII/46
Poi che fu desto, e che de l'ora tarda, XVII/115
Poi che fu quattro o cinque giorni appresso, XXXII/14
Poi che fur giunti a piè de l'alta ròcca, II/48
Poi che furon d'daccordo, ritornosse, XXXI/106
Poi che gittar mi vidi i prieghi invano, XIII/28
Poi che gran pezzo al caso intervenuto, I/71
Poi che, inchinando le ginocchia, fece, XXXVIII/33
Poi che l'altro matin la bella Aurora, XXIII/52
Poi che l'augel trascorso ebbe spazio, VI/19
Poi che l'empio pagan molto ha sofferto, XXIX/5
Poi che l'ha seco in solitario loco, XXV/29
Poi che l'ordine suo vide esequito, XXXXIII/167
Poi che l'un quinci e l'altro quindi giunto, XXXI/110
Poi che la donna preso ebbe il sentiero, VIII/35
Poi che la figlia al vecchio par matura, XXXXIII/17
Poi che la luce candida e vermiglia, IV/68
Poi che la notte scelerata venne, XXI/48
Poi che la prima botta poco vale, X/102
Poi che le cerimonie finite hanno, XXXVIII/88
Poi che le parve aver fatto soggiorno, XIX/37
Poi che le racontò la maggior parte, XIII/74
Poi che mi fu, per questo mezzo, aviso, XXXIV/41
Poi che narrato ebbe con altro scritto, XXXV/57
Poi che non c'è Ruggier, che la contesa, XXXXVI/57
Poi che non parla più Lidia infelice, XXXIV/44
Poi che, orribil come era e spaventosa, XII/52
Poi che passò l'esercito di Spagna, XIV/17
Poi che più cose imaginate s'ebbe, XXV/85
Poi che più in alto il sole il camin prese, XXXXIII/145
Poi che quivi alla briglia alcun nol prende, XXXXIII/149
Poi che revisto ha quattro volte e cinque, XII/19
Poi che Ruggier fu d'ogni cosa in punto, X/68
Poi che s'affaticar gran pezzo invano, I/18
Poi che senza rimedio si comprende, XXXXI/18
Poi che sì ad alto vien, ch'un picciol punto, IV/50
Poi che si fece la notte più grande, XXV/57
Poi che si fur posati un giorno e dui, X/65
Poi che si vide il traditore uscire, II/72
Poi che si vide tor, come di furto, XVI/62
Poi che son d'arme e d'ogni arnese in punto, XXXXI/34
Poi che venne il cugin per la risposta, XXXXII/39
Poi che vestiti furo e bene armati, XXV/95
Poi, come gli è più presso, e vede in fronte, XVIII/65
Poi con gran pianto seguitò, dicendo, XI/58
Poi con risposte più beigne molto, XIV/60
Poi confortollo che no niega il cielo, XXXXI/56
Poi dice: -- Conosco io pur queste notte, XXIII/104
Poi disse: "A questo termine son io, V/35
Poi disse al conte: -- Uomo non vidi mai, XIII/34
Poi disse, come già disse Sileno, XXXIX/60
Poi disse lor: -- Facendo noi la via, XXII/46
```

Poi fattasi arrecare una sua veste, XXV/55
Poi gli rispose: -- Io sono il duca inglese, XX/66
Poi gli sovien ch'egli le avea promesso, XXV/84
Poi la donzella e sé richiama in chiesa, III/21
Poi la pregò che seco oltr'a quell'acque, XX/109
Poi le fece veder, come non fusse, XXIV/89
Poi li strascina fuor de la spelonca, XIII/41
Poi lo fe' rimontar su quello alato, XXXVIII/26
Poi lor convenzion ratificaro, XXVII/107
Poi mirando Odorico: -- Io vo' che sia, XXIV/40
Poi monta il volatore, e in aria s'alza, XXXIV/48
Poi mostra Cesar Borgia col favore, XXXIII/37
Poi mostra ove il duodecimo Luigi, XXXIII/34
Poi ne sceglie un che de' casi d'amore, XXXXII/35
Poi non conviene all'importanzia nostra, XXII/56
Poi quando in sella vòlse risalire, XXVII/115
Poi ritorna in se alquanto, e pensa come, XXIII/114
Poi rivolgendo a caso gli occhi, mira, I/77
Poi se ne vien dove col capo giace, XVIII/176
Poi se ne ritornò verso il pagano, XXXI/99
Poi seguì, dimandandole novella, XVII/40
Poi seguita, ch'essendo a tal partito, XXV/87
Poi seguitò, volendo dar consigli, XXII/60
Poi si feccion promettere ch'a quanti, XXXVII/116
Poi si vedea d'imperiale alloro, XXVI/34
Poi si vide sudar su per la scorza, VI/32
Poi volto a Ferraù, disse: -- Uom bestiale, XII/40
Pon mente ancor, che quando così aiti, XX/53
Poniamo ancor, che, come a vi pur pare, XXXII/104
Porta in azzurro una dorato sbarra, X/85
Portava Mandricardo similmente, XXVI/100
Portava quei ch'al periglioso ponte, XXXIX/30
Portòci alla sua tana il mostro cieco, XVII/33
Poscia ch'Argeo non conosciuto giacque, XXI/50
Poscia ch'egli restar vede l'entrata, XIV/49
Pose due volte il nostro campo in rotta, IX/30
Posti lor furo et allacciati in testa, XXX/47
Posto avea il genial letto fecondo, XXXXVI/77
Posto ch'ebbe alle liti e alle contese, XXVIII/85
Poté con queste e con miglior ragioni, XVI/39
Potea aver l'ippogrifo similmente, VII/78
Potea così scoprirlo al primo tratto, IV/22
Poteasi dar di somma astuzia vanto, XVIII/84
Potrai mandare un che Marfisa prieghi, XXVII/98
Potria in ogn'altro tempo esser creduto, XXV/82
Potria poco giovare e nuocer molto, XXXXIII/7
Potuto avrian pigliar la via mancina, XV/93
Pregar non val, né far di premio offerta, XXI/65
Pregato ho alcun guerrier, che meco sia, IX/54
Prendi quest'altra via, prendila, figlio, XV/46
Prese la strada all sinistra il conte, XII/56
Prese nuovo consiglio, e fu il migliore, X/107
Presi e montati c'hanno i lor cavalli, XVIII/121
Preson del campo; e come agli altri avvenne, XXXV/79

Presso alla porta ove Grifon venìa, XVII/119
Presto si volge, e nel voltar, cercando, XXII/88
Prima avendo spacciato un suttil legno, XXXVIII/36
Prima ch'altro disturbo vi si metta, IX/43
Prima ch'indi si partan le guerriere, XXXVII/115
Prima che parti, ne farai la prova, XXXXIII/29
Prima, credendo d'acquistar Marfisa, XXVI/107
Prima, di guadagnarla t'apparecchia, XXVII/59
Prima ne fur decapitati molti, XX/31
Proferte senza fine, onore e festa, XXXXIV/9
Promesso gli ho, non già per osservargli, XXI/43
Prora in terra non pon; che d'esser carca, IX/10
Proteo marin, che pasce il fiero armento, VIII/54
Provate mille abbiamo, e tutte belle, XXVIII/73
Può esser, vita mia, che non ti doglia, XXXXIV/57
Pur ch'io non resti fuor, non me ne lagno, XXXX/53
Pur ch'uscir di là su non si domande, IV/32
Pur, che non gli ha tolto anco le calcagna, XV/85
Pur chiude alquanto appresso all'alba i lumi, XXXIII/60
Pur ci passano alcuni, ma si rari, XX/61
Pur io vedrò di far che tu l'ottenga, XX/45
Pur la colpa potea dar al cavallo, XVII/90
Pur, per salvar l'onor, non solamente, XXXVIII/3
Pur, quando io avessi fatto solamente, XXXXV/88
Pur se ti par che non ci sia il tuo onore, XXXVIII/61
Pur si ritrova ancor su la riviera, I/24
Pur si torce e dibatte sì, che viene, XXXXVI/139
Pur suo talora o tre schiudon le labbia, XXXIX/76
Pur tra quei boschi il ritrovarsi sola, I/50
Pur vo' tanto cercar prima ch'io mora, XXVII/124
Pure Agramante la pugna sostiene, XXXIX/67
Purgati de lor colpe a un monasterio, XV/99


Q


Qua su lasciasti una citta vicina, XXXXIII/11
Quadi radendo l'aurea Chersonesso, XV/17
Qual buono astor che l'anitra o l'acceggia, XXIV/96
Qual cauto ucellator che serba vivi, IX/67
Qual con salnitro, qual con oglio, quale, XIV/132
Qual dì e la notte e mezzo l'altro giorno, I/35
Qual duro freno o qual ferrigno nodo, XXXXII/1
Qual Ettorre et Enea sin dentro ai flutti, XXXVI/6
Qual fa la lepre contra i cani sciolti, XXV/17
Qual istordito e stupido aratore, I/65
Qual lo stagno all'argento, il rame all'oro, XIII/70
Qual mensa trionfante e suntuosa, VII/20
Qual ne le alpine ville o ne' castelli, XV/50
Qual nomade pastor che vedut'abbia, XXXXII/7
Qual pargoletta o damma o capriuola, I/34
Qual per le selve nomade o massile, XVIII/22
Qual raggion fia che 'l buon Ruggier raffrene, XI/2

```
Qual sagra, qual falcon, qual colubrina, XI/25
Qual serpe che ne l'asta ch'alla sabbia, XXXVII/78
Qual soglion l'acque per umano ingegno, XVIII/154
Qual sotto il più cocente ardore estivo, XXXII/108
Qual su le mosse il barbaro si vede, XXXXV/71
Qual talor, dopo il tuono, orrido vento, XXXXV/72
Qual venir suol nel salso lito l'onda, XXIV/9
Quale al ceder de le cortine suole, XXXII/80
Quale è colui che prima oda il tumulto, XVI/88
Quale il canuto Egeo rimase, quando, XXXXVI/59
Quando allo scontro vengono a trovarsi, XXXXI/69
Quando allo scudo e quando al buono elmetto, XXXXV/76
Quando Angelica vide il giovinetto, XIX/20
Quando apparir Zerbin si vide appresso, XXIII/64
Quando aspettava che di Nicosia, XVI/11
Quando, cedendo Morini e Picardi, XIV/3
Quando conobbe non si apporre in fallo, XXVII/73
Quando crede cacciarlo, egli s'arresta, II/7
Quando di dritto e quando di riverso, XVIII/63
Quando di taglio la donzella, quando, XXXXV/74
Quando ella si fuggì dal padiglione, II/21
Quando ella venne a Mandricardo in mano, XVIII/29
Quando fallir sia quel che si fa a forza, XXI/23
Quando fu noto il Saracino atroce, XVI/21
Quando fu per passare, avea trovato, XXXIX/40
Quando gli parve poi, volse il destriero, II/50
Quando Gradasso il paladin gagliardo, XXXI/95
Quando il garzon sicuro de la vita, XXV/19
Quando io ti confortava a stare in pace, XXXVIII/49
Quando io v'avea in prigione, era da farme, XXII/79
Quando la vita a voi per voi non sia, XXX/36
Quando lo vide Ferraù cadere, XVI/73
Quando lo vide l'altro cavalliero, XXXXII/64
"Quando ne sarà il tempo, avisarotti", V/42
Quando nuocer pensai più alle tue squadre, XXXVIII/14
Quando oggi egli portò qui la tua gente, XVII/42
Quando Origille udi l'irata voce, XVIII/80
Quando pur vede che 'l pregar non vale, XXXVI/50
Quando Ruggier la vede tanto accesa, XXXVI/37
Quando si vede Ariodante quinto, V/55
Quando si vide in tante parti rosse, XXXXVI/121
Quando si vide sola in quel deserto, VIII/38
Quando uccidiate Orlando, e noi venuti, XXXXI/41
Quando un pianto s'udì da le vicine, XXXVI/84
Quando vicini fur sì, ch'udir chiare, XXIV/97
Quando vide la timida donzella, II/11
Quando vide scoprire alla marina, X/48
Quando vincer de l'impeto e da l'ira, XXX/1
Quante volte uscirai alla campagna, XXXVIII/59
Quanti prieghi la notte, quanti voti, XXV/44
Quanto che darà lor l'inclita prole, III/50
Quanto dovea parergli il dubio buono, XXXXIII/120
Quanto dura un de' velli, tanto dura, XXXIV/90
Quanto fia meglio, armandola tu ancora, I/20
```

Quanto il navilio inanzi era venuto, IX/17
Quanto mancò più la speranza, crebbe, XXXXV/79
Quanto più cerca ritrovar quiete, XXIII/117
Quanto più su l'instabil ruota vedi, XXXXV/1
Quanto potea più forte, ne veniva, I/15
Quanto Ruggier l'era nel core impresso, XXIII/29
Quanto utilmente, quanto con tuo onore, XXI/31
Quantunque debil freno a mezzo il corso, XI/1
Quantunque il simular sia le più volte, IV/1
Quantunque io sappia come mal convegna, XXXVIII/38
Quantunque sia debitamente mia, XXIII/81
Quasi ascosi avea gli occhi ne la testa, XXIX/60
Quasi de la montagna alla radice, XXXIII/127
Quasi Rinaldo di cercar suaso, XXXXII/104
Quasi sul collo del destrier piegosse, XXIV/68
Quegli ornamenti che divisi in molti, XXXV/9
Quei cavallier, con animo disposto, XVIII/191
Quei ch'a Rinaldo e a Carlo dier le spalle, XXXI/89
Quei ch'egli uccise e quei che i suoi fratelli, XXXI/85
Quei che la mensa o nulla o poco offese, XIII/40
Quei da le mura, che stimar non sanno, XXXV/73
Quei di Bellamarina, che Gualciotto, XIV/25
Quei di Dudone, a cui possanza e ardire, XXXIX/82
Quei di Tolledo e quei di Calatrava, XIV/14
Quei giorni che con noi contrario vento, IX/24
Quei rispondean ne la sbarrata piazza, XVII/85
Quei tutti che sapeva e gli era detto, IX/46
Quel baron molti armati seco tolse, XVII/128
Quel cade, e Mandricardo in piedi giuzza, XXIV/106
Quel ch'a Rinaldo in mille e mille imprese, XXXXII/48
Quel ch'a te dico, io dico al tuo vicino, XVII/78
Quel ch'era utile a dir, disse; e quel tacque, IV/10
Quel ch'in pontificale abito imprime, III/56
Quel ch'or mi dite, era da dirmi quando, XXXXV/111
Quel che d'Orlando agli altri far non lece, XI/51
Quel che fosse dipoi fatto all'oscuro, XIV/63
Quel che la tigre de l'armento imbelle, XVI/23
Quel che più fa che lor si inchina e cede, X/59
Quel Costantin di cui doler si debbe, XXXXVI/84
Quel d'Antiochia, più d'ogn'altro vile, XVII/71
Quel d'Antiochia, un uom senza ragione, XVII/86
Quel dì e la notte, e del seguente giorno, XXXXIV/15
Quel donò già Morgana a Ziliante, XIX/38
Quel fe' tre balzi; e funne udita chiara, XXIX/26
Quel fugge per la selva, e seco pota, XXIII/95
Quel giorno e mezzo l'altro segue incerto, XIV/38
Quel giorno in India lo provò, che tolto, XXII/27
Quel gli urta il destrier contra, ma Ruggiero, XXXXVI/126
Quel ladro non si stende a tutto corse, XXII/13
Quel letto, quella casa, quel pastore, XXIII/124
Quel liquor di secreto venen misto, I/79
Quel lodava Ruggier, che sì se avesse, X/45
Quel monstro lui ferir vuol d'una lancia, VI/65
Quel popul sempre stato era nimico, IX/83

```
Quel re che si tenea spacciato al tutto, XVIII/158
Quel sciocco, che del fatto non s'accorse, XV/84
Quel se gli appressa, e forte lo percuote, VIII/8
Quel signor disse lor: -- Vo' che sappiate, XXXIII/6
Quel tanto al Redentor caro Giovanni, XXXIV/58
Quel tuttavia più va perdendo il sangue, XXIV/71
Quel venne in piazza sopra un gran destiero, XIX/79
Quell'altra schiera è la gente di Bolga, XIV/24
Quell'era armata del più fin metallo, VII/3
Quell'era omo di Scozia, Almonio detto, XIII/22
Quella benigna e saggia incantatrice, VII/39
Quella ch'a piè rimase, dispettosa, XXII/51
Quella che gli avea detto il Padre eterno, XIV/82
Quella che quivi Orlando avea condutto, IX/85
Quella che tolto avea, come io narrava, XIV/115
Quella donna gentil che t'ama tanto, VII/68
Quella rara bellezza il cor gli acesse, VIII/31
Quella servò, come servar si debbe, XX/3
Quella vittoria fu più di conforto, XIV/6
Quelle c'hanno per scorta cavallieri, XXXVII/84
Quelle che i lor mariti hanno lasciati, XXVIII/81
Quelle due belle giovani amorose, VI/77
Quelli che entraro in mar, contati foro, XXXIX/29
Quelli promiser farlo volentieri, XXIII/99
Quello ippogrifo, grande e strano augello, VI/18
Quest'altro comparir ch'Adonio fece, XXXXIII/114
Quest'arte, con che i nostri antiqui fenno, XXXIII/5
Quest'era il re d'Algier, che per lo scorno, XXXXVI/102
Quest'era una fortezza ch'ad Amone, XXXXIV/73
Questa bestia crudele uscì del fondo, XXVI/40
Questa che forse è maraviglia a voi, XXXVII/38
Questa cittade, e intorno a molte miglia, II/64
Questa conclusion fu la secure, XXIII/121
Questa condizion contiene il bando, XXXXV/23
Questa è l'antiqua e memoriabil grotta, III/10
Questa è la cruda e avelenata piaga, XXXI/5
Questa è la vecchia che solea servire, XX/107
Questa era Fiordiligi, che sì acceso, XXXIX/39
Questa era quella Ippalca a cui fu tolto, XXVI/55
Questa imaginazion sì gli confuse, IX/15
Questa lor fu per dieci giorni stanza, XX/20
Questa Melissa, come so che detto, XXXXVI/20
Questa mia ingratitudine gli diede, XXXIV/43
Questa pietà ch'egli alla patria mostra, XV/33
Questa speranza dunque la sostenne, XXXII/27
Queste, ch'andar per la non ferma sabbia, X/38
Queste cose là dentro eran secrete, VII/30
Queste et altre parole ella non tacque, XXIII/8
Queste gli disse e più parole invano, XXI/9
Queste non son più lacrime, che fuore, XXIII/126
Queste parole e simile altre usai, XXXIV/30
Queste parole et altre assai, ch'Amore, XIV/59
Queste parole et altre dicea Orlando, XXXXIII/175
Queste parole et altre suggiungendo, XXXXVI/45
```

Queste parole et altro seguitando, XX/79
Queste parole han qui fatto venire, XXXII/59
Queste parole una et un'altra volta, XII/16
Questi ch'indizio fan del mio tormento, XXIII/127
Questi che noi veggiàn pittori, e quelli, XXXIII/3
Questi con l'altro esercito pagno, XII/70
Questi et ogn'altro che la patria tenta, XV/34
Questi guerrier, e più di tutti Orlando, XXXX/28
Questi parole et altre, ch'interrotte, XXXXV/102
Questi, quantunque d'amicizia poco, XXXXIV/3
Questi tre, la cui terra non vicina, XXXII/55
Questi vedendo il generoso figlio, XXXVI/25
Questo Brunel sì pratico e sì astuto, III/70
Questo ch'io v'ho narrato, in parte vidi, XVII/68
Questo ch'or a nui viene è il secondo Azzo, III/29
Questo da me più colte Polinesso, V/21
Questo debito a lui parea di sorte, XXXXIV/8
Questo destrier via più che fiamma rossi, XXXIV/69
Questo dicendo e molte altre parole, XXXXV/91
Questo disir, ch'a tutti sta nel core, II/36
Questo è ben veramente alto principio, VII/59
Questo è il buon cavallier, di cui dicea, XXXIII/48
Questo è il buon cavalliero il qual difeso, XXXXVI/54
Questo è il destrier che fu de l'Argalia, XV/41
Questo e l'annel ch'ella portò già in Francia, XI/4
Questo era un nuovo e disusato incanto, XII/21
Questo Ermonide disse, e più voleva, XXI/67
Questo et altro dicendo, in lei risorse, XXXXIII/164
Questo guerriero era Guidon Selvaggio, XXXI/29
Questo il pagan, troppo in suo danno audace, XV/3
Questo Lurcanio al padre l'ha accustata, IV/58
Questo, perché mille fiate inante, XV/104
Questo principe avrà quanta eccellenza, XXVI/47
Questo resta sul mar tanto possente, XIX/52
Questo sì presso l'una all'altra fero, XXXIX/13
Questo vi può bastar; né vi bisogna, XXXIII/73
Questo volgo (per dir quel ch'io vo' dire), XXXXIV/51
Qui consiste il ben vostro; né consiglio, XXXXI/40
Qui de la istoria mia, che non sia vera, XXXII/20
Qui, dove con serena e lieta fronte, VI/74
Qui la donzella il suo parlar conchiuse, IX/57
Qui la tenea; che 'l luogo avuto in dono, XXXII/84
Qui parve a lei fermarsi, e far vendetta, XX/27
Qui riman l'elmo, e là riman lo scudo, XXIII/133
Qui Rinaldo fe' fine, e da la mensa, XXXXIII/50
Quinci e quindi venir si vede il bianco, XXX/48
Quinci il Cataio, e quindi Mangiana, X/71
Quindi a levante fe' il nocchier la fronte, XVIII/75
Quindi avvien che tra principi e signori, XXXXIV/2
Quindi cercando Bradamente gia, II/33
Quindi espediti seguendo la strada, XXXVII/97
Quindi fui tratta alla galea spalmata, XIII/14
Quindi né cavallier né donna passa, XXII/48
Quindi partì Ruggier, ma non rivenne, X/69

Quindi partito, venne ad una terra, XXX/10
Quindi presso a dua miglia ritrovaro, XXIII/44
Quindi scopria de la regina tutta, XXVIII/34
Quindi seguendo il camin preso, venne, XXV/7
Quindi si parte, avendo già concetto, XXXI/77
Quindi si parte; ma prima rinuova, XXXX/64
Quindici o venti ne tagliò a traverso, XVIII/20
Quivi a Ruggier un gran corsier fu dato, VI/76
Quivi ad alcuni giorni e fatti sui, XXXIV/82
Quivi adattolla in modo in su l'arena, XV/59
Quivi arrivando in su l'aprir del giorno, XXXXIII/96
Quivi assedionne Alceste; et in non molto, XXXIV/23
Quivi attendiamo infin che steso all'ombra, XVII/58
Quivi Bardin di soma d'anni grace, XXXXIII/168
Quivi con Grifon stando il paladino, XVIII/124
Quivi d'estrano cavallier sembianza, XX/108
Quivi dei corpi l'orrida mistura, XVIII/183
Quivi divenne intrinseco e fratello, XXI/14
Quivi è Gradasso, quivi è Sacripante, IV/40
Quivi ebbe Astolfo doppia meraviglia, XXXIV/71
Quivi entra, che veder non la puo il mago, XII/26
Quivi era la Discordia impaziente, XXIV/114
Quivi era un uom d'età, ch'avea più retta, XXVIII/76
Quivi erano baroni e paladini, XIV/102
Quivi erano d'Apamia duo germani, XVII/96
Quivi fortificar facea le mura, XXXXV/12
Quivi Fortuna il re da tempo guida, XVII/39
Quivi fu assunto, e trovò compagnia, XXXIV/59
Quivi giunto Ruggier, Frontin conobbe, XXVI/92
Quivi gran parte era del populazzo, XVII/9
Quivi il bramoso cavallier ritenne, X/114
Quivi il caldo, la sete, e la fatica, VIII/21
Quivi il crudo tiranno Amor, che sempre, XIII/20
Quivi il nocchier, ch'ancor non s'era accorto, XXXIX/31
Quivi il tutto cercò, dove dimora, IX/6
Quivi l'audace giovane rimase, III/64
Quivi le Grazie in abito giocondo, XXXXVI/85
Quivi lo trovan che disegna a fronte, XV/96
Quivi mirabilmente transmutosse, VII/51
Quivi non era Bradamante allora, XX/102
Quivi non era Federico allora, XXXXIII/148
Quivi non si trovando altra mercede, XIX/40
Quivi odono il medesimo ch'udito, XVIII/140
Quivi parendo a lei d'esser sicura, I/36
Quivi pensando quanta ingiuria egli abbia, XXXXVI/27
Quivi per forza lo tirò d'incanto, IV/19
Quivi retruova che crudel battaglia, XV/67
Quivi rimase Ullania; e Marganorre, XXXVII/121
Quivi ritrova una picola chiesa, XXVIII/93
Quivi s'indugiar tanto, che Marfisa, XXXVII/120
Quivi sentendo poi che 'l vecchio Otone, XXII/8
Quivi si ferma il corridore al fine, XXIII/91
Quivi si vede, come il fior dispensi, XXXXVI/89
Quivi stando, il destrier ch'avea lasciato, VI/26

Quivi surgea nel lito estremo un sasso, X/23
Quivi trovar che s'era un altro legno, XXXX/46
Quivi trovò che di catena d'oro, XXII/24
Quivi un vecchio pastor, che di cavalle, XI/10
Quivi una bestia uscir de la foresta, XXVI/31
Quivi Zerbin tutte raguna l'arme, XXIV/57


R


Raccolse il cavallier cortesemente, XXV/73
Radoppia il colpo il valoroso conte, XXXXI/77
Ragion gli dimostrò il pericol grande, XXI/54
Ragionando tra sé, dicea Marfisa, XIX/99
Ragionerem più ad agfio insieme poi, XXXIV/57
Re Carlo intanto avendo la promessa, XXXXV/22
Re Fieramonte, che passò primiero, XXXIII/8
Re Fieramonte gli prestò tal fede, XXXIII/11
Re Nornadin, che temperato e saggio, XVIII/94
Re Norandin con la sua corte armata, XVIII/60
Religion non giova al sacerdote, XVI/25
Renduto ha il vostro Orlando al suo Signore, XXXIV/64
Renduto il nappo al sacerdote, lieto, XXXVII/70
Resti con lo scrittor de l'evangelo, XXXV/31
Ricciardo, Alardo, Ricciardetto, e d'essi, XXX/94
Riconobbe il messaggio i cavallier, XXIV/109
Riconosce Marfisa per sorella, XXXVI/67
Ricordati, pagan, quando uccidesti, I/27
Rifulse lo splendor molto più chiaro, XVIII/186
Riman di tanta cortesia Ruggiero, XXXXV/51
Riman la preda e 'l campo ai vincitori, XXVI/26
Riman Leon sì pien di maraviglia, XXXXVI/38
Rimase a dietro il lido e la meschina, X/20
Rimedio a questo il buon nocchier ritruova, XIX/53
Rimontò sul destriero, e ste' gran pezzo, XXIII/96
Rinaldo al Saracin con molto orgoglio, II/3
Rinaldo avea da Carlo e dal re Otone, VIII/27
Rinaldo che esaltar molto si vede, XXXVIII/67
Rinaldo, che non ha simil pensiero, XXIX/2
Rinaldo, che si vide la sorella, XXXXIV/75
Rinaldo, come accade ch'un pensiero, XXXXIII/64
Rinaldo disse al re: -- Magno signore, V/83
Rinaldo e 'l re Gradasso, che patire, XXXIII/89
Rinaldo il credette anco, e gran parole, XXXIII/86
Rinaldo inanzi agli altri il destrier punge, XVI/43
Rinaldo intanto e l'inclito Ruggiero, XXXVIII/74
Rinaldo l'altro e l'altro giorno scórse, IV/51
Rinaldo m'accennava, e similmente, VI/41
Rinaldo mai di ciò non fece meno, II/27
Rinaldo molto non lo tenne in lunga, XXXI/18
Rinaldo nostro n'ho avisato or ora, XXV/76
Rinaldo per Dalinda impetrò grazio, VI/16
Rinaldo se ne va tra gente e gente, V/82

Rinaldo si cacciò ne l'acqua a nuoto, VI/42
Rinaldo un giorno al padre fe' sapere, XXXXIV/35
Rinaldo vuol trovarsi con Orlando, XXXXII/69
Ringrazio anco, che la tua Issabella, XXIV/28
Rise Rinaldo, e disse: -- Io vo' tu senta, XVIII/152
Rispose Astolfo: -- Né l'angel di Dio, XXXIII/117
Rispose Ferraù: -- Tenete certo, XXXVI/13
Rispose il cavallier: -- La bella festa, XVII/25
Rispose il cavallier: -- Non ti rincresca, XXXXII/60
Rispose il cavallier: -- Tu vòi ch'io passi II/61
Rispose il nano: -- Né più tua né mia, XVIII/33
Rispose il re, non si voler partire, XVII/44
Rispose il Saracin: -- Che puoi tu farmi, XXVII/140
Rispose l'empia: "Io voglio che tu spenga, XXI/46
Rispose la Discordia: -- Io non ho a mente, XIV/86
Rispose Mandricardo: -- Indarno tenta, XXIV/98
Rispose quel, ch'era occupato il loco, XXXII/70
Rispose Rodomonte: -- Ottener questo, XXVI/115
Rispose Sacripante: -- Come vedi, I/69
Risposongli ch'errando in quelli boschi, IV/56
Risposto gli avea Amon, che da sé solo, XXXXIV/13
Ritarnando io da quelle isole estreme, VI/34
Ritornò il cavallier nel primo duolo, II/58
Ritrovar poche tempre e pochi ferri, XVI/50
Rivolge gli occhi orribili, e pon mente, XVIII/18
Rivolse poi con si efficaci preghi, XXXXVI/64
Rivolve tuttavia tra sé Rinaldo, XXXI/23
Rodomonte a quel segno ove fu colto, XXIV/104
Rodomonte a Ruggier dietro si spinge, XXVI/119
Rodomonte alla giostra s'apparecchia, XXXV/48
Rodomonte, ch'in mano ancor tenea, XXXXVI/127
Rodomonte, che 'l re, suo signor, mira, XXVII/82
Rodomonte col figlio d'Agricane, XXVII/6
Rodomonte crudel, poi che levato, XXIX/8
Rodomonte, del quale un più orgoglioso, XXVII/75
Rodomonte non già men di Nembrotte, XIV/119
Rodomonte per questo non s'arresta, XXXXVI/124
Rodomonte pien d'ira e di dispetto, XXXXVI/133
Rompe eserciti alcuno, e ne le porte, XXXXIII/3
Roppe il velo e squarciò, che gli copria, XXII/85
Rotta che se la vede, il gran troncone, XIV/45
Rotta l'asta, Rinaldo il destrier volta, XVI/49
Rotta la lancia, quella spada strinse, IX/70
Rotto a Pavia l'un campo, l'altro ch'era, XXXIII/54
Ruggier, che conosciuto avea per fama, VI/54
Ruggier, che questo sente, et ha timore, XXXXIV/76
Ruggier, che sempre uman, sempre cortese, XXII/37
Ruggier, che tolta avria non solamente, XXII/35
Ruggier che gli ama, sofferir non puote, XXXX/74
Ruggier che la donzella a mal partito, XXVI/126
Ruggier che stato era in esilio tanto, XXXXIV/16
Ruggier che vide il comite e 'l padrone, XXXXI/19
Ruggier, come di sopra vi fu detto, XXVI/3
Ruggier, come in ciascun suo degno gesto, XXXXI/4

Ruggier come gli alzò gli occhi nel viso, XXV/9
Ruggier (come io dicea) dissimulando, VIII/3
Ruggier da l'altra parte, ancor che molto, XXXVIII/68
Ruggier fu tratto di quel loco oscuro, XXXXV/49
Ruggier fuggito, il suo guardian strozzato, XXXXV/50
Ruggier, Gradasso, Iroldo, Bradamante, XXII/20
Ruggier, Gradasso, Sacripante, e tutti, IV/44
Ruggier non cessa, e spinge il suo cavallo, XXX/59
Ruggier non cessa: or l'una or l'altra prende, XXXVI/51
Ruggier non conoscendo ancor chi fosse, XXXV/80
Ruggier non perde il tempo, e di grande urto, XXXXVI/131
Ruggier non vuol cessar fin che decisa, XXVI/133
Ruggier non vuol ch'in altra pugna vada, XXX/20
Ruggier per la vittoria ch'avea avuto, XXXXV/5
Ruggier promette, se de la tenzone, XXXVIII/87
Ruggier pur d'ogn'intorno riguardava, XI/7
Ruggier, qual sempre fui, tal esser voglio, XXXXIV/61
Ruggier, quel dì che troppo audace ascese, XXIII/27
Ruggier riguarda Bradamante, et ella, XXII/32
Ruggier riman confuso e in pensier grande, XXXV/64
Ruggier rispose lor, che capitano, XXXXIV/98
Ruggier rispose: -- Gl'invitati ancora, XXVI/11
Ruggier rispose: -- Non ch'una battaglia, VI/80
Ruggier scontra Grifone, ove la penna, XXII/84
Ruggier se ne ritorna ove in disparte, XXVI/135
Ruggier, se ti guardò, mentre che visse, XXXVI/64
Ruggier si stava vergognoso e muto, VII/65
Ruggier sul capo al Saracin tempesta, XXVI/121
Ruggier tenne lo 'nvito allegramente, XXXVI/12
Ruggiero a quel parlar ritto levosse, XXXXVI/107
Ruggiero a quel parlar salito in piede, XXVI/61
Ruggiero accettò il regno, e non contese, XXXXVI/71
Ruggiero accortamente le rispose, XXXVI/80
Ruggiero, al fin constretto, il ferro caccia, VIII/9
Ruggiero al vecchio domandò, chi fosse, XXII/64
Ruggiero alla sorella non ascose, XXXVI/68
Ruggiero, ancor ch'a par di Bradamante, XXXXVI/99
Ruggiero andò due volte a capo chino, XXXXVI/123
Ruggiero in questo mezzo avea seguito, XXVI/88
Ruggiero incominciò, che da' Troiani, XXXVI/70
Ruggiero intanto, poi ch'ebbe gran pezzo, XI/13
Ruine di cittadi di castella, XXXIV/79


S

S'a disfidar s'ha Orlando, son quell'io, XXXX/52
S'a quella etade ella in Arimino era, XXXXVI/6
S'acconcia il mostro in guisa al fiero assalto, XXXXII/49
S'acquisito c'è, tu 'l sai. Trentadui fummo, XXXVIII/53
S'affatica Agramante, ne disciorre, XXX/19
S'al fiero Achille invidia de la chiara, XXXVII/20
S'appiglia al fin, come a miglior partito, XXVII/104
S'appresentò Ruggier con l'augel d'oro, XXXXVI/52

S'attendete, signori, al mio consigli, XXXX/44
S'attonito restasse e malcontento, XXVIII/22
S'ebbero un tempo in urta e in gran dispetto, XXXI/41
S'era accostato Pinabello intanto, XXII/71
S'era partito disarmato e a piede, XXXV/55
S'erano assisi, e porre alle vivande, XXXII/97
S'imagini che tal, poi che cadendo, IX/79
S'impalidisce, e tutta cangia in viso, XXXII/101
S'impetrar lo potrò, vo' che 'l suo nome, XXXX/78
S'in altro conto aver vuoi a far meco, XX/123
S'in poter fosse stato Orlando pare, XII/3
S'incrudelisce e inaspra la battaglia, XII/50
S'io ci fossi per donna conosciuta, XX/78
S'io non sarò al mio padre ubbidinte, XXXXIV/46
S'io ti parvi esser degna d'una morte, XXXXIII/142
S'odon lor colpi dispietati e crudi, XXXI/21
S'odon ramaricare i vecchi giusti, XIV/101
S'un medesimo ardor, s'un disir pare, IV/66
Sa ch'ogni poco più ch'ivi rimane, VIII/10
Sa dove è saldo e da dove è piu molle, XXXI/72
Sa questo altier ch'io l'amo e ch'io l'adoro, XXXII/19
Salito Astolfo sul destrier volante, XXIII/16
Salta a cavallo, e per diversa strada, XXX/8
Salta a cavallo, e vien spronando in fretta, XXXVI/17
Salta ora in questa squadra et ora in quella, XXVI/16
Saltaro a piedi, e con aperte braccia, XXIV/19
Salvossi il Ferruffin, restò il Cantelmo, XXXVI/7
Sansonetto all'incontro al duca diede, XV/98
Sapea ben al virtù de la sua spada, XXXVI/55
Sapea che di grazvissimo periglio, XXXXIV/7
Sappi, signor, che mia sorella è questa, XVIII/82
Sappiate che costor che qui scritto hanno, XXVI/39
Sarà possibil mai che nome regio, XXXXIV/58
Saria la legge, ch'ogni donna colta, XXVIII/82
Satanasso (perch'altri esser non puote), XVI/87
Sbrigossi dalla donna il mago alora, IV/39
Scarpello si vedrà di piombo o lima, XXXXIV/62
Sceglie de' suoi scudieri il più fedele, XXXXIV/78
Sceglieronne una; e sceglierolla tale, XXXVII/16
Scende alla spalla; e perché la ritrovi, XXXXI/76
Scende la tomba molti gradi al basso, XII/90
Sceso era Astolfo dal giro lucente, XXXVIII/24
Sceso nel lito il cavallier d'Anglante, XXXXI/36
Schiavon crudele, onde hai tu il modo appreso, XXXVI/8
Scioglie il nochier, come venir lo vede, X/44
Sciolto che fu il pagan con leggier salto, II/8
Sciolto era l'elmo e disarmato il collo, XXXXII/9
Scontraro il dì seguente inver la sera, XXXI/8
Scontrò presso a Damasco il cavalliero, XVI/6
Scontrossi col re d'Africa Oliviero, XXXXI/71
Scordendo il legno uomini in acqua dotti, XXXXIII/189
Scorrendo il duca il mar con sì fedele, XV/18
Scòstati un poco, scòstati da casa, XXXXIII/26
Scrive l'autore, il cui nome mi taccio, XXIV/45

Scrive Turpino, come furo ai passi, XXXXIV/23
Scuotesi Orlando, e lungi dieci passi, XXXIX/50
Sdegnata e malcontenta la via prese, XII/65
Sdegnosa piu che vipera, si spicca, XXXVI/46
Se 'l dubbio di morir ne le tue tane, XVII/77
Se 'l sol si scosta, e lascia i giorni brevi, XXXXV/38
Se 'l vi ricorda quel ch'avete udito, XX/135
Se Balisardo lo giungea pel dritto, XXX/55
Se béi con questo, vedrai grande effetto, XXXXII/103
Se ben di Carlo in questo mezzo intese, XXXXVI/103
Se ben di quante io n'abbia fin qui amate, XXVII/123
Se ben m'avesse ucciso, tormentato, XXXXV/90
"Se ben non mi conosci, o cavalliero, XXXXIII/97
Se ben non veggon gli occhi ciò che vede, XXXI/3
Se bene uso von gli altri cortesia, XXXVI/21
Se Bireno amò lei come ella amato, X/4
Se chi sian queste, e di ciascuna voglio, XXXVII/15
Se, come il viso, si mostrasse il core, XIX/2
Se, come in acquistar qualch'altro dono, XXXVII/1
Se conosciute il re quell'arme avesse, XVII/83
Se Cristianissimi esser voi volete, XVII/75
Se d'avarizia la tua donna vinta, XXXXIII/48
Se d'aver meco a far non ti dà il core, XXXI/97
Se d'ogn'altro peccato assai più quello, XXXII/41
Se da Gradasso vi fosse condutto, XXXIII/92
Se da Iocondo il re bramava udire, XXVIII/40
Se de l'animo è tal la nobiltate, XXXXVI/23
Se de l'aspra donzella il braccio e grave, XIX/97
Se di disio non vuol morir, bisogna, XIX/30
Se di Gradasso la ragion prevale, XXVII/61
Se di lontano o splendor d'arme vede, XXXII/15
Se di portarne il furto ascosamente, XXIII/42
Se di provarti c'hai fatto gran fallo, XXVI/97
Se di sangue vedessino una goccia, XXIV/51
Se di scoprire avesse avuto aviso, VI/67
Se di te duolmi e di quest'altri tuoi, XIX/103
Se dieci o venti più persone a un tratto, XX/35
Se donavan gli antiqui una corona, XVI/36
Se, dopo lunga prova, a gran fatica, IV/2
Se dunque da far altro non mi resta, IX/51
Se duo, tre, quattro o più guerrieri a un tratto, XXXII/67
Se Fortuna di me non ebbe cura, XXXXIII/12
Se fosse stata a quell'ostel d'Atlante, XXIV/55
Se fosse stata ne le valli Idee, XI/70
Se fu quel letto la notte dinanti, XXV/69
Se gli accosta all'orecchio, e pianamente, XIV/95
Se gli è amico o nemico non comprende, I/39
Se gli fe' incontra, e con sembiatne altiero, VIII/5
Se gli spiccano il capo, Orrilo scende, XV/71
Se i nomi e i gesti di ciascun vo' dirti, III/23
Se in Almonte e in Troian non ti potevi, XXXVI/77
Se l'affogniarmi in mar morte non era, VIII/44
Se l'intricati rami e l'aer fosco, I/73
Se l'onor vostro, e queste tre vi sono, XXXVII/42

Se la donna s'affligge e si tormenta, XXXXIV/48
Se Laodamìa, se la moglier di Bruto, XXXVII/19
Se lo porta il destrier per la campagna, XXVI/118
Se mai d'aver veduto vi raccorda, XXVI/17
Se mal si seppe il cavallier d'Anglante, I/57
Se mi domanda alcun chi costui sia, I/45
Se molti non si fossero interposti, XXVII/67
Se n'accorse uno, e ne parlò con dui, XXII/40
Se ne va in questa e in quella parte errando, XXI/38
Se non basta ch'Argeo mi tenga preso, XXI/33
Se non ti muovon le tue proprie laudi, VII/60
Se non ti par questo partito buono, XX/125
Se Norrandino il simil fatto avesse, XVIII/3
Se parve al re vituperoso l'atto, XXVIII/44
Se per adietro abbiàn perduto, io temo, XXXVIII/56
Se per amar, l'uom debbe essere amato, XIV/58
Se per mangiare o ber quello infelice, XXXIII/108
Se però presa son per non avere, XXXV/100
Se, poi che Carlo avrà lo scudo avuto, XXXII/58
Se pur ad aiutarti i duri fati, XXXXIII/162
Se pur volevi, Amor, darmi tormento, XXV/35
Se, quando arriva un cavallier, si trova, XXXII/66
Se quanto dir se ne potrebbe, o quanto, XXXVII/21
Se questi il fior, se questi ognuno stima, XXXXIV/47
Se Ruggier qui s'affligge e si tormenta, XXXXV/95
Se sei (dicea) sì ardito e sì cortese, XXXV/36
Se stava all'ombra o se del tetto usciva, XIX/35
Se tacito Ruggier s'affligge et ange, XXXVIII/70
Se tu m'avessi posto alla difesa, XXIV/31
Se tu m'occidi, è ben ragion che deggi, XXXVI/33
Se tu sai che fedel la moglie sia, XXXXII/101
Se turbarete coi l'ordine in parte, XXVII/62
Se vuoi saper se la tua sia pudica, XXXXII/102
Seco avrà la sorella Beatrice, XIII/62
Seco chiamollo, e vòlse che prendesse, V/45
Seco dicea: -- Non è Ruggier costui, XIII/77
Secondo il luogo, assai contento stava, XXXXI/60
Sedeva in tribunale amplo e sublime, XXVII/50
Sedici mila sono, o poco manco, X/89
Segue la terza schiera di Marmonda, XIV/18
Seguendo, si partir de la fontana, XXXIII/90
Seguia Ruggiero in fretta il Saracino, XXVI/91
Seguitò l'eremita riprendendo, XXXXI/55
Seguitò la vittoria, et a sue spese, XXXIV/36
Seguon gli Scotti ove la guida loro, XIX/16
Sei cavallier con lor ne lo steccato, V/81
Sei giorni me n'andai matina e sera, II/41
Semplicemente disse le parole, XXXV/77
Sempre che l'inimico è più possente, XXIV/32
Sempre ha in memoria, e mai non se gli tolle, XXXXII/44
Sempre ha timor nel cor, sempre tormento, XXXXI/33
Senapo imperator de la Etiopia, XXXIII/102
Sentendo il re Agramante a che periglio, XXXVIII/37
Sentendo poi che gli gravava troppo, XXIX/70

```
Sentia il maggior piacer, la maggior festa, VIII/81
Sento venir per allegrezza un tuono, XXXXVI/2
Senza aspettar risposta urta il destriero, XX/129
Senza che tromba o segno altro accennasse, XXXIII/79
Senza dir altro, o più notizia darsi, XXXI/9
Senza indugio al nocchier varar la barca, XXVIII/87
Senza mai riposarsi o pigliar fiato, XXIV/101
Senza molti scudier dietro o davante, XVIII/90
Senza nocchieri e senza naviganti, XXXX/61
Senza pensar che sian l'imagin false, VIII/84
Senza più indugio alla città ne vanno, XVIII/105
Senza prender riposo erano stati, XXXIII/83
Senza risponder altro, la donzella, XXII/58
Senza scudiero e senza compagnia, IV/54
Senza scudiero e senza compagnia, XXXII/49
Senza smontar, senza chinar la testa, XXXXVI/104
Senza strepito alcun, senza rumore, XVI/40
Senza trovar cosa che degna sia, XIII/44
Settecento con lui tenea Rinaldo, XXXI/56
Si buono è quella piastra e quella maglia, XXVI/84
Sì ch'avea causa di venir Brunello, XIV/21
Si ch'essendo dipoi preso e condutto, XXXXVI/62
Sì che continuando il primo detto, XXXV/30
Si che i navili che d'Astolfo avuti, XXXIX/80
Si che né più si puon calar di sopra, XI/38
Sì che non è per mai trovarsi stanco, XXXVII/10
Sì che non pur la gente che gli chiede, XXXVIII/28
Sì che, o chiaro fulgor de la Fulgosa, XXXXII/22
Si che per dare ancor più maraviglia, X/91
Sì che, per rimediarvi, in fretta manda, XXXXIII/130
Sì che prima ch'entrassero in viaggio, XV/94
Si che s'avete, cavalier, desire, IX/11
Si che, salvando una città, non soli, XVI/34
Sì che, temprando il suo rigore un poco, XX/30
Si come il lupo che di preda vada, XXXVII/95
Si dice che 'l soldan, re de l'Egitto, XXXIII/106
Si fe' Agramante la cagione asporre, XXVII/68
Si fe' quivi arrecar piu d'una fune, XXXIX/54
Sì forte ella nel mar batte la coda, X/106
Si fu propizio il vento, si fu l'ora, XX/19
Sì l'occupa il dolor, che non avanza, XXXII/26
Si levan quindi, e poi vanno all'altare, XXXVIII/85
Si maraviglia la donzella, come, XIX/108
Sì poco, e quasi nulla era di luce, XXXIV/8
Si rallegra Mongrana e Chiaramonte, XXXXVI/67
Si ricordò del bando, e si ravvide, XXXV/78
Si rivolta ai compagni, e dice: -- Io sono, XXIV/38
Si sentono venir per l'aria, e quasi, XXXIII/121
Si tira i remi al petto, e tien le spalle, XI/32
Si tosto a pena gli sferraro i piedi, XVII/135
Si vede altrove, a gran pensieri intento, XXXXVI/95
Si vede per gli essempii di che piene, XXXV/4
Si vennero a incontrar con esso al varco, XXIX/52
Sia quel che puo, più tosto vuol morire, VI/68
```

Sia vero o falso che Ginevra tolto, IV/64
Sia vile agli altri, e da quel solo amata, I/44
Siatemi testimoni, ch'io prometto, XXXVIII/83
Sicuramente Fiordiligi intanto, XXIX/49
Siede Parigi in una gran pianura, XIV/104
Siedono al fuoco, e con giocondo e onesto, XXXII/82
Signor, far mi convien come fa il buono, VIII/29
Signor mio (disse al fin), quando saprai, XXXXVI/34
Signor, ne l'altro canto io vi dicea, XXIV/4
Signor, non voglio che vi paia strano, II/20
Signor, queste eran quelle gelide acque, XXXXII/61
Signor, qui presso una città difende, XXXXIII/32
Signoreggia Forbesse il forte Armano, X/87
Simil battaglia fa la mosca audace, X/105
Simile esempio non credo che sia, XXXVI/10
Simula anch'ella; e così far conviene, IV/3
Simula il viso pace; ma vendetta, XXXVII/60
Sin alle stelle il volator trascorse, II/52
Slegate il cavallier (gridò), canaglia, XXIII/58
Smonta con pochi, ove in più lieve barca, XXXX/8
Smonta il Circasso et al destrier s'accosta, I/74
So ch'io m'appiglio al torto; e al torto sia, VI/11
So che i meriti nostri atti non sono, XIV/72
So quanto, ahi lassa! debbo far, so quanto, XXXXIV/43
So scudo e lancia adoperare anch'io, XXVI/80
Sobrin che di tanto uom vede l'assalto, XXXXI/74
Sobrin che molto sangue avea perduto, XXXXII/16
Sobrin gli era a man manca in ripa a Senna, XIV/108
Sobrin redoppia il colpo, e di riverso, XXXXI/88
Sol per lui visitar, che gravemente, XXXII/34
Sol per signori e cavallieri e fatto, XXIX/42
Soletto lo trovò, come lo volle, VII/53
Solo senza te son; né cosa in terra, XXXXIII/171
Sommamente ebbe Astolfo grata questa, XVIII/103
Son cinque cavallier c'han fisso il chiodo, XXVII/102
Son, come i cigni, anco i poeti rari, XXXV/23
Son dunque (disse il Saracino), sono, I/80
Son fatti in questa legge disuguale, IV/67
Son pochi dì ch'Orlando correr vidi, XXXI/45
Son simile all'avar c'ha il cor sì intento, XXXXV/34
Sono altri esposti, altri tenuti occulti, XX/12
Sono appoggiate a un tempo mille scale, XIV/116
Sono omai dieci giorni (gli soggiunse), XXIII/73
Sopra di lei più lance rotte furo, XIX/84
Sopra gli altissimi archi, che puntelli, X/61
Sopra gli altri il signor di Montalbano, XXXXIV/6
Sopra gli altri ornamenti ricchi e belli, XXXXII/78
Sopra Gradasso il mago l'asta roppe, II/51
Sopra il sanguigno corpo s'abbandona, XXIV/86
Sopra ogn'altr'arme, ad espugnarlo, molto, XXVI/46
Sopra tutti i rumor, strepiti e gridi, XXVII/90
Sopravien l'oste, e di colui l'informa, XVII/116
Soriani in quel tempo aveano usanza, XVII/73
Sorrise amaramente, in piè salito, XIII/35

Sospira e geme, non perché l'annoi, I/66
Sotto il castel ne la tranquilla foce, X/53
Sotto la fede entrar, sotto la scorta, XV/32
Sotto la negra selva una capace, XIV/93
Sotto quel sta, quasi fra due vallette, VII/13
Sotto sue negri e sottilissimi archi, VII/12
Soviemmi che cantare io vi dovea, XXXII/1
Spera ch'in Francia, alla famosa corte, XXXII/54
Spera, per forza di piedi e di braccia, XXXXI/22
Spera, s'alquanto il tien da sé rispinto, XXXXI/90
Spesso di cor profondo ella sospiera, XXIII/7
Spesso in difesa del biasmato absente, XVIII/2
Spesso in poveri alberghi e in pocciol tetti, XXXXIV/1
Spesso la voce dal disio cacciata, XXXXII/98
Spinge il cavallo, e ne la turva sciocca, XVIII/113
Spinge l'augello: e quel batte sì l'ale, VIII/6
Spingonsi inanzi, e via più chiaro il suon ne, XXXVII/26
Spinse a un tempo ciascuno il suo cavallo, XVI/52
Spinse il demonio inanzi al mesto figlio, XXXIX/5
Spirando il vento prospero alla poppa, VIII/26
Splende lo scudo a guisa di piropo, II/56
Sprona Frontin che sembra al corso un vento, XXXXIV/85
Sta Bradamante tacit, né al detto, XXXXIV/39
Sta la cruda Anassarete più al basso, XXXIV/12
Sta Polinesso con la faccia mesta, V/88
Sta su la porta il re d'Algier, lucente, XVII/11
Stando ella quivi, il principe, il signore, XXX/90
Stando in questo pensoso il cavalliero, XXXIII/67
Stando quivi suspesa, per ventura, XXIII/18
Standosi quivi, e di gran spazio essendo, XIII/46
Standovi un giorno il Saracino pensoso, XXVIII/95
Stassi Caligorante in su la porta, XV/51
Stassi d'Amon la sbigottita figlia, III/13
State, vi priego per mia verde etade, XVIII/50
Stati che sono in gran piacere e in festa, XVIII/133
Stato era il cavallier sempre in un canto, XIX/88
Stato era in campo, e inteso avea di quella, I/47
Stava ella nel sepulcro; e quivi attrita, XXXXIII/185
Stava il pastore in assai buona e bella, XIX/27
Stava Marfisa con serena fronte, XXXVI/75
Stava mirando se vedea venire, XXII/30
Stava Ruggier, com'io vi dissi, in atto, XXXVII/25
Stava Ruggiero in tanta gioia e festa, VII/33
Stendon le nubi un tenebroso velo, XVIII/142
Stero in questo travaglio, in questa pena, XIX/50
Steron taciti al detto d'Agramante, XXX/23
Stese le mani, et abbraciar lo volle, XXXIX/44
Stete fra gli altri un giorno a veder, ch'ella, XXVIII/38
Stette alquanto a pensar; poi si risolse, XXIII/22
Stette sei mesi che non messe piede, XXI/35
Stimando non aver Gradasso altrove, XXXX/57
Stordilano e Tesira e Baricondo, XIV/13
Stordito de l'arcion quel re stramazza, XII/84
Streptio ascolta e spaventevol suono, XI/16

Stringe Fusberta, poi che l'asta è rotta, XVI/82
Stringonsi insieme, e prendono la via, XXVII/18
Studisi ognun giovare altrui; che rade, XXIII/1
Stupida e fissa nella incerta sabbia, VIII/39
Stupisce Cloridan, che tanto core, XVIII/170
Su la riviera Ferraù trovosse, I/14
Su per la soglia e fuor per le colonne, VI/72
Sua forza o sua destrezza vuol che cada, XXXXVI/128
Subito il paladin dietro lor s[rona, XXXIII/126
Subito s'arma, et a fatica aspetta, XXX/46
Subito smonta, e fulminando passa, XII/9
Sugginse a lei Guidon: -- Tu m'avrai pronto, XX/72
Suggiunse a liu Marfisa: -- Al tuo dispetto, XX/124
Suggiunse a queste altre parole molte, XXXXIV/67
Suggiunse Ferraù: -- Sciocchi voi, quasi, XII/42
Suggiunse il duca: "Non sarebbe onesto, V/40
Suggiunse poi: -- Tu forse avevi speme, XXXI/96
Sul collo inanzi del destrier si pone, XXVII/94
Suonar per gli alti e spaziosi tetti, XVII/13


T

Taccia che loda Fillide, o Neera, XI/12
Tacque Merlino avendo così detto, III/20
Tagliò in due parti il provenzal Luigi, XIV/125
Tagliò lo scritto e 'l sasso, e sin al cielo, XXIII/130
Taglionne quanto ella ne prese, e insieme, XXX/60
Tal Bradamante si dolea, che tolto, XXXXV/40
Tal ne la piazza ho il tuo valor provato, XX/71
Tanacro, che non mira quanto importe, XXXVII/65
Tant'era l'amor grande che Zerbino, XXIV/47
Tante donne, tanti uomini traditi, XXIV/42
Tanto desire il paladino preme, IX/92
Tanto esaltazione e così presta, XXXV/7
Tanto le prese andò mutando il franco, XXXXVI/134
Tanto replica l'un, tanto soggiunge, XXVIII/68
Tanto un giorno et un altro se n'andaro, XXXI/37
Temperando il dolor che gli ardea il petto, XII/62
Tenea la mano al buco de la tana, XVII/55
Tenea quell'Altaripa il vecchio conte, XXIII/4
Tenea Ruggier la lancia non in resta, X/101
Tenendo tuttavia le belle braccia, XXXXIII/93
Tener non poté il conte asciutto il viso, XXXXIII/152
Tenner lo 'nvito senza alcun sospetto, XIX/107
Tenni modo con lei, ch'avea desire, XVIII/83
Tentar, prima ch'accada, si dispone, XXXIV/24
Termine a ritornar quindici o venti, XXX/81
Termine tolse alla risposta, e spene, XXXXII/34
Terrà costui con più felice scettro, III/34
Terran Pugliesi, Calabri e Lucani, III/47
Ti parrà duro assai, ben lo conosco, XIII/53
Timagora, Parrasio, Polignoto, XXXIII/1
Tocca avean nel cader la terra a pena, XIX/96

Tolse il destrier ch'Astolofo aver solea, XXXII/48
Tolte che fur le mense e le vivande, VII/21
Tolto in quel tempo una gran lancia avea, XVIII/44
Tommi la vita, giovene, per Dio, IV/28
Tor penso che la donzella, III/5
Torna al patron con gran vergogna et onta, XXXXIII/127
Torna Ruggiero in Arli, ove ha ritratta, XXXVIII/7
Torna verso Arli; che trovarvi spera, XXXX/69
Tornando a lui la vincitrice in sella, XX/128
Tornaro ad iterar gli abbracciamenti, XXII/33
Tornate a dietro, o pigliate altra via, XII/39
Torniamo a quel di eterna gloria degno, X/57
Tornò Grifon con la medesma antenna, XVII/94
Tornò la fiamma sparsa, tutta in una, XIV/133
Tosto ch'al fin le sante esequie foro, XXXVII/69
Tosto ch'ella ai tre colpo tutti gli ebbe, XXXII/77
Tosto ch'entraro, e ch'ella loro il viso, XXXXIII/157
Tosto ch'essi lui veggiono sul lito, XVII/37
Tosto che 'l buon Ruggiero in se ritorna, XXVI/120
Tosto che 'l castellan di Damiata, XV/90
Tosto che 'l ladro, o sia mortale, o sia, II/38
Tosto che 'l Saracin vide la bella, XXVIII/98
Tosto che fuor del ponte i guerrier vede, XXXII/75
Tosto che furo a terra, udir le nuove, XXXIX/42
Tosto che l'orca s'accostò, e scoperse, XI/37
Tosto che la donzella più vicino, XXXI/42
Tosto che ne la foce entrò lo stanco, IX/18
Tosto che pon dentro alla soglia il piede, XII/18
Tosto che riconobbe Rodomonte, XVIII/32
Tosto che sente il Tartaro superbo, XXX/45
Tosto che son nel borgo, alcuni fanti, XXXVII/99
Tosto che spunti in ciel la prima luce, III/63
Tosto che vede il Tartaro Marfisa, XXVI/70
Tra casa di Maganza e di Chiarmonte, II/67
Tra duri sassi e folte spine gia, VIII/19
Tra gli altri di sua corte avea assai grato, XXVIII/6
Tra Gradasso e Ruggier credo che sia, XXX/22
Tra i cavallier la donna di gran core, XXIV/111
Tra il fin d'ottobre e il capo di novembre, IX/7
Tra la marina e la silvosa schena, XXXIII/100
Tra le purpuree rose e i bianchi gigli, VI/22
Tra lor dicendo: -- Quanto doloroso, XIV/55
Tra lor si donandaron di lor via, XVIII/102
Tra molti mal gli parve elegger questo, XXI/19
Tra noi tenere un uom che sia sì forte, XX/52
Tra questo loco e quel de la colonna, XXXXII/93
Tra sé dicea sovente: -- Or si parte ella, VII/25
Tra sé volve Ruggiero e fa discorso, XXXX/66
Tra sì e no la giovane suspesa, II/65
Trar fiato, bocca aprir o battere occhi, XIX/93
Trascorso avea molto paese il conte, XXIX/51
Trasone intanto, il buon dica di Marra, XVI/55
Trasse la spada, e alla padrona disse, XXXXIII/126
Trassene un libro, e mostrò grande effetto, II/15

Tratti che si fur dentro un picciol seno, X/17
Travestiti cercaro Italia, Francia, XXVIII/48
Tre volte e quattro e sei lesse lo scritto, XXIII/111
Tre volte e quattro il pallido nocchiero, XXXXI/17
Trecento agli altri eran passati inanti, XXXXIII/177
Trecento miglia sarebbe ito e mille, XXVI/95
Tremava, più ch'a tutti gli altri, il core, XXXXVI/113
Tremò Parigi e turbidossi Senna, XXVII/101
Tristano, ancor che lei molto non prezze, XXXII/89
Tristano ci arrivò che 'l sol gia volto, XXXII/84
Troppo fallò che le spelonche aperse, XXXIV/2
Troppo sarà, s'io voglio ir rimembrando, XXXXIII/94
Troppo spiacque a Zerbin l'esser caduto, XX/127
Trovando idonia scusa al priego regio, XVII/130
Trovandosi costui dunque presente, XIV/32
Trovano in su l'entrar de la cittade, XV/95
Trovaro una villetta che la schena, XXXVII/35
Trovato ha Brandimarte il re Agramante, XXXXI/91
Trovò Melissa questa lancia d'oro, VIII/18
Trovò tutto il contrario al suo pensiero, XV/8
Trovolli tutti amabili e cortesi, XXXXIV/5
Truova prima il Silenzio, e da mia parte, XIV/76
Tu déi saper che non si muove fronda, XXXV/18
Tu déi sapere (Andronica risponde), XV/19
Tu dunque avrai da me solazzo e gioia, XXXVII/71
Tu fa come ti par (disse Marfisa), XX/77
Tu fai da discortese e da villano, XXXVI/52
Tu gli va dietro: e come t'avicini, III/74
Tu, gran Leone, a cui premon le terga, XVII/79
Tu guadagnato, e perdita ho fatto io, XXXXIII/172
Tu la mia insegna, temerario, porti, XXVI/102
Tu m'hai lo stato mio, sotto pretesto, X/31
Tu m'hai, Ruggier, lasciata: io te non voglio, XXXII/43
Tu mi pregasti, non sapendo ch'io, XXXXVI/36
Tu non andrai più che sei miglia inante, XV/43
Tu non sie né gentil né cavalliero, X/41
Tu puoi pensar se 'l padre addolorato, V/66
Tu te ne menti che ladrone io sia, II/4
Tu vedi ben quella bandiera grande, X/77
Turbato il re di questa cosa molto, XXXXV/106
Turbossi nel principio ella non poco, XXXXIII/38
Tutta coperta è la strada maestra, XVII/20
Tutta la gente alloggiar fece al bosco, XXXI/50
Tutta la notte per diverso mare, XXXXI/16
Tutta la notte per gli alloggiamenti, XVIII/164
Tutta la sfera varcano del fuoco, XXXIV/70
Tutta sotto acqua va la destra banda, XXXXI/14
Tuttavolta conforta Doralice, XIV/57
Tutte l'altre lasciò pender dai sassi, XXXV/54
Tutte l'antique ingiurie gli remesse, XXXII/8
Tutte le vie, tutti li modi tenta, VIII/50
Tutti cercando il van, tutti gli danno, XII/12
Tutti eravam sì intenti al caso nostro, XVII/57
Tutti gli altri alla spola, all'aco, al fuso, XIX/72

Tutti gli altri animai che sono in terra, V/1
Tutti gli atti crudeli et inumani, XXXVI/3
Tutti i sudditi tuoi, morendo, privi, XXXX/38
Tutti m'aveano tolto così in fallo, XXV/53
Tutto confuso e privo di consiglio, XXXI/81
Tutto ieri et oggi l'ho pregato; e quando, XXVI/60
Tutto il popul correndo si trea, XV/62
Tutto in un corso, senza tor di resta, XXIII/60
Tutto in un tempo il duca di Glocestra, XVI/69
Tutto quel giorno e la notte seguente, XXXX/68
Tutto quel giorno, e l'altro fin appresso, XXXVII/122


# U

Uccise di rovescio in una volta, XIV/123
Ucciso Olindro, ne menò captiva, XXXVII/56
Udì che di bei tetti posta inante, XXXXIII/58
Udì che gli dicea ch'in questo loco, XXXIII/27
Ullania a Bradamante che la porta, XXXVII/34
Ullania che conosce Bradamante, XXXVII/30
Umide avea l'innanellate chiome, VII/55
Un altro poppe, un altro sotto prora, XIX/45
Un ch'avea umana forma i piedi e 'l ventre, VI/64
Un ch'era alla veletta in su la rocca, X/51
Un, detto de la Marca, e tre Angioini, XXXIII/23
Un dì che mi trovò fuor del palagio, XXXXIII/24
Un fraudolente vecchio incantatore, XXVII/9
Un giorno che d'andar per la contrada, XXXVI/63
Un giorno o duo ne la città soggiorna, XXVII/12
Un giovinetto che col dolce canto, XVI/72
Un gran pezzo di notte si dispensa, XVII/69
Un medico trovò d'inganni pieno, XXI/59
Un semplice fanciul nell'urna messe, XXX/24
Un servitor intanto di Ruggiero, Ss/63
Un timor freddo tutto 'l sangue oppresse, XVIII/151
Un tratto d'arco fuor di strada usciro, XXXII/73
Un ventolin che leggiermente all'orza, XXII/9
Un'altra volta pur per questo venni, XXVI/104
Una che d'anni alla Cumea d'Apollo, XIX/66
Una percossa a pena l'altra aspetta, XII/81
Una, senza sforzar nostro potere, XXVIII/51
Una splendida festa che bandire, XVI/8
Una voce medesma, una persona, XII/20
Undici mila et otta sopra venti, XV/4
Ungiardo de la gente, che fuggita, XXXXV/8
Ungiardo era signor di quella terra, XXXXIV/102
Uno elegante Castiglione, e un culto, XXXXII/87
Uno il saluta, un altro se gl'inchina, XXXXIV/97
Uno sul collo, un altro su la groppa, XXXIII/122
Uomo non veggio qui, non ci veggio opra, X/28
Urta, apre, caccia, atterra, taglia e fende, XVIII/57
Urta il cavallo, e vien dietro alla pésta, XXXVI/44
Uscimmo poi là dove erano molte, XXV/56

V

V'è che negli infantili e teneri anni, XXXXVI/88
V'è chi, finito un vello, rimettendo, XXXIV/89
V'era una vecchia; e facean gran contese, XII/92
Va molti giorni, prima che s'abbatta, XXXI/78
"Va pur, non dubitar", disse il fratello, V/46
Vada al traverso, al dritto, ove si voglia, XXXXII/51
Vaghi boschetti di soavi allori, VI/21
Van discorrendo tutta la marina, VIII/60
Van gli altri in rotta ove il timor li caccia, XVIII/4
Vanno affrettando i passi quanto ponno, XVIII/188
Vanno per quella i cavallieri erranti, IV/52
Vanno scorrendo timpani e trombette, XVII/70
Vantaggio ha bene assai de l'armatura, XXXXI/92
Varii gli effetti son, ma la pazzia, XXIV/2
Vattene in pace, alma beata e bella!, XXIX/27
Ve' Nicolò, che tenero fanciullo, III/42
Vebian d'intorno all'ignobil quadriga, XVII/132
Vede inanzi alla porta uno Etiopo, XXXXIII/135
Vede lontan non sa che luminoso, XXIV/49
Vede Ruggier de la sua dolce e bella, XI/19
Vede tra via la gente suo troncata, XVII/7
Vede un villan che con un gran bastone, XXXXIII/78
Vedeasi celbrar dentr'alle porte, XVII/21
Vedendola, fu certo ch'era quella, XXVII/55
Veder Baiardo a zuffa con un mostro, XXXIII/84
Veder torsi Frontin troppo gli pesa, XXVII/113
Vedesi altrove in arme relucente, XXXXVI/96
Vedesi quivi chi è buon cavalliero, XXXXVI/100
Vedessi altrove da la patria riva, XXXXVI/97
Vedete (dice poi) di gente morta, XXXIII/38
Vedete Carlo ottavo, che discende, XXXIII/24
Vedete Clodoveo, ch'a più di cento, XXXIII/14
Vedete gli omicidii e le rapine, XXXIII/55
Vedete il meglio de la nobilitade, XXXIII/52
Vedete in Puglia non minor macello, XXXIII/35
Vedete un altro Carlo, che a' conforti, XXXIII/20
Vedete un Ugo d'Arli far gran fatti, XXXIII/19
Vedi che per pietà del nostro duolo, XXXXV/17
Vedi Folco, che par ch'al suo germano, III/28
Vedi in tre pezzi una spezzata lancia, X/79
Vedi in un bello et amichevol groppo, III/40
Vedi Leonello, e vedi il primo duce, III/45
Vedi poi l'uno e l'altro Sigismondo, III/58
Vedi quel primo che ti rassimiglia, III/24
Vedi qui Alberto, invitto capitano, III/26
Vedi Rinaldo, in cui non minor raggio, III/38
Vedi tra duo unicorni il gran leone, X/84
Veduto aveano intanto il mar de' Persi, XV/37
Veduto avreste i cavallier turbarsi, II/18
Veduto che nol piega e che nol muove, XVIII/171

Veduto ciò, Martana ebbe paura, XVII/88
Veduto fiammeggiar la bella face, XIX/51
Veggiamo una balena, la maggiore, VI/37
Veggiàn che fa quella fedele amante, XXXXII/24
Veggio la santa croce, e veggio i segni, XV/23
Veggio Prosper Colonna, e di Pescara, XV/28
Veggio tanto il valor, veggio la fede, XV/29
"Veggo (dicea Ruggier) la faccia bella, XXV/20
Veggo Nicolò Tiepoli, e con esso, XXXXVI/16
Veggo sublimi e suuprumani ingegni, XXXXVI/17
Veggo un'altra Genevra, pur uscita, XXXXVI/4
Veloci vi correvano i delfini, VI/36
Vendola torre i cavallieri a sorte, XIX/73
Vengo a te per provar, se tu m'attendi, XVIII/149
"Vengon (mi disse il nano) per far pruova, II/46
Venia Grifone e la sua compagnia, XVII/22
Venian conto e cent'altri a diversi usi, XXXXIII/179
Veniano sospirando, e gli occhi bassi, III/61
Venite pure inanzi amenduo insieme, XXVII/65
Veniva da partir gli alloggiamenti, XXIII/23
Venne a incontrare un cavallier guascone, XXXII/28
Venne al cavallo, e lo disciolse e prese, VI/57
Venne alla stalla, e fece briglia e sella, VII/77
Venne Astolfo a Marsilia, e venne a punto, XXXXIV/26
Venne chi la novella al re Agramante, XXVII/81
Venne in pontificale abito sacro, XXXVIII/23
Venne in speranza di lontan Ruggiero, XXXX/73
Venne Rinaldo a Montalbano, e quivi, XXX/93
Venner da le parole alle contese, XXVII/78
Venuta quivi intanto era la nuova, XXXXV/53
Venuto ad Agramante era all'orecchio, XIV/66
Venuto era ove il duca di Labretta, XVIII/179
Ver la palude, ch'era scura e folta, XV/52
Verrà forse anco che prima che muori, XXXII/46
Verria costui sopra un navilio armato, XIII/13
Verso Acquamorta a man dritta si tenne, XXVIII/92
Verso Africa Agramante alzò le vele, XXXIX/75
Verso gli alloggiamenti i segni invia, XVIII/157
Verso la parte ove la donna il conte, XXXI/65
Verso Lidia e Larissa il camin piega, XVIII/77
Verso Provenza per la via più dritta, XXXV/33
Verso quel raggio andando in fretta il conte, XII/88
Vi fu legata pur quella matina, X/94
Vi giunse un messaggier del popul Moro, XXIV/108
Vi saranno altre ancor, ch'avranno il nome, XIII/64
Vi sorge in mezzo un sasso che la cima, IV/12
Via più dolente sol di Bucifaro, XXXIX/22
Via se ne va Ruggier con faccia rossa, XXII/90
Vicino un miglio ho ritrovato Orlando, II/17
Vide gran copia di pannie con visco, XXXIV/81
Vide il periglio il Biscaglino, e a quello, XIII/17
Vide le Gade e la meta che pose, XXXIII/98
Vide lontano, o le parve vedere, X/24
Vide Marocco, Feza, Orano, Ippona, XXXIII/99

Z

# III.
**Torquato Tasso**
*Gerusalemme Liberata*

```
A
A costei la feretra e 'l grave incarco, XI/28
A costui viene Aletto, e da lei tolto, IX/8
A destra ed a sinistra in sé comprende, XVII/6
A fatto ancor nel piano e lento moto, XII/73
A gli atti del primiero ufficio degno, XII/87
A grado sì che gli sarà concessa, XVII/48
A i lor consigli la sdegnosa mente, V/51
"A l'arme! A l'arme!" subito ripiglia, XI/20
A l'essercito avverso eletto in spia, XIX/57
A l'incauto Ademar, ch'era da lunge, XI/44
A l'onesta baldanza, a l'improviso, II/20
A lor né i prandi mai turbati e rotti, VI/4
A lui ch'umil gli s'inchinò, le braccia, XVIII/2
A lui sol di troncar non fia disdetto, XIV/14
A molti poi dicea: "L'Asia campioni, XX/27
A pena ha tocco la mirabil nave, XV/9
A piè del monte ove la maga alberga, XIV/73
A quel grido, a quel colpo, in lui converse, IX/38
A quel parlar chinò la donna e fisse, IV/70
A quel parlar le faci, onde s'adorna, XIII/9
A queste or vien la donna, ed: "Omai sète, XV/37
A questo, che retaggio era materno, I/42
A ragion, dico, al tumido Gernando, V/59
A riguardar sovra il guerrier feroce, XIX/104
A sé dunque li chiama, e lor favella, V/3
A sua retenzion libero vegna, V/56
A tai messaggi l'onorata cura, XIV/29
A voi per grazia e sovra l'arte e l'uso, XV/40
"Abbia sin qui sue dure e perigliose, XIII/73
Ad altri poi, ch'audace il segno varca, IV/89
Ad altri: "O valoroso, or via con questa, XX/25
Aggiungi a questo ancor quel ch'a maggiore, XVI/46
Ah! ma non fia che fra tant'armi e tante, XX/124
Ah! non fia ver, ché non sono anco estinti, IV/15
Ah non, per Dio!, vinci te stesso e spoglia, V/47
Ah non sia alcun, per Dio, che sì graditi, I/27
Ah non sia ver che tanta indignitate, VIII/80
Ah! non sia ver, per Dio, che si ridica, IV/81
Ah perché forti a me natura e 'l cielo, VI/83
Ahi! che s'io allora usciva, o dal periglio, XII/103
Al dipartir del capitan, si parte, XI/57
Al fin colà fermossi ove le prime, XX/13
Al fin giungemmo al loco ove già scese, X/61
Al fin questi su l'alba i lumi chiuse, VIII/59
Al fin tra mille colpi il saracino, VII/92
Al fine un largo spazio in forma scorge, XIII/38
Al giovin Poliferno, a cui fu il padre, VI/108
Al gran concento de' beati carmi, IX/58
Al gran piacer che quella prima vista, III/5
```

```
Al mal difeso carro egli fa scorta, XX/70
Al pagan, poi che sparve il suo conforto, XX/119
Al re gridò: "Non è, non è già rea, II/28
Al silenzio, a l'aspetto, ad ogni segno, VII/60
Al suon di queste voci arde lo sdegno, V/23
Aladin, ch'a lui contra era già sorto, X/53
Aladin detto è il re, che, di quel regno, I/83
Albazàr con la mazza abbatte Ernesto, IX/41
Alcasto il terzo vien, qual presso a Tebe, I/63
"Alcun non sia di voi che 'n questo duro, II/45
Alcun però, dal pio Goffredo eletto, VI/24
Alete è l'un, che da principio indegno, II/58
Alfin lasciò la spada a la catena, XIX/17
Alfin, quando già tutto intorno chete, X/7
Ali bianche vestì, c'han d'or le cime, I/14
Ali ha ciascuno al core ed ali al piede, III/3
Allor gridava: "Oh qual per l'aria stesa, III/10
Allor (né pur tre lustri avea forniti), I/60
Allor ripigliò l'altro: "Il Rege eterno, XIV/16
Allor ristette il cavaliero, ed ella, XVI/42
Allor s'arretra, e dubbio alquanto resta, XIII/34
Allor scioglie la Fama i vanni al volo, XX/101
Allor si ferma a rimirar Rinaldo, XX/121
Allor tutte le squadre il grido alzaro, XVIII/101
Allor vegg'io che da la bella face, VIII/32
Altre fiamme, altri nodi Amor promise, II/34
Altre spiegar le vele, e ne vedieno, XV/12
Altri i tassi, e le quercie altri percote, III/76
Altro che dirvi omai nulla m'avanza, XIV/78
Altrove è la sua morte, e 'l suo destino, XVII/70
Altrui vile e negletta, a me sì cara, VII/10
Alza alfin gli occhi Armida, e pur alquanto, XIX/70
Alza Sofronia il viso, e umanamente, II/30
Alzano allor da l'alta cima i gridi, XX/2
Ama ed arde la misera, e si poco, VI/60
Amici, dura e faticosa inchiesta, XIV/35
"Amico, altri pensieri, altri lamenti, II/36
Amico, hai vinto: io ti perdon... perdona, XII/66
Ancor dubbia l'aurora ed immaturo, XI/19
Ancor guerreggia per ministri, ed have, XVII/8
Andianne, e resti invendicato il sangue, VIII/70
Anzi giudice Dio, de le cui voglie, VII/70
Anzi pregar ti vo' che, quando torni, XIX/83
Anzi un de' primi, a la cui fé commessa, IV/64
Aperta è l'Aurea porta, e quivi tratto, XII/48
Apprestar se lerbetta, ov'è più densa, X/64
Apre allora le luci il pio Buglione, XIV/20
Apre Tancredi gli occhi e poi gli abbassa, XIX/111
Apriva allora un picciol uscio Ismeno, X/34
Aramante al fratel che giù ruina, IX/32
Argante, che non vede alcun ch'in atto, VI/28
Argante il corridor dal corso affrena, VI/35
Argante, il tuo periglio allor tal era, VII/99
Argante qui (né sarà vano il vanto), XII/10
```

Argo non mia, non vide Cipro o Delo, IV/29
"Armati," dice "alto signor; che tardi?, VI/20
Arnalto, un de' più cari al prence estinto, V/33
Arte di schermo nova e non più udita, XX/36
Asciutte le mirate? or corra, dove, XII/83
Assimiro di Mèroe infra l'adusto, XX/54

B

Baldovin poscia in mostra addur si vede, I/40
Bello in sì bella vista anco è l'orrore, XX/30
Ben altamente ha nel pensier tenace, V/13
Ben co 'l lume del dìi ch'anco riluce, XV/45
Ben è da' due guerrier riconosciuto, XVII/59
"Ben oggi il re de' Turchi e 'l buon Argante, XII/3
Ben potete scivar l'aspro mio sdegno, X/69
Ben prego il Ciel che, s'ordinato male, XVII/40
Ben rimirò la fuga; or da lui chiede, XX/122
"Ben," riplicogli Ugon, "tosto raccolto, XIV/8
Ben s'avisaro i Franchi onde de l'ire, XX/3
Ben se l'ode Goffredo e ben se 'l vede, XIII/70
Ben si conosce al volto Attila il fello XVII/69
Ben ti prometto (e tu per nobil pegno, IV/69
"Ben tosto" dice "il predator cristiano, VII/54
Ben tosto fia, se pur qui contra avremo, V/50
"Ben volev'io, quando primier m'accorsi, XII/102
Benché né furto è il mio, né ladra i' sono, II/25
"Buona pezza è, signor, che in sé raggira, XII/5

C

Cade il cristiano, è ben e il colpo acerbo, VI/32
Cade il garzone invitto (ahi caso amaro!), VIII/24
Cader seco Alforisio, ire in essiglio, XVII/72
Calca le nubi e tratta l'aure a volo, XVI/71
Canto l'arme pietose e 'l capitano, I/1
Carlo incomincia allor: "Se ciò concede, XV/38
Cautamente ciascuno a i colpi move, VI/42
Cava grotta s'apria nel duro sasso, X/29
Cavò questa spelonca allor che porre, X/31
Cedean cacciati da le stuol cristiano, III/29
"Cedimi, uom forte, o riconoscer voglia, XIX/21
Cedon le turbe, e i duo legati insieme, II/42
Cercando, trova in sede alta e pomposa, XIX/67
Certo è scorno al tuo onor, se non s'addita, XX/132
Cessa la pioggia al fine e torna il sole, XIII/80
Cessi Dio tanta infamia! Or quel ch'ad arte, VI/10
Ch'al servigio di Dio già non si toglie, IV/80
Ch'avend'io preso di Cilicia il regno, V/48
Ch'avra fame d'oro e sete insieme, IV/58
Ch'un cavalier, che d'appiattarsi in questo, VI/15
Ché 'l reo demon che la sua lingua move, V/25
Ché 'l vostro Piero, a cui lo Ciel comparte, XIV/18
Ché da quel lato de' pagani il campo, XX/71
Ché dal furor de le nemiche spade, XIX/40

Che fa più meco il pianto? altr'arme, altr'arte, XVI/64
Che far dée nel gran caso? Ira e pietade, XX/97
Ché fu, com'ella disegnò creduto, XIV/56
Ché là dove il cadavero giacea, VIII/39
Ché non ambiziosi avari affetti, II/83
Ché poco è il desiderio, e poco è il nostro, VII/11
Ché, poi che legge d'onestate e zelo, IV/73
Che poi distinto in voci: "Ahi! troppo" disse, XIII/42
Ché se 'l nemico avrà due mani ed una, VI/8
Ché se di gemme e d'or, che 'l vulgo adora, VII/16
Ché, se ne 'l sai, ti sono amico; e quanto, XVII/60
Ché sei de la caligine del mondo, XVIII/8
Che sian gl'idoli nostri a terra sparsi?, IV/14
Chi dal fero Goffredo e da la frode, VIII/61
Chi di là giunge e chi di qua, né l'uno, V/85
Chi è dunque costui, che così bene, III/18
Chi sia Rinaldo, è noto; e qui di lui, XVII/46
Chiama gli abitator de l'ombre eterne, IV/3
Chiamano; e te che sei pietra e sostegno, XI/8
Chiamata da Goffredo, indugia e scuse, XIII/30
Chiede: "O Vafrin, qui come giungi e quando?, XIX/114
Chiedo solite cose: ognun qui sembri, XX/19
Chieser questi udienza ed al cospetto, II/60
Chiudesti i lumi, Armida; il Cielo avaro, XVI/61
Cibo non prende già, ché de' suoi mali, VII/4
Cinquanta spade impugna e con cinquanta, XVIII/36
Ciò che sofferto abbiam d'aspro e d'indegno, VIII/64
Ciò detto, l'armi chiede; e 'l capo e 'l busto, V/44
Ciò detto, tace; e la risposta attende, IV/65
Ciò detto, vola ove fra squadre erranti, IX/3
Ciò dice egli di far perché dal volto, IV/60
Clorinda, emula sua, tolse di vita, III/35
Clorinda fui, né sol qui spirto umano, XIII/43
Clorinda intanto ad incontrar l'assalto, III/21
Clorinda intanto incontra a i Franchi e gita, III/13
Clorinda intenerissi, e si condolse, II/43
Co 'l buio de la notte è poi la vasta, XVIII/63
Co 'l duce a destra è il re de gli Indiani, XX/23
Co 'l durissimo acciar preme ed offende, VI/92
Co 'l sangue suo lavi il comun difetto, VIII/81
Colà s'invia l'essercito canoro, XI/11
Colei Sofronia, Olindo egli s'appella, II/16
Colui che sina allor l'animo grande, XX/141
Comanda forse tua fortuna a i venti, II/76
Come al lume farfalla, ei si rivolse, IV/34
Come dal chiuso ovil cacciato viene, X/2
Come destrier che da le regie stalle, IX/75
Come è là giunto, cupido e vagante, XIV/59
Come il pesce colà dove impaluda, VII/46
Come imagin talor d'immensa mole, XVI/70
Come l'alma gentile uscita ei vede, XII/70
Come la nobil coppia ha in sée raccolta, XV/7
Come ne l'Apennin robusta pianta, IX/39
Come olmo a cui la pampinosa pianta, XX/99

Come pari d'ardir, con forza pare, IX/52
Come pastor, quando fremendo intorno, XIX/47
Come per acqua o per cristallo intero, IV/32
Come sentissi tal, ristette in atto, IX/98
Come talor ne la stagione estiva, XIII/76
Come vede talor torbidi sogni, XX/105
Come vide spuntar l'aureo mattino, XX/6
Come volle sua sorte, assai vicini, VI/107
Comincian qui le due feroci destre, XX/48
Composto è lor d'intorno il rogo omai, II/33
Con la destra viril la donna stringe, XX/33
Con orribile imago il suo pensiero, VI/65
Con questi detti le smarrite menti, V/92
Con sottile magistero in campo angusto, XVII/66
Con tali scherni il saracin atroce, VII/75
Con tutte ciò d'andarne oltre non cessa, XVIII/71
Con tutto ciò, se ben d'andar non cessa, III/47
Conduce ei sempre a le maritime onde, I/78
Confusamente si bisbiglia intanto, XII/100
Conobbi allor ch'augel notturno al sole, XIV/46
Conosce il popol suo l'altera voce, XI/77
Consolato ei si desta e si rimette, XII/94
Contra il gran fiume ch'in diluvio ondeggia, XVII/71
Contra il maggior Buglione il destrier punge, XX/138
Corre, e non ha d'onor cura o ritegno, XVI/38
Corre inanzi il Soldano, e giunge a quella, IX/22
Corrono già precipitosi a l'armi, VIII/75
Così al publico fato il capo altero, II/22
Così allora il Soldan vorrira rapire, XX/106
Così cade egli, e sol di lei gli duole, XX/100
Così cantando, il popolo devoto, XI/10
Così ce n'andavamo e come l'alta, X/71
Così, cheto il tumulto, ognun depone, VIII/85
Così ciascun de gli altri anco fu volto, X/67
Così con lor parlando, al loco viene, XIV/48
Così concluse, e i cavalier francesi, XI/25
Così costei, che de l'amor la sete, VI/110
Così costui parlava.  Alcasto v'era, XIII/24
Così credeasi, ed abitante alcuno, XIII/5
Così d'amor, d'onor cura mordace, VII/50
Così dal palco di notturna scena, XIV/61
Così de la battaglia or qui lo stato, XI/68
Così di messaggier fatto è nemico, II/95
Così di naviganti audace stuolo, III/4
Così dice egli, e 'l capitano ondeggia, XIII/50
Così dice egli, e 'l giovenetto in volto, XIX/126
Così dice egli, e per suo di non cessa, XI/37
Così dicea il pagano; e perché il giorno, VII/36
Così dicea quel motto.  Egli era intento, XIII/40
Così dicendo ancor vicino scorse, X/1
Così dicendo, il capo mosse; e gli ampi, XIII/74
Così diceva, e 'l capitano a i detti, V/69
Così diceva, e s'avolgea costui, X/48
Così diss'egli; e già la notte oscura, III/71

Così disse egli; e Guelfo a lui rispose, V/57
Così disse egli, e il cavalier s'offerse, XVIII/4
Così disse egli, e l'aure popolari, XII/105
Così disse ella; e per l'ondose strade, XV/33
Così disse Goffredo; e 'l suo germano, V/6
Così doleasi, e con le flebil onde, XX/134
Così Emiren gli schiera, e corre anch'esso, XX/24
Così fatto lor duce, or d'ogni intorno, IX/7
Così favella; e seco in chiaro suono, IV/82
Così feroce leonessa i figli, IX/29
Così fra lor concluso, ambo gli move, IX/45
Così fuggiano i Franchi, e di lor caccia, VII/120
Così furon disciolti. Aventuroso, II/53
Così gìr ragionando insin che furo, X/25
Così gli disse, e 'l cavaliero allotta, X/33
Così gli disse, e con rifuto altero, XII/13
Così gli disse, e in un medesmo punto, XX/139
Così gli disse; e quel prima in se stesso, XVIII/9
Così gli parla il rigido romito, XI/3
Così gli parla, e intanto ei mira e tace, XIX/84
Così Goffredo impone, il qual desia, XI/86
Così gridando, la cadente piova, XIII/77
Così i Franchi dicean; ma 'l duce greco, XIII/68
Così il consiglia; e 'l cavalier s'appresta, XVIII/11
Così il pagan, che già venir sentia, XIX/48
Così l'iniquo far suo cor ragiona, I/88
Così l'un disse; e l'altro in giuso i lumi, XIV/11
Così la torre sovra, e più di sotto, XI/51
Così languia la terra e 'n tale stato, XIII/64
Così leon, ch'anzi l'orribil coma, VIII/83
Così lo sfida, e di percosse orrende, XX/103
Così me' si vedrà s'al tuo s'agguaglia, III/26
Così mutato scudo a pena disse, XI/54
Così ne va sino al suo albergo, e siede, XVIII/6
Così nel cavo rame umor che bolle, VIII/74
Così parla a l'amante; e no 'l dispone, II/31
Così parla a le turbe, e se n'intese, II/13
Così parla costei, che non prevede, VI/106
Così parla, e le guardie indi dispone, VIII/16
Così parla il gran vecchio, e sproni acuti, VII/66
Così parla quel misero, e gli è detto, XII/80
Così parlando ancor diè per la gola, IX/78
Così parlava, e già vedean là sotto, III/41
Così parlava; e l'altro, attento e cheto, XVII/64
Così parlava, e l'Eremita intanto, X/73
Così parlava il veglio, e le parole, XVII/95
Così parlavan questi; e 'l capitano, III/64
Così parlò il tiranno, e del soprano, XVII/39
Così parlogli, e Gabriel s'accinse, I/13
Così passa costei, meravigliosa, XVII/36
Così pensando, a le più eccelse cime, XVIII/14
Così piuma talo, che di gentile, XV/5
Così pregava il conte, e le preghiere, VII/79
Così pregava, e ciascun altro i preghi, XIV/25

Così pregava, e gli sorgeva a fronte, XVIII/15
Così pregava, e le preghiere ìr vòte, XX/114
Così pregollo, e da colui risposto, II/44
Così pugna naval, quando non spira, XIX/13
Così pugnato fu sin che l'albore, VIII/20
Così quel contra morte audace core, XIII/46
Così ragiona, e in guisa tal s'accende, XI/62
Così ripose, e di pungente rabbia, II/88
Così risolse, e cavalieri e donne, XVI/75
Così risolve; e stimolata e punta, VI/89
Così scendendo del natio suo monte, IX/46
Così se 'l corpo libertà ribbe, VI/58
Così si combatteva, e 'n dubbia lance, XX/50
Così spinge le genti, e ricevendo, VII/118
Così Tancredi allor, qual che si fosse, VII/47
Così tolse congedo, e fe' ritorno, XVII/97
Così trapassa al trapassar d'un giorno, XVI/15
Così vince Goffredo, ed a lui tanto, XX/144
Costei, che figlia fu del re Cassano, VI/56
Costei gl'ingegni feminili e gli usi, II/39
Costui non solo incominciò a comporre, XVIII/43
Costui pronto di man, di lingua ardito, VIII/58
Cotal si vanta al capitano, e tolta, XIII/26
Cresce il gran foco, e 'n forma d'alte mura, XIII/27
Crinita fronte essa dimostra, e ciglia, XV/4
Crollando Tisaferno il capo altero, XIX/73
Crollava il capo e sorridea dicendo, XIII/25
Curate al fin le piaghe, e già fornita, XII/2


D
D'elmi e scudi percossi e d'aste infrante, VII/105
D'essi parte a sinistra e parte a destra, IV/6
D'in su le mura ad ammirar fra tanto, XI/12
D'incontra è un mare, e di canuto flutto, XVI/4
D'ira, di gelosia, d'invidia ardenti, V/76
D'un bel pallore ha il bianco volto asperso, XII/69
D'un mandritto Artaserse, Argeo di punta, XX/34
D'una in un'altra lingua in un momento, V/89
D'una pietosa istroia e di devote, XII/23
Dà fiato intanto al corno, e n'esce un suono, VII/57
Da gli occhi ce mortali un negro velo, VII/115
Da l'altra parte il fero Argante corse, VII/87
Da l'altra parte, il consiglier fallace, VI/73
Da l'impeto medesmo in fuga è vòlto, VII/110
Da l'usbergo lo stral si tragge il conte, VII/103
Da la concava nube il turco fero, X/35
Da le notti inquiete il dolce sonno, XIII/58
Da me presi ed avinti, e da me furo, XVII/45
Da quel giro del campo è contenuto, III/65
Da sì bella cagion dunque sospinto, II/64
Da sì fatto furor commosso, appella, VII/56
Da tai speranze lusingata (ahi stolta!), VI/78
Da' gran perigli uscita ella se 'n viene, XI/84

Dal fianco de l'amante (estranio arnese), XVI/20
Dalli lor tu, ché si mai gli occhi gira, XII/98
Dan fiato allora a i barbari metalli, IX/21
Darà, fanciullo, in varie imagin fere, XVII/91
De la cittade intanto un ch'a la guarda, III/9
De la matura età pregi men degni, XVII/92
De la spada Tancredi e de lo scudo, VI/43
De' figli i figli, e chi verrà da quelli, X/76
Declina il carro il cavaliero e passa, XX/62
Degne d'un chiaro sol, degne d'un pieno, XII/54
Deh! ben fòra, a l'incontra, ufficio umano, VI/76
Deh! che del fallir nostro or qui sia il fine, XVI/55
Deh! che ricerchi tu? privata palma, XI/22
Deh! con quai forze superar si crede, XIII/65
"Deh mira" egli cantò "spuntar la rosa, XVI/14
Deh! poi che sdegni me, com'egli è vago, XVI/22
Deh! spezza tu del predator francese, XI/30
Deh! vanne omai dove il desio t'invoglia, VI/74
Del dì cui de l'assalto il dà successe, XVIII/62
Del letto, ove la stanca egra persona, XIX/120
Del re d'Egitto è la città frontiera, XVII/2
Dentro è di muri inestricabil cinto, XIV/76
Depon Clorinda le sue spoglie inteste, XII/18
Desto il Soldan alza lo sguardo, e vede, X/9
Di Bonifacio parlo; e fanciuletto, XVII/73
Di ligustri, di gigli e de le rose, XIV/68
Di loro indugio intanto è quell'altero, VII/73
Di me medesmo fui pago cotanto, XIV/45
Di nobil pompa i fidi amici ornaro, III/67
Di parte in parte poi tutto gli espose, XIX/127
Di più dirò:  ch'a gli alberi dà vita, XIII/49
Di procurare il suo soccorso intanto, V/60
Di qua di là sollecito s'aggira, XIX/60
Di santo sdegno il pio guerrier si tinse, VII/34
Dice allora il Soldan: "Qual via furtiva, X/30
Dice: "O diletta mia, che sotto biondi, IV/24
Diceva a i suoi lietissimo in sembianza, XIX/51
Dico il corpo di Sveno a cui fia data, VIII/31
Diè più morti che colpi, e pur frequente, XX/55
Difesa incontra al Perso, il qual con tanti, VIII/9
Dimmi, che pensi far? vorrai le mani, V/46
Dimmi: s'a' danni tuoi l'Egitto move, II/71
Dimostratevi in me (ch'io vi perdono, XX/125
Dio messaggier mi manda: io ti rivelo, I/17
Diretro ad essi apparvero i cultori, XVII/20
Disponsi al fin con disperata guerra, VII/41
Disponsi alfin di girne ove raguna, X/4
Diss'ella: "O cavalier, perché quel dono, XIX/74
Disse al suo nunzio Dio: "Goffredo trova, I/12
Disse ch'Aronte i' avea con doni spinto, IV/57
Disse, e a i detti seguì breve bisbiglio, I/29
Disse, e colà portato egli fu posto, XIX/119
Disse, e lieto (credo io) de la vicina, VIII/22
Disse questi: "O signor, già non accuso, X/40

Dissegli Ubaldo allor: "Già non conviene, XVI/41
Ditegli che vederne omai s'aspetti, III/48
Divulgossi il gran caso, e quivi tratto, II/27
"Donna, se pur tal nome a te conviensi, IV/35
Dono infelice, io tu rifiuto; e insieme, XVI/67
Dopo non molti dì vien la donzella, IV/28
Doppia allor Guelfo il colpo e lei non coglie, IX/73
Doppia vittoria a te, signor, bisogna, II/77
Dove in passando le vestigia ei posa, XVIII/23
Drizza pur gli occhi a riguardar l'immenso, XVIII/93
Dubita alquanto poi ch'entro sì forte, VII/30
Dudon di Consa è il duce; e perché duro, I/53
Due squadre de' cristiani intanto al loco, XII/47
"Dunque" a lei replicava il cavaliero, XV/29
Dunque accesi tuguri e greggie e buoi, IX/10
Dunque gli eroi compagni, i quai non lunge, I/19
Dunque il fatto sin ora al rischio è molto, I/24
Dunque il Signor che v'indirizza e move, V/91
Dunque il titolo tu d'esser pudica, VI/72
Dunque io no 'l chiedo e non 'l rifiuto; e quando, V/15
Dunque lo starne o 'l girne i' son contento, V/5
"Dunque ove tu, Signor, di mille rivi, III/8
Dunque, poscia che fian contra i nemici, XI/24
Dunque, prima ch'a lui tal nova apporti, V/68
Dunque stima costui che nulla importe, XIII/66
Dunque suso a Macon recar mi giova, II/51
Duomila fummo, e non siam cento. Or quando, VIII/21
Dura division! scaccia sol quelli, II/55


        E
E 'l Loco e Quella che, qual fumo o polve, IX/57
E 'l bel volto e 'l bel seno a la meschina, XX/129
E 'l crin, ch'in cima al capo avea raccolto, XV/61
E 'l fin omai di quel piovoso inverno, I/7
E 'l possente corsiero urta per dritto, VII/88
E 'l re pur sempre queste parti e quelle, VI/2
E 'l vedean poscia procedendo avante, XV/34
E 'l vulgo, ch'anzi irriverente, audace, VIII/82
E 'n don menàrmi al capitano, a cui, XIX/100
E 'n guisa oprar sapea, ch'amicamente, VI/191
E 'n un momento incontra Raffia arriva, XV/15
E ben allor allor l'invitta mano, XIX/50
E ben cadeva a le percosse orrende, XI/40
E ben due volte il corridor sospinse, VII/121
E ben ei vi facea mirabil cose, XI/82
E ben la vita sua sdegnosa e schiva, XII/71
E ben mastra natura a le montane, XI/73
E ben nel volto suo la gente accorta, I/49
E ben quel fine avrà l'empio desire, IV/61
E ben questo Aquilin nato diresti, VII/77
E ben ragion, s'egli averrà ch'in pace, I/5
E ben rotta la spada aver si crede, VII/94
E ben sei degna a cui suoi sdegni ed ire, XVII/52

```
E certo i' son che perderanla alfine, XIX/55
E ch'ei non crede già, né 'l vuol ragione, VI/113
E ch'essa ha in lui sì certa e viva fede, VI/100
E che 'l medesmo poco poi l'avolse, VIII/55
E che l'insano ardire e la licenza, V/88
E che non solo è di pugnare accinto, VI/16
E che per legge è reo di morte e deve, V/34
E chi sarà, s'egli non è, quel forte, XIV/23
E chiamando il buon Guelfo a sé con mano, XI/56
E chino il capo e le ginocchia, al petto, XVII/38
E cibato di lor, su 'l terren nudo, X/6
E co 'l grave scudo, il qual di sette, XX/86
E come a nostro pro veduto abbiamo, III/70
E come è sua ventura, a le sonati, X/3
E come tratto ho fuor del fosco seno, XVII/87
E cominciàr costor danze e carole, XVIII/28
E con la fronte le sue genti altere, VII/104
E con la men, ne l'ira anco maestra, V/30
E con man languidetta il forte braccio, XX/130
E congiungendo a temerario ardire, VI/46
E contanto iternarsi in tal pensiero, I/10
E d'Aronte il castel, ch'Aronte fue, IV/56
E d'emula virtù l'animo altèro, XVII/82
E da sé la respionge e tien lontana, XI/50
E de non che non era il dì che scritto, VII/114
E del fonte de Lidia i sacri umori, XI/74
E, dentro, il cor gli e in modo tal conquiso, XIII/45
E di corpo Tancredi agile e sciolto, XIX/11
E di machine e d'arme han pieno inante, XI/27
E di sì scerbo lutto a gli occhi sui, IX/36
E dice lor: "Prego ch'alcun racconti, X/59
E dice: "O cavalier, seguendo il grido, XIV/30
E dirò pur (benché costui di morte, X/46
E dirò sol ch'è qui comun sentenza, II/50
E dispiegàr verso gli abissi il volo, IX/66
E disse a lui rivolto: "Ah non sia vero, VII/62
E distendeva incontra a i greci lidi, IX/4
E dolce campo di battaglia il letto, XV/64
E dritto è ben che, se 'l ver mira e 'l lume, X/77
E fama che fu visto in volto crudo, VIII/84
E fama che quel dì che glorioso, I/46
E forza è pur che fra mill'arme e mille, XII/45
E fra le grida e i suoni in mezzo a densa, XVII/41
E fugge Antonio, e lasciar puo le speme, XVI/6
E già fuggiano i Franchi allor che quivi, IX/55
E già l'antico Eròtimo, che nacque, C/70
E già tra' merli a comparir non tarda, XI/58
E gli disse: "Goffredo, ecco opportuna, I/16
E gran canne indiane arman di corte, XVII/22
E i famelici sguardi avidamente, XVI/19
E il picciol Siloè, che puro e mondo, XIII/59
E in atto sì gentil languir tremanti, IX/86
E in lui m'acqueto. Egli comanda e insegna, XIV/47
E in lui versò d'inessicabil vena, XIX/105
```

```
E in quel tempo medesmo il destrier punge, VII/96
E in tal modo comparte i detti sui, V/71
"E insino a quando ci terrai prigioni, VI/3
E l'aspettar del male è mal peggiore, I/82
E l'osa pure e 'l tenta, e ne riporta, V/22
E la bocca sciogliendo in maggio suono, X/74
E là dove battaglia è più mortale, VII/109
E la procurerò, ché non invano, XVII/47
E la spada togliendosi dal finco, VII/72
E la sua mente è tal, che s'appagarti, II/65
E la via più vicina e più spedita, XI/69
E mentre ammira in quell'eccelso loco, XIV/5
E mette in guardia i cavalier de' fanti, XI/32
E mi soggiunse poi ch'a la mia vita, IV/53
E miran d'ogni intorno il ricco fiume, XIV/39
E ne ridica il numero e 'l pensiero, XVIII/57
E non aspetta pur i feri inviti, XX/76
E passa primo i ponte, ed impedita, XVIII/98
E per l'orme di lei l'antico fianco, XII/19
E perché conosciuto avea il rapello, X/58
E perché fra' pagani anco risassi, XIX/89
E però ch'ella de la madre apprese, VI/67
E Pirro, quel che fe' il lodato inganno, VII/67
E più ch'altrove impetuoso fère, VII/39
E poi che 'l rischio è di sì leve danno, V/7
E poi che giunse a la regal presenza, VI/17
E poi su l'ampia fronte il ripercote, VII/42
E presente Vafrino e 'l tutto ascolta, XIX/75
E procurate voi che, mentre ascendo, XVIII/66
E quale allora fui, quando al cospetto, VII/64
E quali sian, tu 'l sai, che lor cedesti, X/45
E quando sembra che più avampi e ferva, XVII/68
E quanto di magnanimo e d'altero, V/24
E quei ch'ivi sorgean vivi sudori, XIV/67
E quel ch'a i Franchi più spavento porge, XI/59
E questi, che son tutti insieme uniti, I/80
E questi di sciagura aspra e noiosa, VIII/48
E questi re di Sarmacante; e 'l manco, XVII/27
E questo antiveder potea ben ella, XIV/54
E qui i suoi Loteringhi e qui dispone, XX/10
E quivi cauto rimirando spia, XI/52
E resiste e s'avanza e si rinforza, XVIII/78
E sarà del legittimo e del dritto, V/55
E scinto e nudo un piè nel cerchio accolto, XIII/6
E scorrer lieti i Franchi, e i petti e i volti, X/26
E se di tal dolcezza entro trasfusa, XV/66
E se ne cinge intorno e impaziente, VI/21
E se, poi ch'altri più non parla o spira, V/21
E se pur anco la prigion ricusi, V/49
E se pur la notturna aura percote, VII/24
E seguì poscia, e la disfida espose, VI/18
E sendo giunto il termine che fisse, V/67
E si mostra in quel lume a i riguardanti, IX/26
E so che fuora andando opre faresti, XII/14
```

```
E sotto i piè mi veggio or folte or rade, XIV/44
E sovra un carro suo, che non lontano, X/15
E sta sospeso in aspettando quale, VI/55
E tra 'l collo e la nuca il colpo assesta, IX/70
E tra sé dice sospirando: "O quanto, VI/82
E veder ponno onde il Po nasca ed onde, XIV/38
E veloce così che tigre or pardo, VI/30
E vèr le piaggie di Tortosa poi, I/15
E volgendosi a quegli, i quai già furo, XVIII/73
Ebbe Argante una spada; e 'l fabro egregio, II/93
Ecco, a voi noto è il mio poste ne dice, X/68
Ecco altre isole insieme, altre pendici, XV/35
Ecco da fera compagnia sequito, XIX/43
Ecco il fonte del riso, ed ecco il rio, XV/57
Ecco io chino le braccia, e t'appresento, III/28
Ecco poi fin da gl'Indi e da l'albergo, XVII/28
Ecco poi là Dudon, che l'alta porta, XVIII/95
Ecco sùbite nubi, e non di terra, XIII/75
Ecco tra via le sentinelle ei vede, IX/20
Ed a lui dice: "In te, signor, riposta, XX/11
Ed a quel largo pian fatto vicino, VI/26
Ed affretto il partire, e de la torta, XVI/35
Ed al supplice volto, il qual in vano, IX/84
Ed amando morro: felice giorno, XII/99
Ed aspramente allora anco fu punto, XI/60
Ed eccitati dal paterno essempio, IX/28
Ed ecco in sogno di stellata veste, XII/91
Ed egli stesso a l'ultimo germano, XVIII/79
Ed ei gli rispondea: "Quel novo aspetto, XIV/6
Ed essi ogni pensier che 'l dì conduce, XIV/2
Ed in due parti o in tre forate e fatte, VII/91
Ed in tua vece una fanciulla nera, XII/25
Ed in vece del dì sereno e puro, IV/10
Ed inferno somiglia a cui vitale, XIII/79
Ed io, bench'a gir curvo mi condanni, VII/63
Ed io, che nacqui in sì diversa fede, IV/40
Ed io giù scendo e ti ricolgo, e torno, XII/32
Ed ischerzando seco, al fero muso, XII/31
Ed oh mia sorte aventurosa a pieno!, II/35
Ed oltre i diece che fur tratti a sorte, VII/59
Ed egli: "E mio parer ch'a i novi albori, XIX/128
Egli al lucido scudo il guardo gira, XVI/30
Egli alza il ferro, e 'l suo pregar non cura, XVIII/35
Egli ancor dal suo lato in fuga mosse, IX/54
Egli, ch'ode l'accusa, i lumi al cielo, VIII/76
Egli, che dopo il grido udì il tumulto, IX/42
Egli dicea, quasi per gioco: "Anch'io, XIX/78
Egli è il prence Tancredi: oh prigioniero, III/20
Egli ferrata mazza a due man prende, XIX/42
Egli in sublime soglio, a cui per cento, XVII/10
Egli, la sua porgendo a la mia mano, XIX/94
Egli medesmo al corpo omai tremante, XVIII/67
Egli medesmo sua fortuna affretta, VIII/12
Egli, seguendo le vestigia impresse, VII/23
```

Ei ch'al cimiero ed al dipinto scudo, III/23
Ei ch'egualmente satisfar desira, V/72
Ei crollando il gran capo, alza la faccia, III/52
Ei dal campo gioioso al saluto, XVIII/40
Ei gli stocchi e le mazze, egli de l'aste, VII/111
Ei molto per sé vede, e molto intese, XIV/31
Ei passò le Colonne, e per l'aperto, XV/26
Ei, presili per man, ne le più interne, XIV/37
Ei si mostra a i soldati, e ben lor pare, I/34
Ei si rivolge e dilatato il mira, XVIII/22
Ella, che 'n essi mira aperto il core, V/70
Ella, che dall'essercito cristiano, IX/2
Ella d'elmo coprissi, e se non era, I/48
Ella d'un parlar dolce e d'un bel riso, X/65
Ella dal petto un gran sospiro apriva, XIX/91
Ella dinanzi al petto ha il vel diviso, XVI/18
Ella è detta immortal perché difetto, XIX/123
Ella gridava a i suoi: "Per noi combatte, VII/117
Ella l'amato medicar desia, VI/68
Ella mostrando già ch'a l'oriente, XV/41
Ella, se ben si duol che non succeda, V/66
Emaùs è città cui breve strada, II/56
Enrico v'era e Berengario; e dove, XVII/74
Entra allor cincitore il campo tutto, XVIII/105
"Entrate," dice "o fortunati, in questa, XV/6
Era il prence Tancredi intanto sorto, XIII/32
Era la notte allor ch'alto riposo, II/96
Era la notte, e 'l suo stellato velo, VI/103
Era la notte, e non prendean ristoro, XII/1
Era ne la stagion ch'anco non cede, XVIII/12
Era tornato ov'è pur anco assisa, XIX/77
Erano essi già sorti e l'arme intorno , XV/2
Erminia, benché quinci alquanto sceme, CC?95
Esce a Tancredi in più d'un loco il sangue, XIX/20
Esce allor de la selva un suon repente, XIII/21
Escon de la cittade e dan le spalle, XIX/8
Escon notturni e piani, e per lo colle, XII/43
Essa veggendo il ciel d'alcuna stella, VI/90
"Essere, o mio fedele, a te conviene, VI/99
Essi van cheti inanzi, onde la guarda, XII/44
Esso il consiglia, e gli ministra i modi, IV/23
Eustazio è poi fra i primi; e i propri pregi, I/54
Eustazio lei richiama, e dice: "Omai, IV/84
Evvi Orindo, Arimon, Pirga, Brimarte, XVII/31


F
Fa nove crespe l'aura al crin disciolto, IV/30
Facea ne l'oriente il sol ritorno, I/35
Fan lor machine anch'essi e con molt'arte, XVIII/47
Fassi inanzi gridando: "Anima vile, VI/37
Fatto intanto ha il Soldan ciò che è concesso, IX/97
Fea l'isteso camin l'occhio e 'l pensiero, IV/55
Felice me, se nel morir non reco, XX/126

```
Fèr le trombe cristiane il primo invito, XX/31
Ferillo ove spendea d'oro e di smalto, XX/42
Fermo il guerrier ne la gran piazza, affisa, XVIII/26
Fermossi, e lui di pauroso audace, III/27
Figlia i' son d'Arbilan, che 'l regno tenne, IV/43
Finalmente ritorna anco ne' vinti, XIX/44
Fine alfin posto al vagheggiar, richiede, XVI/26
Finita l'accoglienza, il re concede, X/54
Fisso è nel Ciel ch'al venerabil segno, IX/64
Folli, perché gettate il caro dono, XIV/63
Forse averrà, se 'l Ciel benigno ascolta, VII/21
Forse (se deve infra celesti arcani, XX/21
Forsennata gridava: "O tu che porte, XVI/40
Forte sdegnossi il saracino audace, VI/12
Fra color che mostraro il cor più franco, IX/27
Fra gli estinti compagni io sol cadei, VIII/25
Fra i segni ignoti alcune note ha scorte, XIII/39
Fra l'ombre de la notte e de gli incanti, VII/45
Fra lo sdegno Tancredi e la vergogna, XIX/15
Fra melodia sì tenera, fra tante, XVI/17
Fra questi è il crudo Alarco ed Odemaro, XVII/30
Fra questi è il valoroso e nobil perso, XIX/125
Fra se stesso pensava: "Oh quante belle, XVIII/13
Fra sì contrarie tempre, in ghiaccio e in foco, IV/93
Fragile è il ferro allor (ché non resiste, VII/93
Freme il circasso irato, e dice: "Or prendi, VII/86
Freme in se stesso Argante, e pur tal volta, III/45
Fu il nome suo con lieto grido accolto, VII/71
Fu stupor, fu vaghezza, e fu diletto, II/21
Fugge Erminia infelice, e 'l suo destriero, VI/111
Fugge, non ch'altri, omai la regia schiera, XX/109
Fuggì tutta la notte, e tutto il giorno, VII/3
Furor contra cirtute or qui combatte, IX/50


        G
Gardo a quel fero scontro è spinto a terra, III/15
Gaza è città de la Giudea nel fine, XVII/1
Geme cruccioso, e 'ncontra il Ciel si sdega, VII/26
Geme il vicino mar sotto l'incarco, I/79
Già 'l sesto anno volgea, ch'in oriente, I/6
Già Carlo ferro stringe e 'l serpe assale, XV/49
Già cedea ciasun altro, e non secreto, VI/25
Già cheti erano i tuoni e le tempeste, VIII/1
Già co 'l più imbelle vulgo anco ritratto, XIX/33
Già di tanti guerrier cinta e munita, XX/117
Già eran giunti in parte assai romita, XIX/86
Già già mi par ch'a giunger qui Goffredo, II/48
Già il mormorar s'udia de le parole, XVIII/88
Già il sole avea desti i mortali a l'opre, XX/1
Già l'aura messaggiera erasi desta, III/1
Già la morte o il consiglio o la paura, XIX/1
Già lassi erano entrambi, e giunti forse, VI/50
Già ne l'aprir d'un rustico sileno, XVIII/30
```

Già non avresti, o dispietato Argante, VI/84
Già non lasciammo i dolci pegni e'l nido, I/22
Già non mira Tancredi ove il circasso, VI/27
"Già non si deve a te doglia né pianto, III/68
Già più da ritardar tempo non parmi, XVIII/54
Già questi seguitando e quei fuggendo, III/33
Già richiamava il bel nascente raggio, XV/1
Giace il cavallo al suo signore appresso, XX/51
Giace l'alta Cartago: a pena i segni, XV/20
Giacea, prono non già, ma come vòlto, VIII/33
Giansi appressando, e non lontano al fianco, XX/45
Gierusalem sovra duo colli è posta, III/55
Gildippe ed Odoardo, i casi vostri, XX/94
Giudicò questi (ahi, cieca umana mente, IV/21
Giunge all'irresoluto il vincitore, XX/107
Giunge in campagna tepida e vermiglia, XX/92
Giungi amante o nemico? Il ricco ponte, XVIII/32
Giungi aspettato a dar salute a l'egra, XVIII/29
Giunse Rinaldo ove su 'l carro aurato, XX/61
Giunse dove sorgean da vivo sasso, VII/25
Giunsero inaspettati ed improvisi, XI/64
Giunsersi tutti seco a questo detto, XVIII/74
Giunta a gli alberghi suoi chiamò trecento, XVI/68
Giunta è tua gloria al sommo, e per l'inanzi, II/67
Giunti nel vallo e l'ordine disciolto, XI/16
Giunto Rinaldo ove Goffredo è sorto, XVIII/1
Giunto a la tomba, ove al suo spirto vivo, XII/96
Giunto il gran cavaliero ove raccolte, XIX/34
Gli accoglie il rio ne l'alto seno, e l'onda, XV/3
Gli aduna là dove sospese stanno, VIII/63
Gli ammonisce quel saggio a parte a parte, V/78
Gli aprì tre volte, e i dolci rai del cielo, III/46
Gli Arabi allora, e gli Etiòpi e i Mori, XX/53
Gli Etiòpi di Mèroe indi seguiro, XVII/24
Gli figura un gran busto, ond'è divio, VIII/60
Gli ordini danno di salire in sella, XIX/85
Gli ordini diede, e posica ei si ritrasse, III/12
Gli rispose colei: "Ben degna in vero, XV/39
Gli rispose colui: "Di qui lontano, VIII/51
Gli soggiunse colei: "Diverse bande, XV/28
Gli uni e gli altri son mille, e tutti vanno, I/44
Goda il corpo sicuro, e in lieti oggetti, XIV/64
Goffredo intorno gli occhi gravi e tardi, VII/58
Goffredo, ove fuggir l'impaurite, IX/47
Gran mole intanto è di là su rivolta, XI/38
Grande è il zelo d'onor, grande il desire, XIX/7
Grande e mirabil cosa era il vedere, XX/28
Grande ma breve aita apportò questi, XX/93
Grida il guerrier, levando al ciel la mano, IX/12
Gridava il re feroce: "A i segni noti, XX/102
"Guarda tu le mie leggi, e i sacri tèmpi, XX/26
Guasco quarto fuor venne, a cui successe, V/75
Guelfo ti pregherà (Dio sì l'inspira), XIV/17
"Guerra e morte avrai;" disse "io non rifiuto, XII/53

"Guerrier di Dio, ch'a ristorar i danni, I/21


   H
Ha da quel lato donde il giorno appare, III/57
Ha la corrazza indosso, e nobil veste, VIII/78
Ho core anch'io che morte sprezza e crede, XII/8


   I
I cavalier per l'alta aspra salita, XV/55
I difensori a grandinar le pietre, III/49
I duo guerrier, in luogo ermo e selvaggio, XV/47
I libici tiranni e i negi regi, XX/56
I pacifici scettri osàr costoro, VI/51
I pietosi scudier già sono intorno, XII/74
I semplici fanciulli, e i vecchi inermi, III/11
Ier poi su l'alba, a la mia mente oppressa, XII/39
Il bel candor de la mutata vesta, XVIII/17
Il buon conte d'Ambuosa in ripa al fosso, XI/43
Il cader dilatò le piaghe aperte, XIX/25
Il capitan, che da' nemici aguati, I/74
Il cavalier, pur come a gli altri aviene, XVIII/19
Il dì sequente, allor ch'aperte sono, I/71
Il fero Argante, che se stesso mira, VI/44
Il feroce circasso uscì di stuol, III/34
Il fiume gorgogliar far tanto udio, XIV/60
Il Guascon ritrandosi cedeva, XX/83
Il maganimo eroe fra tanto appresta, VII/37
Il magnanimo duce inanzi a tutti, XVIII/85
Il mago, poi ch'omai nulla più manca, XIII/12
Il padre, ah non più padre! (ahi fera sorte, IX/35
Il perfido pagan già non sostiene, VII/43
Il più usato sentir lasciò Vafrino, XIX/102
Il popol de l'Egitto in ordin primo, XVII/14
Il popol di Giesù, dietra a tal guida, IX/51
Il primo cavalier ch'ella piagasse, XI/42
Il re ne fa con importuna inchiesta, II/10
Il rettor de le turbe e l'un Roberto, XX/49
Il saggio capitan con dolce morso, III/2
Il simulacro ad Oradin, esperto, VII/100
Impon che sian le tende indi munite, III/66
In disparte giacea (qual che si fosse, XIX/36
In pezzi minutissimi e sanguigni, XVIII/89
In questo mezzo, a la città la torre, XVIII/90
In questo mezzo il capitan d'Egitto, XX/137
In tal guisa parlommi: indi la mano, VIII/28
In tal mio stato, o fosse amica sorte, IV/52
In tutti allor s'impallidìr le gote, XIII/22
In van cerca invaghirlo, e con mortali, V/62
Inalza d'oro squallido squamose, XV/48
Incominciaro a saettar gli arcieri, XVIII/68
Indarno a lui con mille sciere armate, XVII/94
Indi dicea piangendo: "In voi serbate, VII/20

Indi il suo manto per lo lembo prese, II/89
Indi partissi e quella notte intera, XIX/66
Indi tolto il congedo, è da lui ditto, II/94
Infuriossi allor Tancredi, e disse, XIX/26
Ingravida fra tanto, ed espon fuori, XII/24
Intanto Erminia infra l'ombrose piante, VII/1
Intanto il sol, che de' celesti campi, I/73
Intanto noi signoreggiar co' sassi, XIX/56
Io 'l vidi, e 'l vider questi; e da lui porta, X/72
Io crebbi, e crebbe il figlio; e mai né stile, IV/46
"Io, di cui si ragiona, or son presente, X/50
Io, io vorrei, se 'l vostro alto valore, VIII/71
Io la guardo e difendo, io spirto diedi, XII/37
"Io mi son un" risponde il vecchio "al quale, X/10
"Io n'andrò pur," dice ella "anzi che l'armi, XVI/73
"Io per me" gli risponde "or qui mi celo, X/49
Io per me non vuo' già ch'ignobil morte, VI/5
Io piangendo ti presi, e in breve cesta, XII/29
Io pur verrò là dove sète; e voi, XII/79
Io, quanto a me, ne vegno, e del periglio, II/4
Io sarò teco, ombra di ferro e d'ira, VIII/62
"Io son Clorinda": disse hai forse intesa, II/46
Io sterparogli il core, io darò in pasto, XVII/50
"Io te 'l difenderò" colui rispose, V/83
Io te chiamo, in te spero; e in quella altezza, IV/41
"Io vivo? io spiro ancora? e gli odiosi, XII/75
Ite, e curate quei c'han fatto acquisto, C/52
Ivi solo discese, ivi fermosse, VI/23


      L
L'abito di costoro è meno adorno, XVII/21
L'acqua in un tempo, il vento e la tempesta, VII/116
L'altro è il circasso Argante, uom che straniero, II/59
L'angelo, che fu già custode eletto, VII/80
L'antichissima selva, onde fu inanti, XVIII/3
L'approvàr gli altri: esser sue parti denno, I/33
L'arme, che già sì liete in vista foro, XX/52
L'arte sue non seconda ed al disegno, XI/72
L'assalitore allor sotto al coperto, XI/39
L'asta, ch'offesa or porta ed or vendetta, XI/80
L'atto fero e 'l parlar tutti commosse, II/90
L'aurora intanto il bel purpureo volto, IX/74
L'avean già tese, e poco era remota, II/57
L'onorò, la servì, di libertate, VI/57
L'onta irrita lo sdegno a la vendetta, XII/56
L'opra è degna di re, tu nobil vanto, VIII/4
L'orror, la crudeltà, la tema, il lutto, IX/93
L'un così le ragiona: "O verginella, VI/71
L'un l'altro essorta che le piante atterri, III/73
L'un l'altro guarda, e del suo corpo essangue, XII/58
L'un margo e l'altro del bel fiume, adorno, XVIII/20
L'una disse così, l'altra concorde, XV/65
L'uno di servitù, l'altra d'impero, XVI/21

```
Ma capitano i' son di gente eletta, XX/18
Ma Carlo, il quale a lui del regio erede, XVII/83
Ma ch'io scopra il futuro e ch'io dispieghi, X/20
Ma che cerco argomenti? Il Cielo io giuro, VIII/68
Ma che? felice è cotal morte e scempio, VIII/44
Ma che fia, se più tarda? Or su, concedo, X/44
Ma che giovava, oimè!, che del periglio, IV/50
Ma che rinovo i miei dolor parlando?, IV/12
Ma che? son colpe umane e colpe usate, XVI/54
Ma che? squallido e scuro anco mi piaci., XIX/107
Ma chi dà legge al vulgo ed ammaestra, IX/95
Ma ciascun terrà cosa in su l'elmetto, XIX/88
Ma cinquemila Stefano d'Ambuosa, I/62
Ma come a le procelle esposto monte, IX/31
Ma come apparse in ciel l'alba novella, II/8
Ma come essa lasciando il caro amante, XIV/77
Ma come furo in oriente apparsi, XVIII/64
Ma come giunse, e vide in quel bel seno, XII/81
Ma come prima egli ha veduto in piega, IX/94
Ma come vede il ferro ostil che molle, IX/87
Ma con men di terrore e di scompiglio, XX/78
Ma con provido aviso al fin dispone, V/2
Ma contra l'arme di costei non meno, V/65
Ma d'altra parte l'assediate genti, VI/1
Ma da la casta melodia soave, XI/13
Ma di più vago sol più dolce vista, VII/49
Ma dice: "Oh quale omai vicina abbiamo, VIII/15
Ma disteso ed eretto il fero Argante, XIX/12
Ma dove, oh lasso me!, dove restaro, XII/78
Ma duce è un prence armeno il qual tragitto, XVII/32
Ma duro ad impedir viengli il sentiero, VII/107
Ma ecco omai l'ora fatale è giunta, XII/64
Ma ella intanto impaziente, a cui, VI/ 102
Ma forse hai tu riposta ogni tua speme, II/73
Ma fra gli altri" mi disse "Alfonso io sceglio, XVII/90
Ma fu de' pensier nostri ultimo segno, I/23
Ma già distendon l'ombre orrido velo, IX/15
Ma già tolte le mense, ella che vede, XVII/42
Ma già tutte le squadre eran con bella, I/65
Ma giù se 'n viene e grida: "Ove fuggite, XX/85
Ma giunto ove la schiera empia infernale, IX/63
Ma grida al suo nemico: "E dunque frale, IX/37
Ma Guelfo, poi che 'l giovene feroce, V/53
Ma i Franchi, pria che 'l terzo di sia giunto, XVIII/61
Ma il barbaro signor, che sol misura, V/17
Ma il chiaro umor, chi di sì spesse stille, IV/76
Ma il consiglio di tal cui forse pesa, II/68
Ma il fanciullo Rinaldo, e sovra questi, I/58
Ma il feroce pagan, che seco vòle, VII/89
Ma il fortissimo eroe, quasi non senta, XI/55
Ma il giovenetto Eustazio, in cui la face, IV/78
Ma il gran mostro infernal, che vede queti, IX/1
Ma il pietoso Buglion, poi che da questa, III/74
Ma il pio Goffredo la vittoria e i vinti, X/57
```

```
Ma il più giovin Buglione, il qual rimira, V/8
Ma il più saggio fratello, il quale anch'esso, VI/112
Ma il primo lustro a pena era varcato, IV/44
Ma il principe Altamor, che sino allora, XX/69
Ma il sospettoso re stimò periglio, II/54
Ma in questo dir sorrise, e fe' ridendo, XIX/79
Ma in questo mezzo i pio Buglion non vòle, XIII/17
Ma insin dal fondo suo l'imperio ingiusto, X/23
Ma intanto Soliman vèr la gran torre, XIX/39
Ma l'arte mia per sé dentro al futuro, XVII/88
Ma l'empio Ismen, che le sulfuree faci, XVIII/87
Ma l'invitto Tancredi, il qual altrove, XI/67
Ma l'un percote sol; percote e impiaga, XX/116
Ma la destra si pose Alete al seno, II/61
Ma lassa! i' bramo non possibil cosa, VI/86
Ma libero fu dato e venerando, V/38
Ma mentre dolce parla e dolce ride, IV/92
Ma né 'l campo fedel, né 'l franco duca, II/97
Ma ne' suoi rami italici fioriva, XVII/81
Ma nega il saggio offrir battaglia inante, XX/4
Ma no 'l farà: prevenirò questi empi, I/87
Ma non aspettar già che di quell'oste, XIX/121
Ma non eran fra tranto a i saracini, XVIII/46
Ma non fu la percossa in van diretta, XX/65
Ma non lunga stagion volgon la faccia, XX/57
Ma non lunge se 'n va che giunge a fronte, XX/8
Ma non lungi da' merli a Palamede, XI/45
Ma non perciò nel disdegnoso petto, IX/67
Ma non togliea però de la difesa, XVIII/70
Ma non vi spiaccia entrar ne le nascose, XIV/36
Ma nota è questa via solinga e bruna, X/32
Ma pensando che chiesto al pio Goffredo, XIV/22
Ma per le vie ch'al più sublime colle, XIX/31
Ma per le voci altrui già non s'allenta, V/29
Ma perché 'l greco imperator fallace, I/69
Ma perché il tuo valore, armato d'esse, XVII/63
Ma perché il valor franco ha in grande stima, IV/22
Ma perché più lo tuo desir s'avvive, XIV/9
Ma perché più v'indugio? Itene, o miei, IV/16
Ma percorsa è la fama, apportatrice, I/81
Ma più ch'altra cagion, dal molle seno, VI/70
Ma poi ch'alla è passata, il re de' regi, XVII/37
Ma poi ch'ebbe di questi e d'altri cori, I/11
Ma poi ch'Erminia in solitaria ed ima, VI/97
Ma poi ch'il vero intese, e intese ancora, VI/64
Ma poi ch'in ambo il minacciar feroce, VI/39
Ma poi che 'l re crudel vide occultarse, II/11
Ma poi che già le nevi ebber varcate, XV/53
Ma poi che intepidì la mente irata, XII/50
Ma poi che la gran torre in sua difesa, XII/15
Ma poi che quel desio che fu ripresso, XIX/99
Ma poi che si riscote, e che discorre, I/18
Ma pria che 'l pio Buglione il campo ceda, XI/83
Ma pria dimmi il tuo nome, e con qual arte, X/19
```

```
Ma prima ch'egli apertamente loro, IX/6
Ma pur sì fero essercito e sì grosso, XV/52
Ma quando di sua aita sua ella ne privi, II/86
Ma quando in lui fissò lo sguardo e vide, XIV/66
Ma quando l'ombra co i silenzi amici, XVI/27
Ma quando parte il sol, qui tosto adombra, XIII/3
Ma quando pur del valor vostro usato, VI/6
Ma quel che chiedi tu, ch'al tua soprano, V/58
Ma riprovata avendo in van la sorte, IX/5
Ma s'a i meriti miei questa mercede, V/43
Ma s'alcun v'è cui nobil voglia accenda, XIII/31
Ma s'animosità gli occhi non benda, II/70
Ma s'egli averrà put che mia ventura, XII/6
Ma se 'n duce me prendi, entro quel muro, X/12
Ma se Goffredo di credenza alquanto, IV/83
Ma se la nostra fé varia ti move, IV/42
Ma se nel troppo osar tu non isperi, VI/7
Ma se più questi o s'altri a lui simìile, X/51
Ma se prima ne gli atti ella s'accorge, IV/95
Ma se quel nobil tronco è quel ch'io credo, VIII/56
Ma se stimate ancor che mal convegna, V/4
Ma seguitato e preso, a la richiesta, VIII/54
Ma sendo io colà giunto ove dechina, XII/33
Ma si conviene a te, cui fatto il corso, X/41
Ma sì de' cavalier, sì de' pedoni, XIX/122
Ma son, mentr'ella piange, i suoi lamenti, VII/6
Ma sovra ogn'altro feritore infesto, XIX/2
Ma sovra tutti gli altri il fero vecchio, VII/68
Ma Tancredi, dapoi ch'egli non giunge, III/36
Ma tu, che a le fatiche ed al periglio, VIII/45
Ma tutta insieme poi tra verdi sponde, XV/56
Ma tutti gli occhi Arsete in sé rivolve, XII/101
Ma vede in Baldovin cupido ingegno, I/9
Ma veloce a lo schermo ei non è tanto, VII/40
Ma venga in prova pur, che d'ogn'oltraggio, VI/19
Ma venirne Rinaldo in volto orrendo, XVIII/99
Ma verso il mezzogiorno, ove il canuto, XVIII/102
Ma voler e poter che si divida, XX/98
Maggior virtù ti salva; un angiol, credo, XI/75
Mal amor si nasconde.  A te sovente, XIX/96
Mancava ancor la destra, e 'l busto grande, VIII/53
Maraviglie dirò: s'aduna e stringe, X/16
Me l'oro del mio regno e me le gemme, XX/152
Me per ministro a tua salute eletto, VIII/30
Me scelse Amor, te la Fortuna: or quale, V/82
Me su la piaggia di Biserta aprica, XIX/81
Mente, de gli anni e de l'oblio nemica, I/36
Mentra così l'indomita guerriera, IX/71
Mentre Raimondo il vergognoso sdegno, XX/89
Mentre a ciò pur ripensa, un messo appare, V/86
Mentre bisbiglia il campo, e la cagione, VIII/50
Mentre ciò dice, come aquila sòole, XV/14
Mentre con tal valor s'erano strette, XI/41
Mentre ei così dubbioso a terra vòlto, IV/67
```

```
Mentre ei così la gente saracina, IX/91
Mentre ei così ragiona, Erminia pende, VII/4
Mentre ei ragiona ancor, gli occhi e la voce, X/13
Mentre il Soldan sfogando l'odio interno, IX/40
Mentre il campo a l'assalto e la cittade, XVIII/49
Mentre il fanciullo, a cui novel piacere, IX/83
Mentre il latin di sottentrar ritenta, XIX/14
Mentre il tiranno s'apparecchia a l'armi, II/1
Mentre in tal guisa i cavalieri alletta, V/1
Mentre io le piaghe sue lavo co 'l pianto, VIII/34
Mentre la donna in guisa tal favella, XVII/49
Mentre mira il guerriero ove si guade, XVIII/21
Mentre ne van precipitosi al chino, IX/96
Mentre qui segue la solinga guerra, XIX/29
Mentre ragiona a i suoi, non lunge scorse, III/14
Mentre riguarda, e fede il pensier nega, XVIII/25
Mentre son questi a le bell'opre intenti, IV/1
Mentre sono in tal rischio, ecco un guerriero, II/38
Mentre li raggi poi d'alto diffonde, XIII/55
Meraviglie quel dì fe' Tisaferno, XX/112
Meraviglioso foco indi m'apparse, XIII/48
Mesce il mago fellon zolfi e bitume, XVIII/48
"Messaggier, dolcemente a noi sponesti, II/81
Mille Turchi avea qui che di loriche, IX/89
Mille e più vie d'accorgimento ignote, XIX/76
Mille son di gravissima armatura, I/38
Mio giudizio è però che a te convegna, XIX/129
"Mira, Aletto, venirne (ed impedito, VIII/2
Mira di quei che fur campion di Cristo, XVIII/94
Mira egli alquanto pria come sia forte, XIX/59
Mira ne gli occhi miei, s'al dir non vuoi, XX/135
Mira quel grande, ch'è coperto a bruno, III/40
Mirasi qui fra le meonie ancelle, XVI/3
Mirata da ciascun passa, e non mira, II/19
"Mirate" disse poi "quell'alta mole, XV/44
Mirava Argante, e non vedea Tancredi, VII/84
Mirò tutte le cose, ed in Soria, I/8
Misera! ancor presumo? ancor mi vanto, XVI/51
Misera Armida, allor dovevi, e degno, XVI/65
Misera! non credea ch'a gli occhi miei, XIX/106
Misero, di che godi? oh quanto mesti, XII/59
Molti scorta gli furo al capitano, VIII/5
More alcuno, altri cade: egli sublime, XVIII/77
Mortalmente piagollo, e quel fellone, XX/46
Morto il duce Emireno, omai sol resta, XX/140
Mosse l'essempio assai, come al dì chiaro, XIII/69
Mosser le natatrici ignude e belle, XV/59
Mostra il bel petto le sue nevi ignude, IV/31
Mostragli Caio, allor ch'a strane genti, XVII/67
Musa, quale stagione e qual là fosse, XVII/3
```

**N**

```
N'arde il marito, e de l'amore al foco, XII/22
```

```
Né 'l superbo pavon sì vago in mostra, XVI/24
Né cessò mai sin che nel seno immersa, V/31
Né ciò gli parve assai; ma in preda a morte, IV/11
Né, come altrove suol, ghiacci ed ardori, XV/54
Né creder che sia questo il dì primiero, XVII/44
Né credo già ch'al dì secondo tardi, XIX/124
Né de i preghi materni; onde nudrita, XII/38
Né di ciò ben contento, al corpo morto, IX/88
Né già d'andar fra la nemica gente, VI/69
Né già ritorna di Damasco al regno, XIV/69
Né già sì tosto caderà se tali, XII/11
Né giova ad Algazarre il fino usbergo, III/44
Né Guasco né Ridolfa a dietro lasso, I/56
Né impedimento alcun torcer da l'orme, V/63
Né in virtù fatte son d'angioli stigi, XIV/42
Ne l'ira Argante infellonisce, e strada, VI/36
Ne la dolce prigion due lieti mesi, XIX/82
Ne la pugna inegual (però che venti, VIII/18
Ne la squadra che segue è scelto il fiore, XVII/29
Ne le latebre poi del Nilo accolto, XVI/7
Ne le scole d'Amor che non s'apprende?, I/57
Né mancherà qui loco ove s'impieghi, V/11
Né men secura da gli alberghi suoi, XIV/79
Né parlo io già così perch'io dispere, X/38
Né, perch'or sieda ne mio seggio e 'n fronte, IV/59
Né perché senta inacerbir le doglie, X/5
Né pur l'umana gente or si rallegra, XIII/78
Né pur l'usata sua pietà natia, IV/66
Né quelli pur, ma qual più in guerra è chiaro, XVII/53
Né questa è già quell'oste onde la persa, IX/18
Né quivi ancor de l'orride procelle, VII/122
Né sol l'estrane genti avien che mova, VIII/73
Né sol la tema di futuro danno, VI/66
Né solamente disacciò costoro, XX/40
Né sorgea forse, ma in quel punto stesso, III/42
Ne sorride il superbo, e gli risponde, VII/85
Né sotto l'arme già sentir gli parve, XIII/36
"Né te Sofia produsse e non sei nato, XVI/57
Né te, Altamoro, entro al pudico letto, XVII/26
Né v'è fra tanti alcun che non le ascolte, II/63
Né voi che del periglio e de gli affanni, IV/79
Nel corno manco, il qual s'appressa a l'erto, XX/9
Nel curvo lido poi Tunisi vede, XV/19
Nel palagio regal sublime sorge, VI/62
Nel primiero squadron appar la gente, XVII/15
Nel seguente mattino il vecchio accoglie, XI/4
Nel tempio de' cristiani occulto giace, II/5
Nel tronco istesso e tra l'istessa foglia, XVI/11
Nessun più rimanea, quando improvisa, Cc/33
Nessuna a me co 'l busto essangue e muto, XIX/117
"No," gli risponde Otton "fra noi non s'usa, VI/33
"Noi" gli dice ella "or trascorriam le vòte, IX/9
Noi raccorrem molte vittorie in una, XX/15
Noi (se lece a me dir quel ch'io ne sento) X/42
```

Noi trarrem neghittosi i giorni e l'ore, IV/13
Non accusi già me, biasmi se stesso, XVI/74
Non altramente il tauro, ove l'irriti, VII/55
Non ardirieno a lei far i custodi, VI/88
Non aspettàr già l'alme a Dio rubelle, IV/18
Non cala il ferro mai ch'a pien non colga, IX/23
Non ci aspetta egli e non ci teme, e sprezza, IX/11
Non copre abito vil la nobil luce, VII/18
Non creder già che noi fuggiam la pace, II/87
Non di morte sei tu, ma di vivaci, XII/97
Non dico io già che i principi, ch'a cura, IV/79
Non è chi con quel fero omai s'affronte, XX/41
Non è gente pagana insiene accolta, I/75
Non è la turba de' pagan già lenta, XVIII/65
Non è mortal, ma grace il colpo e 'l salto, XI/36
"Non è questa Antiochia, e non è questa, XI/61
Non edifica quei che vuol gl'imperi, I/25
Non entra Amor a rinovar nel seno, XVI/52
Non era il fosso di palustre limo, XI/34
Non esce il sol giamai, ch'asperso e cinto, XIII/54
Non ha poscia la notte ombre più liete, XIII/57
Non lontana è Clorinda, e già non meno, IX/68
Non lunge a l'auree porte ond'esce il sole,  XIV/3
Non lunge un sagacissimo valletto, XIV/55
Non mancàr qui cento ministri e cento, XIV/49
Non meno intanto son feri i litigi, IX/53
Non morì già, ché sue virtuti accolse, XII/68
Non può far quel magnanimo ch'almeno, VII/113
Non regger voi de gli elmi e de gli scudi, IX/77
Non rimaneva i me tanta virtude, VIII/26
Non s'avide esso allor d'aver temuto, XIII/29
Non sbigottir, signor: resisti e fura, XVIII/52
Non schivar, non parar, non ritirarsi, XII/55
Non, se di ferro doppio o d'adamante, III/51
Non si desto fin che garrir gli augelli, VII/5
Non sosterran de le vittorie il nome, XIX/131
"Non tu, chiunque sia, di questa morte, IX/80
Non tu, signor, né tua bontade è tale, IV/72
Non venir seco tu, ma resta appresso, I/70
"Non volsi far de la mia gloria altrui, II/23
"Nostra scentura è ben che qui s'impieghi, XII/60
"Nova cosa parer dovrà per certo, II/49
Nudo ciascuno i piè calca il sentiero, III/7
Nulla mai vision nel sonno offerse, XIV/4
Nulla speme più resta, in van mi doglio, IV/71


                    O

O che sia forse il proveder divino, XX/75
"O chiunque tu sia, che fuor d'ogni uso, X/18
"O chiunque tu sia, che voglia o caso, XIV/58
"O de' nemici de Giesù flagello, XX/14
"O degno sol cui d'ubidire or degni, II/62
"O di gran genitor maggior figliuolo, V/9

O fu di man fedele opra furtiva, II/9
"O giovenetti, mentre aprile e maggio, XIV/62
"O magnanimo re," fu la risposta, X/37
O Musa, tu che di caduchi allori, I/2
"O per mille perigli e mille affanni, V/90
O pur le luci vergognose e chine, IV/94
"O re supremo," dice "anch'io ne vegno, XVII/43
"O sempre, e quando parti e quando torni, XX/131
O sia grazia del Ciel che l'umiltade, VII/9
"O Tancredi, Tancredi, o da te stesso, XII/86
"O tu, che (siasi tua fortuna o voglia), VII/32
O vero a me da la sua destra il fianco, VI/85
Occupa Guelfo il campo a lor vicino, I/41
Odi, Gierusalem, ciò che prometta, XII/104
"Odi qual novo strepito di Marte, IX/44
Ogni campo d'intorno arso e distrutto, II/75
Ogni cosa di strage era già pieno, XIX/30
Oh bella destra che 'l soave pegno, XII/82
Oh come il volto han lieto, e gli occhi pregni, V/74
Oh! con quanto fatica ella sostiene, VI/93
Oh! pur avessi fra l'etade acerba, VII/69
Oh, pur colui che circondolle intorno, XIX/101
Oh quanti appaion mostri armati in guarda, XIII/28
Oh s'avenisse mai che contra gli empio, XVII/93
Oh saggio il re di Tripoli, che pace, X/47
Oltra che men ch'altrove in questo canto, XVIII/103
Ombra più che di notte, in cui di luce, XVI/69
Onde al buon vecchio dice: "O fortunato, VII/15
Onde al ponte rifugge, e sol nel corso, VII/44
Onde così rispose: "I gradi primi, V/14
Onde ei le disse alfin: "Poi che ritorsa, XII/20
Onde per tal cagion discordie e risse, V/35
Onde piace là su che, s'or la parte, VIII/35
Onde Raimondo a i suoi: "Da l'altra parte,", XVIII/104
Onde qui caldo avrem qual l'hanno a pena, XIII/14
Onde rispose: "Poi ch'a Dio non piace, XIV/12
Onde rivolta dice al buon Sigiero, XI/53
Onde se in vita il cor misero fue, VII/22
Onde si ferma; e d'ira e di dispetto, VI/31
Or apparecchia pur l'arme mentite, XIX/65
Or che farà? dée su l'ignuda arena, XVI/62
Or che faremo noi? dée quella mano, VIII/69
Or chi fu il primo feritor cristiano, XX/32
Or chiuderò il mio dir con una breve, XIV/19
Or difetto di cibo, or camin duro, VIII/13
"Or discendine giù, solo o seguito, XIX6
Or lo stato del campo, or il costume, XVII/55
Or mentre egli ne viene, ode repente, IX/43
Or mentre guarda e l'alte mura e 'l sito, III/58
Or mentre in guisa tal fera tenzone, XX/73
Or mira d'uom c'ha il titolo di pio, XIII/67
Or negletta e schernita in abbandono, XVI/39
Or odi dunque tu che 'l Ciel minaccia, XII/40
Or perché, s'io m'appongo, esser dée vòlto, X/11

Or qual arte novella e qual m'avanza, XX/67
Or quando del garzon la rimembranza, VIII/47
Or quando ei solo ha quasi in fuga vòlto, IX/24
Or quando pure estimi esser fatale, II/74
Or questa effegie lor, di là rapita, II/6
Or questo udendo il re, ben s'assecura, XIII/16
Or quivi, allor che v'è turba più folta, V/26
Or rimira colui che, quasi in modo, III/62
Or vi narrerò quel ch'appresso occorse, XIV/51
Ora il mio buon custode ad uom sì degno, IV/47
Ora se in tale stato anco rifiuti, II/78
Ormondo intanto, a le cui fere mani, XX/44
Orrida maestà nel fero aspetto, IV/7
"Ov'e, signor la tua virtute antica?", XIX/41
Ove in perpetuo aprile molle amorosa, XIV/71
Ove un sol non impera, onde i giudìci, I/31


          P
"Padre e Signor, s'al popol tuo piovesti, XIII/71
Par che la sua vilta rimproverarsi, VIII/11
Par fulmine ogni sasso, e così trita, XVIII/69
Pargli che vilipeso egli ne resti, II/32
Parla ei così, fatto di fiamma in volto, XIII/52
Parla il duce a colui: "Dunque securo, XIX/63
Parte ancor poi ne le sue lodi avresti, VI/77
Parte, e porta un desio d'eterna ed alma, V/52
Parte la vincitrice, e quei rivali, V/79
Partesi, e mentre va per dubbio calle, VII/27
"Partimmo noi che fuor de l'urna a sorte, X/60
Partissi alfin con un sembiante oscuro, IV/48
Partomi, e vèr l'Egitto onde son nato, SS/34
Parve ch'aprendo il seno indi traesse, II/91
Parve che nel fornir di tai parole, XX/20
Parve un tuono la voce, e 'l ferro un lampo, V/27
Passa il Buglion vottorioso inanti, XVIII/83
Passa più oltre, e ode un suono intanto, XVIII/18
Passa pur questo petto, e feri scempi, XII/76
Passa veloce allor co 'l piè sinestro, XIX/16
Passati i cavalieri, in mostra viene, I/61
Pensa intanto Vafrin come a l'ostello, XIX/115
"Penso" risponde "a la città del regno, XIX/10
Per che 'l reo non si salvi, il giusto pèra, II/12
Per l'entrata maggior (però che centro, XVI/2
Per le facili vie destra, e corrente, XVIII/45
Per le medesme vie ch'in prima corse, XVII/54
Per lungo disusar già non si scorda, XIII/10
Per me stessa, crudel, spero sottrarmi, XX/133
Per questi piedi ond' i superbi e gli empi, IV/62
Per sì profondo orror verso le tende, IX/16
Perch'egli avea certe novelle intese, I/67
Perché se l'alta Providenza elesse, XIV/13
Percosso, il cabalier non ripercote, III/24
Percotono le spalle a i fuggitivi, VII/119

Però ch'altronde la città non teme, XI/26
Però che 'l celo suo bastar non pote, XIX/113
Però che 'l duce loro ancor discosto, XII/72
Però che dentro a una città commisto, I/84
Però che non ognor lunge dal cielo, XIV/43
Però che quegli armenti e quelle biade, X/43
Però che scende in lor più greve il danno, XI/49
Piacquele assai che 'n quelle valli ombrose, XX/123
Piangendo a me ti porse, e mi commise, XII/26
Piene intanto le mura eran già tutte, VII/83
Pietosa boca che solevi in vita, XIX/108
Più e più ognor s'avicinava intanto, VIII/27
Più non si mostra omai tra gli alti flutti, XV/24
Più suso alquanto il passo a lor contende, XV/50
Poco quindi lontan nel sen del monte, XII/67
Poi ch'ella in sé tornò, deserto e muto, XVI/63
Poi che 'l Soldan, che spesso in lunga guerra, XX/108
Poi che de' cibi il natural amore, XI/17
Poi che di sangue ostil si vede asperso, XX/47
Poi che lasciàr gli aviluppari calli, XVI/9
Poi che le dimostranze oneste e care, XVIII/5
Poi che sdegnossi in fuggitivo dorso, XX/59
Poi che stati sospesi alquanto foro, XVII/57
Poi, come lupo tacito s'imbosca, XII/51
Poi cominciò: "Non aspettar ch'io preghi, XVI/44
Poi Damiata scopre, e come porte, XV/16
Poi dolce la consola e sì l'accoglie, VII/17
Poi due regi soggetti anco venieno, XVII/25
Poi fa ritrarre ogn'altro, e in basse note, V/54
Poi gli dice infingevole, e nasconde, III/19
Poi la plebe di Barca, e nuda, e inerme, XVII/19
Poi le risponde: "Armida, assai mi pesa, XVI/53
Poi nel castello istesso a sorte venne, X/70
Poi rimirando il campo ella dicea, VI/104
Poi sforzato a ritrarsi ei cesse i regni, XVIII/42
Poi, sì come ella a quei pensier s'invole, IV/91
Poi vedi, in guisa d'uom ch'onori ed ami, XVII/79
Poich'una scorta è lunge e l'altra uccisa, XX/90
Porta il Soldan su l'elmo orrido e grande, IX/25
Porta sì salda la gran lancia, e in guisa, III/17
Poscia che ribellante al greco impero, XVII/4
Poscia gira da questa a quella parte, VII/97
Poscia il consola; e perché il tempo giunge, XII/42
Poscia in cima del colle ornan l'altare, XI/14
Poscia Tedaldo, e Bonifacio a canto, XVII/77
Posero in resta e dirizzaro in alto, VI/40
Posto su 'l letto, e l'anima fugace, XII/84
Precipitò dunque gli indugi, e tolse, VIII/8
Prende Goffredo allor tempo opportuno, XX/72
Prendete in guardia questa selva, e queste, XIII/8
Prendi, s'esser potrà, Goffredo a l'esca, IV/26
"Prendi" volea già dirgli "un'altra spada,", VII/95
Preparatevi dunque ed al viaggio, I/66
Presa è la bella donna, e 'ncrudelito, II/26

Presa è la rocca, e su per l'alte scale, XX/91
Presagi sono e fanciulleschi affanni, X/75
Presagio ahi troppo vero!" E qui le ciglia, III/61
Prese i nemici han sol le mura e i tutti, XIX/54
Preser commiato, e sì il desio gli sprona, XIV/32
Preso dunque di me questi il governo, IV/45
Prima i Franchi mostràrsi: il duce loro, I/37
"Principe invitto," disse "il cui gran nome, IV/39
Principi, io vi protesto (i miei protesti, I/28
Propria l'altrui difesa, e propria face, XX/37
Punge il destrier, ciò detto, e là si volce, IX/48
Pur a fatica avien che si ripari, XIX/49
Pur di novo l'affonta e pur ricade, XX/80
Pur guardia esser non può ch'in tutto celi, II/15
Pur l'oste che dirà, s'indarno i' riedo ?, XIII/35
Pur lusingato da speranza ardita, VII/13
Pur non gì tutto in vano, e ne' confini, III/30
Pur non tornò, né ritentando ardio, XIII/47
Pur sì fra gli altri Sveno alza la fronte, VIII/19
Pur tragge al fin la spada, e con gran forza, XIII/41
Pur vinto avrebbe a lungo andar la prova, XIX/46


Q
Quai le mostra la scena o quai dipinte, XVIII/27
Qual capitan ch'oppugni eccelsa torre, VII/90
Qual cauta cacciatrice, Armida aspetta, XIV/57
Qual dopo lunga e faticosa caccia, VII/2
Qual feroce destrier ch'al faticoso, XVI/28
Qual gran sasso talor, ch'o la vecchiezza, XVIII/82
Qual i fumi sulfurei ed infiammati, IV/8
Qual in membro gentil piaga mortale, XII/85
Qual l'alto Egeo, perché Aquilone o Noto, XII/63
Qual l'inferno talor ch'in sogno scorge, XIII/44
Qual lupo predatore a l'aer bruno, XIX/35
Qual matutina stella esce de l'onde, XV/60
Qual Meandro fra rive oblique e incerte, XVI/8
Qual musico gentil, prima che chiara, XVI/43
Qual ne l'alpestrei selve orsa, che senta, VI/45
Qual semplice bambin mirar non osa, XIII/18
Qual sonno o qual letargo ha sì sopita, XVI/33
Qual uom da cupo e grave sonno oppresso, XVI/31
Qual vento, a cui s'oppone o selva o colle, XX/58
Quali cose tralascio o quai ridico?, XVI/58
"Quali stolte minaccie e quale or odo, VIII/79
Quando di non so donde esce un falcone, XVIII/50
Quanta e qual sia quell'oste, e ciò che pensi, XVIII/59
Quante mormorò mai profane note, XVI/37
Quanto devi al gran Re che 'l mondo regge!, XVIII/7
Quanto è vil la cagion ch'a la virtude, XIV/10
Quanto me' fòra in monte od in foresta, XII/4
Quasi in quel punto in fronte egli percosse, XX/43
Quasi in quel punto mille spade ardenti, V/28
Quasi in quel punto soliman percote, XI/81

Quattro volte era apparso il sol ne l'orto, XV/23
Quegli ancor al cui penna o la favella, XI/9
Quegli con larghe rote aggira i passi, VII/38
Quegli italico parla: "Or là m'invio, VII/28
Quei che incontra verranci, uomini ignudi, XX/16
Quei che prima ritrova il turco atroce, XX/77
Quei di fine arme e di se stesso armato, VII/98
Quel capitan che cinto d'ostro e d'oro, XX/17
Quel ch'a lui rivelò luce divina, XVII/89
Quel di Dudon aventurier drapello, III/37
Quel doppia il colpo orribile, ed al vento, XIX/24
Quel si dilegua, e questi acceso d'ira, III/31
Quella che terza è poi, squadra non pare, XVII/17
Quella lui mira in un lieta e dolente, XVIII/31
Questa bellezza mia sarà mercede, XVI/66
Questa ha noi mossi e questa ha noi condutti, II/84
Questi, appressando ove lor seggio han posto, XIII/20
"Queste arme in guerra al capitan francese, XIX/64
Queste fur l'arti onde mill'alme e  mille, IV/96
Queste son le cagion, ma non già sole,", XIX/90
Questi (che che lor mova, odio o disegn), XIX/87
Questi e molti altri, ch'in silenzio preme, XX/35
Questi ha nel pregio de la spada eguali, III/38
Questi or Macone adora, e fu cristiano, II/2
Questi or co' Turchi, or con le genti perse, XVII/7
Questi ristretti insieme in ordin folto, IX/90
Questi sgrida in suo nome il troppo ardire, III/53
Questi un fu di color cui dinazi accesse, VI/29
Questi, veggendo armato in cotal modo, XI/21
Questo è il porto del mondo; e qui è il ristoro, XV/63
Questo è lo stagno in cui nulla di greve, X/62
Questo finto dolor da molti elice, IV/77
Questo lor ragionar ne l'altrui mente, VIII/46
Questo pensier la ferità nativa, I/85
Questo popolo e quello incerto pende, VI/49
Questo sol tiene Erminia a lei secreto, VI/80
Questo su 'l Tago nacque, ove talora, VII/76
Qui chinò vinti i lumi e gli alzò poi, XVIII/97
Qui comincia il tiranno a risdegnarsi, II/24
Qui dal soggetto vinto il saggio Piero, X/78
Qui del monte Seir, ch'alto e sovrano, I/77
Qui disdegnoso giunge e minacciante, XI/78
"Qui," disse il vecchio "appresso a i fidi amici, VIII/4
Qui fa' prova de l'arte, e le saette, VII/101
Qui greggia alcuna cercavam che fosse, VIII/52
Qui il vulgo de' pagani il pianto estolle, II/37
Qui l'asta si conserva onde il serpente, VII/81
Qui menerai (non temer già di morte, VII/48
Qui mille immonde Arpie vedresti e mille, IV/5
Qui non fallaci mai fiorir gli olivi, XV/26
Qui s'adunan le streghe, ed il suo vago, XIII/4
Qui si fermano entrambi, e pur sospeso, XIX/9
Qui si tacque il tedesco, e gli rispose, VIII/43
Qui tace, ed ei risponde: "Or ti sia noto, XI/23

Riman da i colpo d'Altamoro ucciso, XX/39
Rimanean vivi ancor Pico e Laurente, IX/34
Rimanti in pace, i' vado; a te non lice, XVI/56
Rimedon, questa insegna a te non diedi, XX/110
Rinaldo ha nome; e la sua destra irata, III/39
Rinaldo han morto, il qual fu spada e scudo, VIII/67
Rinaldo intanto irresoluto bada, XVIII/72
Ripon Tancredi il ferro, e poi devoto, XIX/27
Risolve al fin, benché pietà non spere, III/25
Risponde: "Ercole, poi ch'uccisi i mostri, XV/25
Risponde il capitan: "Come hai per uso, XIX/130
Risponde il capitan: "Da i più sublimi, V/37
Risponde il re pagan: "Ben ho di lui, III/60
Risponde: "Il tuo lodar troppo alto sale, IV/36
Risponde l'indian: "La fronte mesta, XIX/71
Risponde la feroce: "Indarno chiedi, XII/61
Risponde: "Sète voi nel grembo immenso, XIV/41
Rispose egli al guerriero: "A i cieli piaccia, XVII/84
Rispose l'indo faro: "Io mi son uno, XVII/51
Ritirollo, e parlò: "Riconosciuto, XIX/80
Ritornan gli Aquitani e tutti insieme, XX/88
Rodi e Creta lontane inverso al polo, XV/17
Rota Aletto fra lor la destra armata, VIII/72
Rugiadosa di manna era ogni fronda, XVIII/24
Ruppe l'aste e gli intoppi, il violento, XX/60


S
S'alcun giamai tra frondeggianti rive, XIII/60
S'ami che salva i' sia, perché mi privi, V/84
S'apre lo scudo al frassino pungente, XI/79
S'immaculato è questo cor, s'intatte, XII/27
"S'in servigio di Dio, ch'a ciò n'elesse, IV/68
S'ode l'annunzio intanto, e che s'appresta, II/17
S'offerse a gli occhi di Goffredo allora, XVIII/92
Sai che là corre il mondo ove più versi, I/3
Sai quanto ciò rilevi e se conviene, VIII/3
Salta Argante nel mezzo agile e sciolto, VII/106
Sana tu pur Argante, acciò che poi, VI/75
Sappi che tanto abbiam sin or sofferto, II/82
Sarò qual più vorrai scudiero o scudo, XVI/50
Sbigottìr gli altri a l'apparir di tante, VI/61
Scende egli giù per le abbattute mura, XX/82
Sceso Gernando è da' gran re norvegi, V/16
Scorge poscia Altamor, ch'in cerchio accolto, XIX/69
Scorre più sotto il re canuto a piede, XI/29
Se ben raccolgo le discordie e l'onte, I/30
Se fosse in me quella virtù, quel sangue, VII/65
Se gli altri sciolse, ei serva ed ei sostegna, XIV/52
Se m'odii, e in ciò diletto alcun tu senti, XVI/45
Se non giuri d'andar con gli altri sui, VII/33
Se scorge alcun che sal suo amor ritiri, IV/88
Se tu medesmo non t'invidii il Cielo, XII/93
Secondan quei che posti invèr l'aurora, XVII/16

Sedea colà dond'Egli e buono e giusto, IX/56
Segue egli la vittoria, e la trafitta, XII/65
Segue Eustazio il primiero, e pote a pena, V/80
Segue il buon genitor l'incauto stuolo, IX/30
Segue il suo stuolo, ed Aradin con quello, XVII/35
Segue la coppia il suo camin veloce, XV/51
Seguì fra gl' altri Ormusse, il qual la sciera, X/55
Seguia la gente poi candida e bionda, I/43
Seguia parlando, e in bei pietosi giri, XVIII/33
Seguian molti altri la medesma inchiesta, XIX/116
Sembra d'alberi densi alta foresta, XX/29
Sembra il ciel ne l'aspetto atra fornace, XIII/56
Sembra quasi familica e vorace, XX/79
Sente la donna il cavalier che geme, XIX/110
Senza molto mirarle egli le prende, VII/52
Sfortunato silenzio! avessi almeno, XIX/97
Sì canta l'empia, e 'l giovenetto al sonno, XIV/65
Sì ch'a trovarne il mio signo io mossi, XIX/98
Sì ch'ignoto è 'l gran mar che solchi: ignote, XV/27
Sì ch'incontra al castello, ove in un prato, VII/31
Sì che non può capir dentro al suo letto, XIV/33
Si come cerva ch'assetata il passo, VI/109
Sì come soglion là vicino al polo, XIV/34
Si commette la mole e ricompone, XVIII/44
Sì disse, e 'l persuase; e impaziente, II/7
"Sì dunque impenetrabile è costui, XX/66
Si grida "A l'armi! a l'armi!", e Sveno involto, VIII/17
Si movon quegli ad esseguir l'effetto, XIX/45
Sì parla e prega, e i preghi bagna e scalda, XX/136
Si parla il re canuto, e si ristringe, XII/12
Sì potrò, sì, ché mi farà possente, VI/87
Si prepara ciascun, de la novella, XX/5
Si vedea fiammeggiar fra gli altri arnesi, VII/82
Si volse Armida e 'l rimirò improviso, XX/128
Sia dal Cielo il principio; invoca inanti, XI/2
Sia destin ciò ch'io voglio: altri disperso, IV/17
Sia questa pur tra le mie frodi, e vaglia, XVI/47
Sibila il teso nervo, e fuore spinto, VII/102
Sieda in pace il mio campo, e da secura, VII/61
"Signor," dicea "senza tardar se 'n viene, II/3
Signor, gran cose in picciol tempo hai fatte, II/66
"Signor, non è di noi chi più si vante, XIII/23
Signor, non sotto l'ombra in piaggia molle, XVII/61
"Signor, tu che drizzasti incontra l'empio, VII/78
Silvestre cibo e duro letto porse, VIII/42
Smontaro allor del carro, e quel repente, X/28
Soggiunse a questo più che, da le navi, V/87
Soggiunse al fin come già il popol franco, VIII/10
Soggiunse allor Goffredo: "Or riportate, II/92
Soggiunse allor Tancredi: "Or ti soverna, V/36
Soggiunse allora Ismeno: "Attender piaccia, XII/17
Soggiunse appresso: "Or cosa aggiungo a queste, XIII/13
Soggiunse il prence: "A la città regale, XIX/118
Soggiunse l'altro allora: "E tu prometti, VI/53

Soggiunse poi: "Bench'io sembianza esterna, V/41
Soggiunse poi: "Girsi pur Fortuna, X/24
Soggiunse poi: "La notte a me fatale, XIX/92
Soggiunse poscia: "Io là, donde riceve, II/29
Soggiunse poscia: "O padre, or che d'intorno, VII/8
Sol con la faccia torva e disdegnosa, X/56
Sol contra il ferro il nobil ferro adopra, XIX/32
Sol dal regno e'Egitto e dal contorno, XV/13
Sol de i colpi il rimbombo intorno mosse, VI/41
Sol di Tripoli il re, che 'n ben guardate, I/76
Sola esclusa ne fu perché in quell'ora, XII/49
Soletta a sua difesa ella non basta, XX/68
Soleva Erminia in compagnia sovente, VI/79
Soliman, che di la non molto lunge, IX/85
"Soliman, ecco il loco ed ecco l'ora, XI/63
"Soliman, Solimano, i tuoi sì lenti, X/8
Soliman Sveno uccise, e Solimano, VIII/36
Solo ch'io segua te mi si conceda, XVI/48
Somiglia il carro a quel che porta il giorno, XVII/34
Sommessi accenti e tacite parole, III/6
Son cinquanta guerrier che 'n puro argento, IX/92
Son fra' lodati Ubaldo anco, e Rosmondo, I/55
Son già là dove il mar fra terra inonda, XV/22
Son già sotto le mura: allor Rinaldo, XVIII/75
Sopra il turbato ciel, sotto la terra, XVIII/37
Sorge non lunge a le cristiane tende, XIII/2
Sorge più tardi e un gran fendente, in prima, XIX/19
Sorgea la notte intanto, e sotto l'ali, VIII/57
Sorridea quegli, e: "Non già, come credi, XIV/7
Sorrise allor Rinaldo, e con un volto, V/42
Sorrise il buon Tancredi un cotal riso, XIX/4
Sorse a pari co 'l sole, ed egli stesso, III/72
Sorse amor contra l'ira, e fe' palese, XX/63
Sorse la notte oltra l'usato oscura, IV/54
Sospirò dal profondo, e 'l ferro trasse, X/27
Sotto, folta corona al seggio fanno, XVII/13
Sotto ha un destrier che di candore agguaglia, IX/82
Sovente, allor che su gli estivi ardori, VII/19
Sovra gli altri ferisce e trona e svena, XX/81
Sovra i confusi monti a salto a salto, IX/49
Sovra un arbore i' salsi e te su l'erba, XII/30
"Sovra una lieve saettia tragitto, I/68
Spenta è del cielo ogni benigna lampa, XIII/53
Spesso l'ombra materna a me s'offria, IV/49
Spietatamente è cauto, e non oblia, I/90
Spinge il destrier in questo, e tutto oblia, VI/34
Spinse il suo contra lui, che in atto scerse, XX/115
Spira spiriti maschi in nobil volto, XVII/78
Sprezzata ancella, a chi fo più conserva, XVI/49
Squadra d'ordine estrema ecco vien poi, I/52
Stannogli, a destra l'un, l'altro a sinistra, XVII/12
Stassi appoggiato, e con secura faccia, XI/71
Stassi tal volta ella in disparte alquanto, IV/90
Stavasi il capitan la testa ignudo, XIX/62

Stette arronito alquanto e stupefatto, XX/74
Stimi (sì misto il culto è co 'l negletto, XVI/10
Stupidi i guerrier vannno, e ne le nove, XIV/40
Stupido il cavalier le ciglia inarca, X/17
Stupido lor riguardo, e non ben crede, VIII/29
Stupido sì, ma intrepido rimane, XIII/37
Stupisce Argante, e ripercosso il petto, XII/7
Su 'l muro aveano i Siri un tronco alzato, XIX89
Su su, venite: io primo aprir la strada, IX/19
Subito il nome di ciascun si scrissse, V/73
Suona il corriero in arrivando il corno, VII/29
Svelte notar le Cicladi diresti, XVI/5
"Sveno, del re de' Dani unico figlio, VIII/6


                    T
T'alzò natura inverso il ciel la fronte, XVII/62
T'essorteranno a seguitar la strada, II/69
Taccio ch'ove il bisogno e 'l tempo chiede, VIII/65
Tacciono sotto i mar securi in pace, XV/43
Tace, e in colui de l'un morir la tema, XII/89
Tace, e la guida ove tra i grandi eroi, IV/38
Tace, e senza indugiar le turbe accoglie, IX/13
Tace, ed a' suoi costodi in cura dallo, XX/143
Taciti se ne gian per l'aria nera, XVII/86
Tacque, ciò detto; e 'l re, bench'a pietade, II/52
Tacque ciò detto; e poi che furo armati, VI/22
Tacque, e 'l Buglion rispose: "Oh quanto grato, XIV/15
Tacque, e 'l nobil garzon restò per poco, XVI/34
Tacque; e 'l pagano, al sofferir poco uso, VI/38
Tacque, e concorde de gli augelli il coro, XVI/16
Tacque, e dal Cielo infuso ir gra le vene, VIII/77
Tacque, e disse sorgendo il guerrier dano, XIV/27
Tacque, e per lochi ora sublimi or cupi, VIII/41
Tacque, e poi se n'andò là dove il conte, XIX/53
Tacque, e rispose il re: "Giovene ardente, VI/9
Tacque; e rispose il re: "Qual sì disgiunta, II/47
Tai fur gli avolgimenti e tai le scosse, XIX/18
Tal che 'l maligno spirito d'Averno, V/18
Tal Cleopatra al secolo vetusto, XX/118
Tal ei parlava, e la parole accolse, V/40
Tal fean de' Persi strage, e via maggiore, XX/38
Tal gran tauro talor ne l'ampio agone, III/32
Tal ne l'arme ei fiammaggia, e bieche e torte, VII/53
Tal ne viene Argillano: arde il feroce, IX/76
Tal saetta costei. Goffredo intanto, XI/46
Tal si fece il garzon, quando repente, XVI/29
Tale i' son, tua mercé: tu me da i vivi, XII/92
Tale inciampa la torre, e tal da quella, XI/85
Tancredi, cui dinanzi il cor sospese, VI/114
Tancredi, in sé raccolto, attende in vano, VI/47
Tancredi intanto i feri spirti e 'l core, V/45
Tanti di qua, tanti di là fur mossi, XI/48
Tanto e sì fatto re l'arme raguna, XVII/9

Tanto sol disse il generoso Argante, X/39
Tarde non furon già queste preghiere, XIII/72
Tardi riedi, e non solo; io non rifiuto, XIX/3
"Tartarei numi, di seder più degni, IV/ 9
Tatin regge la schiera, e sol fu questi, I/51
Te Genitor, te Figlio eguale al Padre, XI/7
Te, la cui nobilità tutt'altre agguaglia, V/10
"Teco giostra Rinaldo: or tanto vale, V/19
Temea, lassa!, la morte, e non avea, IV/51
Tempo è da travagliar mentre il sol dura, VI/52
"Tempo è" dicea "di girne ove t'attende, XVII/85
Tempo forse già fu che gravi e strane, VIII/66
Tempo già fu, quando più l'uom vaneggia, VII/12
Tempo verràa che fian d'Ercole i segni, XV/30
Tempra dunque il fellon la rabbia insana, I/89
Tenera ancor con pargoletta destra, II/40
Teneri sdegni, e placide e tranquille, XVI/25
Tien su la spada, mentre ei sì favella, X/52
Tolser essi congedo, e manifesto, XI/18
Tondo è il ricco edificio, e nel più chiuso, XVI/1
Torna l'ira ne' cori, e li trasporta, XII/62
Torna la turba, e misera e smarrita, XIII/19
Tornàr le schiere indietro, e da i nemici, III/54
Torni Rinaldo, e da qui inanzi affrene, XIV/26
Tornò sereno il cielo e l'aura cheta, XVIII/38
Torria ben ella che il quadrel pungente, XX/64
Tosto Rinaldo si dirizza ed erge, XX/129
Tosto ciascun, da gran desio compunto, I/72
Tosto fia che qui giunga; or se fra tanto, VI/11
Tosto gli dèi d'Abisso in varie torme, IV/4
Tosto la preda al predator ritoglie, III/16
Tosto, spiegando in vari lati i vanni, IV/19
Tragge egli fuor l'essercito pedone, XI/31
Trar molto il debil fianco oltra non pote, XIX/28
Trascorre oltre Ascalona ed a mancina, XV/10
Trascorser poi le piaggie ove i Numidi, XV/21
Trasse le squadre fuor, come veduto, XX/22
Tratto al tumulto il pio Goffredo intanto, V/32
Travesti ne vanno, e la più ascosa, VI/94
Tre volte il cavalier la donna stringe, XII/57
Trovarete, del fiume a pena sorti, XIV/72
Tu, celeste guerrier, che la donzella, XII/28
Tu, come al regio onor più si conviene, XII/16
Tu, cui concesse il Cielo e dielti in fato, IV/63
Tu drizzarai, Camillo, al tempo stesso, XVIII/56
Tu l'adito m'impetra al capitano, IV/37
Tu, magnanimo Alfonso, il qual ritogli, I/4
Tu questa destra invitta, a cui già poco, X/21
Tu, Raimondo, vogl'io che da quel lato, XVIII/55
Tu spiegherai, Colombo, a un novo polo, XV/32
Tu vincerai sedendo, e la fortuna, XIII/15
Turbossi udendo il glorioso nome, VII/35
Turchi, Persi, Antiochia (illustre suono, I/26

U

Ubaldo incominciò parlando allora, XVI/32
Uccide Ormanno, piaga Guido, atterra, VII/108
"Udite, udite, o voi che da le stelle, XIII/7
Ultimi vanno, e l'impeto seguente, III/43
Umili intorno ascoltano i primieri, XI/15
Un fonte sorge in lei che vaghe e monde, XIV/74
Un paggion de Soldan misto era in quella, IX/81
Un uom de la Liguria avràa ardimento, XV/31
Un'isoletta la qual nome prende, XIV/70
Una selva di strali e di ruine, XVIII/76
Urtò la trave immensa, e così dure, XVIII/81
Usa la sorte tua, chè nulla io temo, XIX/22
Usa ogn'arte la donna, onde sia colto, IV/87
Uscì dal chiuso vallo, e si converse, XI/76
Usciva omai dal molle e fresco grembo, XIV/1


V

V'è Guelfo seco, è gli e d'opre leggiardre, III/63
V'è l'aura molle e 'l ciel sereno e lieti, X/63
V'era Almerico; e si vedea già fatto, XVII/75
Va Piero solo inanzi e spiega al vento, XI/5
Va seco Aletto, e poscia il lascia e veste, IX/14
Va', dille tu che lasci omai le cure, IX/59
Vafrin, tu sai che timidetta accorsi, XIX/93
Vanne al campo nemico: ivi s'impieghi, IV/25
Vassene al mirto; allor colei s'abbraccia, XVIII/34
Vassene, e tal è in vista il sommo duce, XX/7
Vassene il valorosi in sé ristretto, XIII/33
Vassi a l'antica selva, e quindi è tolta, XVIII/41
Vattene pur, crudel, con quella pace, XVI/59
Vede che 'l m al da la stanchezza nasce, XIX/112
Vede, e conosce ben l'immensa mole, VIII/49
Vede, mirando qui, sdrucita tela, XIX/61
Vede or che sotto il militar sembiante, VI/98
Vedeasi in alto il fier elvezio asceso, XI/35
Vedele incontra il fero Adrasto assiso, XIX/68
Vedendo quivi comparir repente, VII/7
"Vedete là di mille furti pieno, IX/17
Vedi Alberto il figliuolo ir fra' Germani, XVII/76
Vedi appresso spiegar l'alto vessillo, I/64
Vedi globi di fiamme oscure e miste, XII/46
Vedi le membra de' guerrier robuste, XIII/61
Vedrai de gli avi il divolgato onore, XVII/65
Veduti Ubaldo in giovenezza e cerchi, XIV/28
Veggia il nemico le mie spalle, e scherna, IX/99
"Veggio" dicea "de la letizia nova, I/86
Veggio o parmi vedere, anzi che lustri, X/22
Veggion che per dirupi e fra ruine, XV/46
Veggiono a un grosso tronco armi novelle, XVII/58
Veloce sovra il natural costume, XV/8
Venga altri, s'egli teme; a stuolo a stuolo, VII/74

Vengane a te quasi celeste messo, VI/13
Vengon sotto Gazèl quei che le biade, XVII/18
Venia per far nel barbaro omicida, III/50
Venia scotendo con l'eterne piume, IX/62
Venian dietro ducento in Grecia nati, I/50
Venie poscia il Buglion, pur come è l'uso, XI/6
Venieno innumerabili, infiniti, XIII/11
Venne a Gierusalemme, e quivi accolta, VI/59
Venne colui, chiamato; e poi ch'intese, XVIII/58
Vennero i duci, e gli altri anco seguiro, I/20
Vennevi un giorno ch'ella in altra parte, VI/81
Veramente è costui nato a l'impero, III/59
Vergine era fra lor di già matura, II/14
Vezzosi augelli infra le verde fronde, XVI/12
Vide ei Rinaldo; e benché omai vermigli, XX/113
Vide tende infinite e ventillanti, XIX/58
Vien contro al foco il turbo; e indietro volto, XVIII/86
Vien poi Tancredi, e non è alcun fra tanti, I/45
Viene aventando la volubil mole, XI/47
Viene or costei da le contrade perse, II/41
Vienne in disparte pur tu ch'omicida, XIX/5
Vinca egli o perda omai, ché vincitore, V/20
Vinta de l'ira è la ragione e l'arte, VI/48
Virtù, ch'a' valorosi unqua non manca, XX/84
Vistommi poi spesso, e 'n dolce suono, XIX/95
Vivi beata pur, ché nostra sorte, III/69
Vivrò fra i miei tormenti e le mie cure, XII/77
Voglion sempre seguirla a l'ombra al sole, V/77
Vola fra gli altri un che le piume ha sparte, XVI/13
Volea gridar: "Dove, o crudel, me sola, XVI/36
Volge il tergo a la forza ed al furore, VII/112
Volgendo gli anni, il regno è stabilito, XVII/5
Volgendo il guardo a terra i naviganti, XV/11
Volgendo in Tisaferno il dolce sguardo, XIX/72
Vuol ne l'armi provarla: un uom la stima, XII/52

# IV.
# Pietro Bembo
## *Rime*

## A

A cui più ch'altri mai servi e devoti, CXVI
A dunque m'hai tu pur in sul fiorire, LXXXIV/1
A lei; che l'Appennin superbo affrena, LXXXIII/12
A pie de l'alpi, che parton Lamagna, LII/3
A quai sembianze Amor Madonnna agguaglia, LXXIV/1
A questa fredda tema, a questo ardente, XIII/1
A questo confortando il popol tutto, CXVIII
A tal opra in disparte ora son volto, cxxviii/2
Accingetivi dunque a lalta impresa, CXXV
Adunque, m'hai tu pur, in sul fiorire, cxliii/1
Ahi poco degno è ben d'alta fortuna, CXLVI, 32
Ahi quanto aven di quello, onde si dice, LI/2
Ahi quanto indegni son di lor fortuna, CXLVI
Alcun è; che de suoi più colti campi, LI/4
Alhor senza sospetto il vano e folle, XLVIII/2
Alma cortese; che dal mondo errante, LXXXIII/1
Alma se stata fossi a pieno accorta, LXVII/1
Alta Colonna e ferma a le tempeste, cxxvi/1
Altro da indi in qua, che pene e guai, XCVII/2
Altro non si potea, fuor che piangendo, LXVIII/2
Ambe le chiavi del celeste regno, cxxxix/2
Amor; che meco in quest'ombre ti stavi, VI/1
Amor è gratiosa e dolce voglia, CXXXI
Amor è graziosa e dolce voglia, CXXXI, 17
Amor la punse, e poi scolpoi l'adorna, lxxxii/2
Amor, mia voglia, e'l vostro altero sguardo, LXXVI/1
Amore è Donne care un vano e fello, XXXIII/1
Amore, io non mi pento, xvi/2
Anchor direi; ma temo non tal volta, CLXIV
Anima, che da' bei stellanti chiostri, lxxviii/1
Anime; tra cui spatia hor la grand'ombra, CXIII/1
Anime, tra cui spazio or la grande ombra, CXIII/1, cxlvi/1
Anzi non pur Amor le vaghe stelle, CXXXIII
Arsi Bernardo in foco chiaro e lento, CIV/1
Avea per sua vaghezza teso Amore, clxii/3
Avess'io almen penna più ferma o stile, clxii/5

## B

Beato se, ch'altrui beato fai, LXXX/2
Bella guerriera mia perché sì spesso, XXVIII/1
Ben devrebbe Madonnna a sé chiamarme, cliv/1
Ben devria farvi honor d'eterno essempio, LXXVII/1
Ben ho da maledir l'empio Signore, LI/1
Ben la scorgo io sin di là su talora, clix/2
Ben le dice mio cor: "chi t'assecura?, cxlix/2
Ben son degni d'onor gl'inchiostri tutti, cxxiv/2
Breve spario che dure il vostro orgoglio, XCVIII/2

## C

Cantai un tempo, e se fu dolce il canto, xlv/1
Cantar, che sembra d'harmonia divine, VIII/2

Canzon e vo ben dir cotanto avanti, LXXIII/4
Canzon qui vedi un tempio a canto al mare, LXXXIII/11, cxlii/
Canzon qui vedi un tempio accanto al mare, LXXXIII/11
Carlo, dunque venite a le mie rime, cxxviii/1
Caro e sovran de l'età nostra onore, cxxvii/1
Caro sguardo sereno, in cui sfavilla, lxxxii/1
Casa, in cui le virtuti han chiaro albergo, cxli/1
Casso e privo son io d'ogni mio bene, LII/2
Cerco fermar il sole, arder la neve, XL/2
Certo ben mi poss'io dir pago homa, LVII/1
Ch'i' non so volger gli occhi a parte, ov'io, clxi/2
Ch'io scriva di costei, ben m'hai tu detto, X/1
Ch'io sperarei de la pietate anchora, VII/2
Ch'ogni pena per voi gli sembra gioco, cxxiii/2
Ché come audace lupo suol de gli agni, CVI/2
Ché con l'altra restai morto in quel punto, LXXXIII/8, cxlii/
Ché con laltra restai morto in quel punto, LXXXIII/8
Ché da ciascun suo raggio in un momento, cxxxiv/2
Ché da la chiara et gran virtute vostra, XVII/2
Che da spiegarlo stile in versi o 'n rime, cxxvii/2
Che detta il mio collega: il qual n'ha mostro, XCVI/2
Ché già sarebbe oltra l'Ibero e 'l Gange, clvii/2
Che giova posseder cittadi e regni, CLVI
Che giova saettar un, che si more, LIII
Che gioverà da l'alma avere scosso, CVII/1, cxviii/1
Che gioverà da lalma havere scosso, CVII/1
Che mi giova mirar donne e donzelle, clxi/1
Ché non arei veduto il mio gran danno, cxliii/2
Ché non harei veduto il mio gran danno, LXXXIV/2
Che parli o sventurato?, LII/4
Ché poi che di quel ben son privo e casso, XLIII/2
Ché poi che Pisa n'ha disciolti e privi, XCV/2
Ché potranno talhor le genti accorti, I/2
Che potranno talor gli amanti accorti, I/2, i/2
Ché sai tra quanto scaldi e quanto giri, XCII/2
Ché son sì stanco; e tu più forte giungi, XLI/2
Che ti val saettarmi, s'io già fore,   LIII, lvii
Cingi le costei tempie de l'amato, cxxv/1
Cola mentre voi sete in fesca parte, LXIX/1
Colei, che guerra a' miei pensieri indice, lxi/1
Colui; che nacque in su la riva, d'Arno, LXXII/2
Come havrian posto al nostro nasciamento, CLIII
Come si converria, de' vostri onori, XVII/1, xviii/1
Come si convienia, de vostri honori, XVII/1
Come, a cui vi donate voi, disdice, CXLVIX
Con la ragion nel suo bel vero involta, XLVIII/1
Correte fiumi a le vostre alte fonti, XLII/1
Cosa dinanzi a voi non pò fermarsi, CXXXVIX
Cosa non vada più come solea, XLII/2
Così 'l sostegno mio da voi mi vene, XXXV/2, xxxviii/2
Così 'l sostegno mio da voi ne vene, XXXV/2
Così convien ch'io pensi e parli e scriva, LXIX/2
Così detto disparve; e le sue chiome, CXXVI
Così mi renda il cor pago e contento, cxxiv/1

Così mi struggo: e pur, s'io non m'inganno, LXXVI/2
Così più d'un error versa dal fonte, CXLIII, 29
Così più dun'error versa dal fonte, CXLIII
Così sol per virtù di questo lume, XVI/5
Così voi vi trovate altrui cercando, CLXII
Crin d'oro crespo et d'ambra tersa et pura, VIII/1


D
Da l'altra speme al vento, e tema invano, XXXII/2, xxxiv/2
Da l'altro speme al vento, e tema in vano, XXXII/2
Da laltra parte un suo ben leve sdegno, LXXIII/2
Da que bei crin; che tanto più sempre amo, XI/1
Da torvi a gliocchi miei s'a voi diede ale, XCV/1
Da torvi agli occhi miei s'a voi diede ale, XCV/1, cx/1
Dal vulgo intanto m'allontano e celo, CIII/2, cxiii/2
De la gran quercia, che bel Tebro adombra, XXV/1
Deh che non mena il sole homai quel giorno, CXIV/2
Deh, perché inanzi a me te ne sei gita, clvi/1
Del cibo; onde Lucretia e l'altre han vita, XXIII/1
Di nessun danno mio molto mi doglio, LI/7
Di que' bie crin, che tanto più sempre amo, XI/1, ix/1
Di riaprirsi Amor questo rinchiuso, CVIII/2
Dinanzi a te partiva ira e tormento, LXXXIII/3
Diranno: et già non sete noi sì vostra, XXIX/2
Dirò di lei, ch'a quella gelosia, lxxviii/2
Donna, che fosti oriental Fenice, clv/1
Donna, cui nulla è par bella né saggia, cxxxii/1
Donna, de' cui begli occhi alto diletto, clxii/1
Donne; c'havete in man l'alto governo, XXXVIII/1
Dura strada a fornir hebbi dinanzi, XLV/2


E
E 'l terzo vi stia inanzi a tutte l'hore, XXIII/2
E come donna in vista dolce, umile, XIX/2, xix/2
E d'un oscuro nembo ricoperse, XCIII/2, cii/2
E fo come augellin, che si fatica, XCIX/2, cviii/2
E forse ancora un amoroso ingegno, cxli/1
E già negli occhi miei feriva il giorno, LXXXII/2, xc/1
E guidemi per man; che sa 'l camino, LXXXIII/9, cxlii/9
E io ne prego lei, e chi mi strinse, LIV/2, lix/2
E la vostra bellezza quasi un orto, CXLV
E ne lo specchio mirarete un'altra, LXXVIII/2, lxxxviii/2
E per bocca di lui chiaro vi dico, CXLIV, 30
E poi che non pote uom senza lo spirto, XCIV/2, ciii/1
E prima fia di stelle ignudo il cielo, XVI/6, xvii/6
E quei, come dicesse: "Io men' vo' gire, XXVI/2, xxv/2
E se pur fia che le mie insegne sante, CXX, 6
E so ch'io movo indarno, o penser casso, xciv/2
E son or questi, ch'io v'addito e mostro, CXXVIII, 14
E tanto in quel sembiante ella mi piacque, V/2, xi/2
E vanno argomentando che si deve, CXXIII, 9
Ecco, l'erbetta e i fior lieti e soavi, VI/2, vi/2

Ecco, ove giunse prima, et poi s'assise, VI/2
Eletto ben hai tu la miglior parte, LXXV/2
Era Madonna al cerchio di sua vita, clx/1
Et come Donna in vista dolce humile, XIX/2
Et d'un oscuro nembo ricoperse, XCIII/2
Et fo come augellin; che s'affatica, XCIX/2
Et già ne gliocchi miei feriva il giorno, LXXXII/2
Et guidemi per man; che sa 'l camino, LXXXIII/9
Et io ne prego lei, e chi mi strinse, LIV/2
Et ne lo specchio mirarete un'altra, LXXVIII/2
Et per bocca di lui chiaro vi dico, CXLIV
Et poi che non pote huom senza lo spirto, XCIV/2
Et prima fia di stelle ignudo il cielo, XVI/6
Et quel; come dicesse io men'vo gire, XXVI/2
Et se mercé de lor fidi scrittori, XLVI/2
Et se pur fia che le mie insegne sante, CXX
Et son hor questi chio v'addito e mostro, CXXVIII
Et tanto in quel sembiante ella mi piacque, V/2
Et vanno argomentando che si deve, CXXIII


        F
Farò, qual peregrin desto a gran giorno, LXXXVI/2
Fedeli miei che sotto l'Euro havete, CXVIX
Felice Imperador; ch'avanzi gli anni, LXXIX/1
Felice lui, ch'è sol conforme obietto, cxxv/2
Felice stella il mio viver segnava, XXVI/1
Fiume; delqual armato Antenor bebbe, XCIII/1
Fiume, onde armato il mio buon vicin bebbe, XCIII/1, cii/1
Foco son di desio, di tema ghiaccio, XVI/4
Fornito hai bella donnna il tuo viaggio, LX/2
Fornito hai, bella donna, il tuo viaggio, cxlviii/2
Forse fia questo aventuroso tempo, XVI/2
Forse non degna me di tanto honore, X/2
Fortuna, che sì spesso indi mi svia, LXXV/2
Fredda era più che neve: né 'n quel punto, XXVII/2
Frisio; che già da questa gente a quella, LXXV/1, liv/1
Fu, perch'io 'l miro in vece et in sembianza, LXXXV/2, xcl/2
Fu, perchiol miro in vece et in sembianza, LXXXV/2


        G
Gela, suda, chier pace e move guerra, cvii/2
Già donna, hor dea; nel cui virginal chiostro, LXXXIX/1
Già donna, or dea, nel cui verginal chiostro, LXXXIX/1, xcvii
Già m'hai veduto a questo fido horrore, III/2
Già vago, hor sovr'ognialtro horrido colle, LXXIV/1
Già vago, or sovr'ogni altro orrido colle, LXXIV/1, lxxx/1
Giaceami stanco, e'l fin de la mia vita, LXXXII/1
Gioia m'abonda al cor tanta e sì pura, LXXIII/1
Giovio, che i tempi e l'opre raccogliete, cxxxviii/1
Girolamo, se 'l vostro alto Quirino, cxxix/1
Gran tempo fui sott'esso preso e morto, CX/2
Grave duol certo: Pur io mi consolo, CXII/2

Grave, saggio, cortese, alto signore, XXI/1, xxi/1
Grazie del ciel, via più ch'altri non crede, cxxxii/2


H
Hor; c'ho le mie fatiche tante e gli anni, XLIII/1
Hor, che non s'ode mormorear di venti, XVI/1
Hor dico, che di me; sì come il Sole, XVI/3
Hor hai colto del mondo il più bel fiore, LX/1
Hor veggo, e dirol chiaro in ciascun loco, LI/3


I
I chiari giorni miei passar volando, XCI/1
I' miro ad or ad or nel suo bel viso, lxxxiii/2
Il pregio d'honestate amato e colto, CL
Il qual errando in questa e'n quella parte, CLII
Il Signor; che piangete, e morte ha tolto, LVI/2
In poco libertà con molti affanni, XC/1
In questa piango: e poi ch'al mio riposo, LXII/2
In questa uscìo de la sua bella spoglia, clviii/2
In tanto al vulgo mi nascondo e celo, CIII/2
Io ardo dissi; et la risposta in vano, XXVII/1
"Io ardo" disse, e la risposto invano, XXVII/1, xxvii/2
Io, che di viver sciolto havea pensato, II/1
Io, che già vago e sciolto avea pensato, II/1, ii/1


L
L'alta cagion, che da principio diede, XXXV/1
L'alto mio dal Dignor tesoro eletto, cl/1
L'entrar precipitoso e l'uscir erto, XXXIII/12, xxxv/12
L'intrar precipitoso, e luscir erto, XXXIII/12
La donna, che qual sia tra saggia e bella, cxxxv/2
Là dove 'l sol più tardo a noi s'adombra, LXXIV/2, lxxiii/2
Là dovel sol più tardo a noi s'adombra, LXXIV/2
La fera che scolpita nel cor tengo, xciv/1
La mia fatal nemica è bella e cruda, XXXI/1
La mia leggiadra e candida angioletta, xvi/1
La nostra e di Iesu nemica gente, C/1
La pena è sola; ma la gioia mista, XII/2
La qual hor cinta di silentio eterno, CXXXVII
La qual in somma è questa: ch'ogni uom viva, CXVII, 3
Laqual in somma è questa, ch'ognun viva, CXVII
Lasso ch'i piango; e'l mio gran duo non move, XLI/1
Lasso me, ch'ad un tempo e taccio e grido, XL/1
Lasso, né manca de' tuoi figli ancora, cxxi/2
Le guerre spesse haver, le pavi rare, XXXIII/11
Le Piramidi e Memphi poi lasciate, CXXVII
Legga le dotte et onorate carte, cxxxvii/2
Leonico, che 'n terra al ver sì spesso, cxliv/1
Lieta e chiusa contrada; ov'io m'involo, LVIX/1
Luna ha 'l governo in man de le contrade, CXXII
Lungi da lei di mio voler sen' vanno, CV/2

M

Ma che non giova haver fedeli amanti, CLVII
Ma dove drizzan ora i caldi rai, cxxxi/2
Ma l'imagine sua dolente e schieva, CIV/2, cxiv/2
Ma limagine sua turbata e schieva, CIV/2
Ma non perviene a la mia Donna il pianto, LXXXVII/2
Ma poi ch'errante e cieco mi guidasti, CVII/2
Ma s'ella il nodo a l'alma non discoglie, cliv/2
Ma se con l'opre, ond'io mai non mi satio, XVIII/2
Ma sì m'abbaglia il vostro altero lume, XXXIX/2
Ma sia, che pò: dopo 'l gelo ritorno, LI/5, lv/5
Ma sia, che puo: dopo 'l gelo ritorna, LI/5
Ma tu sanavi quei, c'havean desire, XLIX/2
Mentre 'l fero destin mi toglie e vieta, LXXXV/1, xci/1
Mentre di me la verde abile scorza, xcv/1
Mentre i duo poli e 'l lucido Orione, clvi/2
Mentre navi e cavalli e schiere armate, CIII/1
Mentrel fero destin mi toglie e vieta, LXXXV/1
Mira le genti strane e la raccolta, XXXVII/2
Mira'l Settentrion Signor gentile, LXXIX/2
Mirando a la sua fede ferma e pura, XLVII/2, li/2
Mirando a la sua fede interna e pura, XLVII/2
Mirate quando Febo a noi ritorna, CLIV, 40
Mirate quando Phebo a noi ritorna, CLIV
Misero, che sperava esser in via, xlv/2
Moderati desiri, immenso ardore, IX/1
Molza che fa la Donna tua, che tanto, XCVI/1
Morte m'ha tolto a la mia dolce usanza, cliii/2
Mostrami Amor da luna parte in schiera, XXXII/1
Mostrommi amor da l'una parte, ov'era, XXXII/1, xxxiv/1
Mostrommi entro a lo spatio dun bel volto, LXXV/1


N

Nacque ne l'alma in tanto un fero ardore, II/2
Nacque ne l'alma inseme un fero ardore, II/2, ii/2
Nasce bella sovente in ciascun loco, LXXIV/3
Navaier mio; ch'a terra strana volto, CXII/1
Né fia per tutto ciò; che quella voglia, LXXIII/3
Ne i vostri sdegni, aspra mia morte et viva, XXIX/1
Ne l'odorato e lucido oriente, CXV
Né men di quel, che santamente adopra, cxl/2
Né men, dove ch'io vada, odo et intendo, lxxxiii/3
Né sì viva riluce a l'età nostra, cxxxvi/2
Né teme di saetta o d'altro inganno, IV/2
Né Tigre sé vedendo orbata e sola, LXV/1
Nega un parlar, un atto dolce umile, XLV/2, xlix/2
Nel mille cinquecento e diece havea, XXXVIII/2
Nel mille cinquecento e dieci avea, XXXVIII/2, xli/2
Niega un parlar, un atto dolce humile, XLV/2
Non è gran meraviglia, s'una o due, CLI
Non membrar le mie colpe, e poi ch'adietro, clxiv/2
Non si nega Signore, CXI/3
Non son, se ben me stesso e te risguardo, LXXXVIII/2

Non sospirate: il meritar gli onori, cxxix/2
Non ti doler di noi; che ne convene, XVIII/2
"Non ti doler di noi, che ne convene, xiii/2
Non vi mandò qua giù l'eterna cura, CXLVIII


O                                        see also H
O alma, in cui riluce il casto e saggio, cxxii/2
O ben nato e felice, o primo frutto, XXXVII/1
O d'ogni mio penser ultimo segno, lxiv/1
O Donna in questa etade al mondo sola, CXXIX, 15
O Donna in questa etate al mondo sola, CXXIX
O Hercole; che travagliando vai, XXI/2
O imagine mia celeste et pura, XIX/1
O; per cui tante in van lacrime e 'nchiostro, XLVI/1
O pria sì cara al ciel del mondo parte, cxxi/1
O quanto è dolce, perch'Amor la stringa, CLVIX
O Rossigniuol; che 'n queste verdi fronde, LII/1
O Sol, di cui questo bel sole è raggio, clxiii/1
O superba e crudele, o di bellezza, LXXVIII/1
Occhi leggiadri, onde sovente Amore, XVIII/1
"Occhi leggiadri, onde sovente Amore, xiii/1
Omai la scorga il tuo celeste lume, clxiii/2
Ombre, in cui spesso il mio sol vibra e spiega, ci/1
Ond'io, Padre celeste, a te mi volgo, CVIX/2, cix/2
Ond'io vi do con se questo consiglio, CLXIII
Ondio Padre celeste a te mi volgo, CVIX/2
Or che non s'odon per le frondi i venti, XVI/1, xvii/1
Or hai de la sua gloria scosso Amore, cxlviii/1
Or sete giunta tardo a le mie rime, cxxxiii/2
Ov'è, mia bella e cara e fida scorta, cxlix/1
Ove romita e stanca e sedea, V/1, xi/1
Ove tutta romita si sedea, V/1


P
Parmi veder ne la tua fronte Amore, XX/2
Pasce la pecorella i verdi campi, CLV
Per appoggiarli al tuo sinistro corno, XXII/2
Per cui d'amaro pianto il cor si bagna, clv/2
Per far tosto de me polvere et ombra, XCVIII/1
Per la via, che 'l gran Tosco amando corse, lxi/2
Perché, dicea, la tua vita consume, LXXXI/2
"Perché" dicea "la tua vita consume, LXXXI/2, lxxxix/2
Perché se 'l Tosco, che di Laura scrisse, xxxvi/2
Perché sia forse a la futura gente, LXXXVI/1
Però che non la terra solo, e'l mare, CXXXII
Però che voi non sete cosa integra, CLXI
Però vorrei ch'andaste a quelle fere, CXXIV
Phrisio; che già da questa gente a quella, LXXV/1
Piacciavi dir, quando il nostro hemispera, CXIII/2
Piansi et cantai la perigliosa guerra, I/1
Piansi et cantai lo strazio e l'aspra guerra, I/1, i/1
Pianta gentil; ne le cui sacre fronde, XXV/2

Picciol cantor, ch'al mio verde soggiorno, III/1, iv/1
Più gioverà mostrarvi humile et piano, XIV/2
Poi ch'ogni ardir mi circonscrisse Amore, VII/1
Poi chel costr'alto ingegno, e quel celeste, LXX/1
Poi chel suon tace, è tolto a gran vergogna, LI/6
Poi com'io torni a la prima figura, LXXVIII/2
Pon Febo mano a la tua nobil arte, CI/1, cxi/1
Pon Phebo mano a la tua nobil arte, CI/1
Por si pò ben nemica e dura sorte, LXXIV/2, lxxx/2
Por si puo ben nemica e dura sorte, LXXIV/2
Porto, che'l piacer mio teco ne porti, CXIV/1, cxlvii/1
Porto; chel mio piacer teco ne porti, CXIV/1
Porto se'l valor vostro arme et perigli, XIV/1, xiv/1
Porto sel valor vostro arme et perigli, XIV/1
Prima ch'io scorga in quel bel viso un segno, XXXI/2
Privo in tutto son io dogni mio bene, XLIX/2
Puossi morta chiamar quella, di cui, CLX


     Q
Qual alga in mar, che quinci e quindi l'onde, clx/2
Qual credenza d'haver senz'Amor pace, CXXX
Qual da la mensa uom temperato e sazio, cxliv/2
Qual fora un uom, se l'una e l'altra luce, CXLVII, 33
Qual fuora un huom, se luna e laltra luce, CXLVII
Qual meraviglia, se repente sorse, LVIII/1
Qual pianser già le triste e pie sorelle, LXXXIII/7
Quando 'l mio sol, del qual invidia prende, LXXVII/1, lxxxvi
Quando 'l mio sol, delqual invidia prende, LXXVII/1
Quando ebbe più tal mostro umana vita, lxiv/2
Quando ecco due man belle oltra misura, XI/2
Quando, forse per dar loco a le stelle, LXI/1
Quanti vi dier le stelle doni a prova, cxxvi/2
Quanto alma è più gentile, xxxvi/1
Quanto esser vi dee caro un huom, che brami, CLVIII
Quanto in mill'anni il ciel devea mostrarne, CXL
Quanto sia dolce un soltario stato, LIX/2
Quanto soffiano i venti, et volge il cielo, XVI/7
Quasi stella del polo chiara e ferma, LXXXIII/4
Quel dolce suon, per sui chiaro s'intende, cxxiii/1
Quella, che co' begli occhi par che 'nvoglie, cxxxvii/1
Quella per cui chiaramente alsi et arsi, clix/1
Questa del nostro lito antica sponda, LXXXVII/1
Questa fe Cino poi lodar Selvaggia, CXXXVI
Questa fe dolce ragionar Catullo, CXXXV
Questa fe' Cino poi lodar Selvaggia, CXXXVI, 22
Questa fe' dolce ragionar Catullo, CXXXV, 21
Questa novellamente ai padri vostri, CXXXVIII
Questa per vie sovra 'l pensier divine, CXXXIV, 20
Questa per vie sovral pensier divine, CXXXIV
Questa risplenderà, come bel sole, cxxxviii/2
Questo infiammato e sospiroso core, XLIX/1
Qui tra le selve e i campi e l'herbe e lacque, XC/2

R
Raro pungente stral di ria fortuna, LXXXIII/2
Re de gli altri superbo et sacro monte, XXII/1
Rime leggiadre, che novellamente, LV/1
Risponde, voi non durareste in vita, XIIII/2
Risponde: "Voi non durereste in vita, XIIII/2, xxx/2
Rose bianche e vermiglie ambe le gote, CXLI


S
S'al vostro amor ben fermo non s'appoggia, cliii/1
S'Amor m'avesse detto: "ohimè, da morte, clvii/1
S'en dir la vostra anglica bellezza, LXXII/1
Sallo Amore, ch'io vorrei ben farvi honore, LV/2
Sanale; che pòi farlo: e dammi aita, LXXXIX/2
Santo saggio cortese alto Signore, XXI/1
Sappia ogniun, ch'io vorrei ben farvi honore, LV/2, lx/2
Sdegni di vetro, adamantina fede, IX/2
Se 'l viver men che pria m'è duro e vile, LXXXI/1, lxxxix/1
Se col liquor che versa, non pur stilla, cxxx/1
Se come già ti valse, hora ti cale, LXXXIII/10
Se dal più scaltro accorger de le genti, XXXIX/1
Se de le mie ricchezze care e tante, CV/1
Se deste a la mia lingua tanta fede, LIV/1
Se già ne l'età mia più verde e calda, clxiv/1
Se in me, Quirina, da lodar in carte, cxxxvi/1
Se la più dura quercia, che l'alpe haggia, XCVII/1
Se la via da curar glinfermi hai mostro, LXXVI/1
Se lo stil non s'accorda col desio, lxxvii
Se mai ti piacque, Apollo, non indegno, cxxv/1
Se ne monti Riphei sempre non piove, LVI/1
Se ne' Rifei sempre non piove, LVI/1, lxii/1
Se non ch'al suo sparir m'agghiaccio; e poi, LXXVII/2
Se non fosse il penser crudele et empio, CXLII, 28
Se non fosse il penser, ch'a la mia donna, lxxxiiii/1
Se non fosse il pensier crudele et empio, CXLII
Se qual è dentro in me, chi lodar brama, cxl/1
Se stata foste voi nel colle Ideo, cxxxiii/1
Se tu stessa, canzone, clxii/6
Se tutti i miei prim'anni a parte a parte, LXXXVIII/1
Se vòi ch'io torni sotto 'l fascio antico, XLVII/1, li/1
Se voi sapete che'l morir ne doglia, XCIV/1
Se vuoi ch'io torni sottol fascio antico, XLVII/1
Sel viver men che pria m'è duro e vile, LXXXI/1
Sento l'odor da lunge, e'l fresco e l'ora, XCII/1
Sento un novo piacer possente e forte, XCI/2
Sento una voce fuor dei verdi rami, ci/2
Sì come là, dove 'l mio buon Romano, CXXI, 7
Sì come là, dovel mio buon Romano, CXXI
Sì come più di me nessuna in terra, clxii/2
Sì come quando il ciel nube non have, XXX/1
Sì come sola scalda la gran luce, XXXIV/1
Sì come suol, poi che'l verno aspro et rio, IV/1
Sì dirà poi sanato ad hora ad hora, LXXVI/2

Sì divina beltà Madonna onora, cxxxiv/1
Sì levemente in ramo alpino fronda, cvii/1
Si vi s'arroge il corpo, in cui beltade, XLV/2, lxx/2
Si vi s'arroge il corpo; ove beltade, XLV/2
Signor; che parti e tempri gli elementi, CVI/1
Signor; che per giovar sei Giove detto, CVIII/1
Signor del ciel, s'alcun prego ti move, CX/1
Signor, poi che fortuna in adornarvi, cxxxix/1
Signor quella pietà; che ti constrinse, CXI/1
Sogno; che dolcemente m'hai furato, LXXX/1
Solingo augello si piangendo vai, XLIV/1
Son questi quei begli occhi, in cui mirando, XX/1
Son tal; che page a mille amanti offesi, LVII/2
Son tali; che quetar ben mille offesi, LVII/2, lxiii/2
Sovra le notti mie fur chiaro lume, clxii/4
Sovra' l tuo sacro e onorato busto, LXXXIII/6, cxlii/6
Sovral tuo sacro e honorato busto, LXXXIII/6
Speme; che gli occhi nostri veli e asaci, L/1
Spiegando in rime nove antico foco, XLVI/2
Stendi l'arco per me, se vòi ch'io viva, xcv/2
Surge la speme, e per le vene un caldo, xxviii/2


        T
Taccian per laere i venti; e caldo o gelo, XXXVI/2
Tacquimi già molt'anni, e diedi al tempio, cxxx/2
Tal che leggiera e di quel nodo sciolta, cl/2
Tal io da speme honesta e pura scorto, XXX/2
Tal io; mentre fra via londe avolgendo, CII/2
Talhor m'assido in su la verde riva, XXIV/2
Talhor vengo a glinchiostri; e parte noto, LXIV/2
Tanta gratia del ciel chi legge altrove, XXXIV/2
Tanta grazia del ciel chi vedd altrove, XXXIV/2, xxxvii/2
Tanto è ch'assenzo e fele rodo e suggo, XCIX/1, cviii/1
Tanto è l'assenzo e'l fel, chio rodo e suggo, XCIX/1
Tenace e saldo, e non per che m'aggrave,CII/1
Thomaso i venni, ove l'un Duce Mauro, XXIV/1
Tomaso, i' venni, ove l'un duce mauro, XXIV/1, v/1
Torceste 'l voi, signor dal corse ardito, LXXVII/2, lxxvi/2
Torcestel voi Signor dal corse ardito, LXXVII/2
Torna col chiaro sguardo, che'è 'l mio sole, CI/2
Tosto che 'l dolce sguardo Amor m'impetra, LXXVIII/1, lxxix
Tosto che la bell'Alba solo e mesto, LXIII/1
Tosto chel dolce sguardo Amor m'impetra, LXXVIII/1
Trifon, che 'n vece di ministri e servi, cxxii/1
Tu m'hai lasciato senza sole i giorni, LXXXIII/5
Tu Padre ne mandasti, CXI/4
Tu, che ne sembri Dio, raffrens: e domo, C/2
Tutto quel, che felice et infelice, XV


        U
Un a gli amici suoi chiuder le parte, XXXIII/5, xxxv/1
Un agliamici suoi chiuder le porte, XXXIII/5

Un anno intero s'è girato a punto, clviii/1
Un ben; che le più volte more in fasce, XXXIII/4
Un cacciar Tigri a passo infermo e lento, XXXII/10
Un cibo amaro, e sostegno aspro e grave, XXXIII/6
Un consumarsi dentro a parte a parte, XXXIII/8
Un desiar; ch'in aspettando un giorno, XXXIII/2
Un dinanzi al suo foco esser di neve, XXXIII/7
Un falso imaginar; che sì ne 'ngombra, XXXIII/3
Un, perché mille volte il di si moia, XXXIII/9
Usato di mirar forma terrena, XII/1
Uscito fuor de la prigion trilusre, CVIX/1


V
Varchi, le vostre pure carte e belle, cxxxi/1
Vattene a i liete e fortunati amanti, L/2
Vattene ai liete e fortunati amanti, L/2, liv/2
Vedi Padre cortese, CXI/2
Vego augelletto; ch'al mio bel sogiorno, III/1
Verdeggi a l'Appennin la fronte e'l petto XXXVI/1, xxxviii/2
Verdeggi al'Appennin la fronte e'l petto XXXVI/1
Viva mia neve e caro e dolce foco, xxviii/1

# V.
## Giovanbatista Strozzi
## (Giovanni Battista Strozzi, the Elder)
### *Madrigali*

## A

A bel fior presso langue, CXLV/1
A che pur folle ammiri, XIII
A che pur t'affatichi, XCII/5
A disasprir sì aspro, XXXI
A primi Amor le labbra, e deh tu spiega, CVI
A quante sueglia violette, e gigli, CXI
A quest'alma d'Amor FACE divina, VIII/2
A tante fiamme, ch'io son già di foco, LXXX/15
A terra sparso il mio ricco tesoro, CXLIV/1
A tutto ardermi il sen candida mano, LXXX/6
A verga a verga tremo, e 'ndietro a passo, CXXXVIII
Abbandona i fioriti colli s'Arno, CVII
Abronzi vita, e marmi, XCVII
Ahi come hor fosco, hor chiaro, CXXVIII
Ahi scelerata inestinguibil sete, XCII/1
All'apparir del'odorato MAGGIO, LXXXVI/4
Alla mia PERLA o perle itene in seno, XXI/5
Alle dolci ombre di si bella, e bianca, CLV/6
Alle piante io pur narro, a' fiori, all' erbe, CII
Alto piacer, che dall'accese stelle, LXXXVII/3
Altra gentil, ma viva, LXXX/14
Altra Neve, e più fresca a sì gran fiamma, LXXX/13
Altre più dolce ripsate olive, CLXXIII
Altri 'n quella, altri 'n questa, CLV/3
Alza Filli il bel viso, e gigli, e rose, CLVI
Amor, che mai non vide, LII
Amor, e 'l sogno in braccio, LXXI/1
Angeletta gentil cinta di mirto, V
Annova guerra, e nuova, LXXX/5
Ape, che si soave mormorando, XXXVIII
Ardo al più lungo, et ardo, LXXX/10
Ardo, e sì dolce ardendo mi disfaccio, CXXII
Asperso di mercede, XVIII/12
Aspre quante d'invidia, e spine, e stecchi, XXXIX
Atra hebb'io scorza, e si stridula, e vile, XCV
Aura de' miei sospiri, CV
AURE del ben seren lucido velo, XI/11
AURE dell'angoscioso viver mio, XI/2
AURE sempre di fiori, XI/6

## B

Beato il Ciel, che mille e mille luci, XLI/5
Bel FIOR tu mi rimembri, XXXV
Bel vago della Luna, XLI/1
Bel vetro (ma qualcun de' miei sospiri, LXVIII
Bel viso, che le stelle, e che l'Aurora, IX
Bianca man, che pur Neve, LXXX/12
Bronzi, e marmi già quanti, XXVIII

## C

Cacciata ohimè da si crud'orche, e belve, CLXVII

Dormiami, e si dormiva, LXXI/9
Dormiasi la mia Filli, e 'nsieme Amore, LXXXVII/1
Dormito hai bella Donna, CLI/1


        E
E' semplicetta pastorella, e dura, CXXXI
Ecco l'alba col di, suegliati bella, XCVIII
Ecco l'Alba, ohimè che nuovo campo, LIX
Ecco MAGGIO, inchinatevi Arboscelli, LXXXVI/6
Ecco MAGGIO seren, chi l'ha vestito, LXXXVI/5
Ecco MAGGIO, un sì bel puepuero nembo, LXXXVI/7
Ella, che ben s'accorse, LXXVIII/2
Entra in questi occhi lassi, LVI/7
Eran le guance, di ch'io piango, e scrivo, CXLVII
Erasi al Sole il mio bel Sole assiso, LXV
Erbe, e fior, lauri, e mirti, CXXVI
Errai, ma frodi, e 'ngiurie, e falli quanti, CLXIV
Esci del chiaro seno, LVI/2


        F
Faticoso viaggio, CLXXIV
Felice lui, che 'n prezioso nembo, CXXIV
Felici, che sì dura alpe d'affanni, CLXIX
Fermate Ore, fermate, CLXXV
Ferro crudel, ma quanto, XCII/7
Fetonte odo, che 'n Pò, quell'altro in mare, CLV/2
Fiamma del Ciel su le tue merci piova, XCII/6
Filli mia, Filli dolce, oh sempre nuovo, XLVII
Foco, e fiamma in tal guisa ardente Sole, LXXX/8
Foss'io fresca Neve hora, LXXX/11
Foss'io lieve augellin; ma qual s'affretta, CXXXIII
Fuggirei volentier, ch'io non più scorgo, CX


        G
Gelido suo ruscel chiaro, e tranquillo, X
Già 'l novello anno del bel verde acerbo, XI/1
Grazie da render, grazie io non ritrovo, CLV/9

        H
Ha benuto soverchio, XCIII/3
Ha di serpe il velen, di lupa il morso, XVII
Hor che 'l Ciel tutto, che suol arder sempre, LXXX/3
Hor che 'l prato, e la selva si scolora, LVI/9
Hor chi Filli beata, L
Hor chi m'inostra, e'mpiuma, VIII/3
Hor come un scoglio stassi, XVI
Hor lieve Ape foss'io / Se non trepid'auretta fugitiva, XXXVI
Hor lieve ape foss'io, che tanto andrei, XXXVII
Hor se tal m'arde, e 'nfiamma, LXXII

on perdonò quest'empia a' figli suoi, XII
on sa (tanto piacer l'abbaglia, e'ncende, LV
ostro avversario, e suo quell'alto Padre, XCII/8
uova io non so, se stella, III
uovo SMERALDO, hor nuovo, e più gentile, CXX


                 O                    see also H
» begli anni dell'oro, o secol divo, CLVI
» benedetto mio gentil pensiero, CXIII
» nuova esca gentil, che m'assimigli, CXII
» più che l'ombra, e l'ora al Sole ardente, LXXV
»cchi miei 'l vostro pianto, LXXXIII
»cchi piangete, poi / Che di pianto si pasce, e si nodrica, LXXXV
»cchi piangete, poi/Che di sua man v'asciuga il Signor .., LXXXIV
»himè lasso, e quando, LVI/5
»mbra io seguo, che piagge, e monti cuopre, LXIII
»mbra io seguo di sempre fuggitivo, CLXIII
»nd'havran più le stelle, CXLVIII
»stro, e nettar, beate, LXX
»ve stelle fugaci, LXXI/10


                 P
»acifiche, ma spesso in amorosa, XI/10
»allide vecchiarelle rannodate, CXLV/6
»astorella angosciosa, CLIV
»er consiglio di vostro amico sdegno, XVIII/6
»er simigliarti il bel sempre sereno, LI
»erdonami Signore, CLV/7
»iangendo mi baciaste, XVIII/16
»iangete, lassi, ma che giova il pianto?, CXLIX
»iansero il fulminato, CXLV/2
»iù non duolmi il mio duol, tanto m'addoglia, LXXXII
»iume hor tutte di lagrime cosparte, LXXI/4
»osa amica gentil, che 'l mondo ignaro, LVIII
»OSA tranquilla, POSA, LVI/4
»osemi Amor d'angoscia, LXXVIII/1
»resso un limpido rio, ch'ambe le sponde, CXVI
»rimavera gentil, ma che giamai, XLV/1


                 Q
»uando la bianca luce, XLI/4
»uando sarai tu stanco, XCII/4
»uante volte il mattin, quante la sera, XCI/1
»uanti ha Cerberi, e Furie, e belve crude, XVIII/9
»uanto è più bello il Ciel Filli mia cara, XVIII/11
»uel nodo ch'io pensai, ch'ognor più forte, XVIII/1
»uel più che neve bianco, LXXVI
»uella neve gentil, ch'arder mi face, LXXIV
»uesta ordio 'l laccio, questa, LXIV
»ueste a' bei nodi biondi, I
»ui si rivolse indietro, XLVI

# VI.
## Luigi Cassola
### *Madrigali*
### *del*
### *Magnifico Signor Cavallier*
### *Luigi Cassola Piacentino*

A

A che biasmar il laccio, che mi lega, LXII/2
A che dolermi donna, CXXV/1
A che gettar in quelle fiamme ardenti, CCLXXXI/1
A che lagnar ti dei, CCCLXXII/2
A che mostrar la fede in fronte scritta, CCLVIII/2
A che mostrarmi donna un tanto sdegno, CCXXIII/1
A che servir cor mio?, CCLVIII/1
A l'ombra usata de la sacre frondi, X/1
A questi abbattimenti arditi, et pronti, CCCXCI
A suo mal grado io bramo, CI/2
A tuo mal grado Amore, LXXVIII/2
Adunque il proprio inferno è l'amor mio, XXVI/2
Ah del mio honor colonna, CX/2
Ahi Carlo quinto honor di nostra etade, CDX
Ahi che ben vero è il detto, CCCLXXI/1
Ahi cieca morte, et sorda, CCCLXXVII/2
Ahi cor afflitto mio tuo puoi ben dire, CC/2
Ahi dispietata sorte, CLXXXVI/2
Ahi dispietato amore, CCCLXX/1
Ahi dolce esca d'amor, hai dolci pene, CVI/2
Ahi gran legge d'amor quanto sei vana, CCCX/2
Ahi spirito gentil lasciate l'ira, CCLI/2
Alhor i dico; ahi sventurati amanti, CCLXXX/2
Alhor più penso come mai parola, CCXXXVII/2
Allhor ringratio l'amorosa guerra, CLXX/2
Alma angelica, et bella, CXXVI
Alma ben nata a gran valor non guarda, CXCII/1
Alma ben nata, se mi duol, et dolse, CLXXXII/1
Alma diletta sposa, CX/1
Alma felice, o felice alma mia, CLXXVI/1
Alma gentil, et bella, CCXXI/1
Alma gentil, s'in voi piet[ fu mai, LXVII/1
Alma gentil, s'un vostro sguardo ha forza, CCIV/1
Alma real che per largo destino, CCCLXXIV/1
Alma serena, et bella, CCXXIX/1
Almo mio sol, s'io faccio parlo o scrivo, CCXXXV/1
Alte superbe mura, CXLIX/1
Altra pace, altro bene, altro refugio, CCCLII/2
Altri d'amor si duole; et io ringratio, CCXLIV/1
Altro non è il mio amor, ch'il propio inferno, XXVI/1
Alzate gli occhi al cielo, CCLXVI/1
Amar un sol amante è vero amore, CCCXXXV/1
Ameni colli, et voi fioriti campi, CCXXVII/1
Amo madonna assai vostra beltate, CXXIV/1
Amor, hor ben comprendo, et chiaro veggio, XVII/1
Amor i miei sospiri, CCLXXXV/2
Amor i moio, Aime che ti da morte?, CCLVI
Amor, io sento un respirar si dolce, XVI
Amor, io son si lieto, LXX/2
Amor, io veggo se di voi mi doglio, LXII/1
Amor, poi che madonna, CCLXV/1
Amor quando fia mai, CCCVI/1
Amor, quanto tu puoi, CCXVIII/1

Amor, s'il foco cresce, XIV/1
Amor, se mai vi piacque il mio servire, C/1
Amor, se notte, e giorno, XCIX/2
Amor; se ogni amar tosco, VI/1
Amor, se per amamr madonna, et voi, CCLXXXV/1
Amore, io non credea, CXCVII/1
Anima bella honor di nostra etate, CCLXXXVII/1
Anima bella, sol de gli occhi miei, CCIX/1
Anzi per sempre bramo, LXVI/2
Anzi sforzar vorrei vostra fortezza, CCCXLV/2
Anzi vo dir ch'in vita amor mi tiene, CCXVI/2
Arde la donna mia hor d'altro ardore, CXCVI/2
Ardo sol di quel foco; et non vorrei, CCII/2


        B
Bel petto, a cui nullo altro si somiglia, XXV/2
Bella Diana fu, bella Minerva, CCCXLVIII/2
Ben ch'io volessi più di quel, ch'io voglio, LXIII/1
Ben mille volte al ciel questi occhi giro, CLXI/1
Ben mille volte, et piut duolmi del cielo, XLVII/1
Ben mille volte fra me stesso giuro, XL/1
Ben mille volte già vi dissi amore, CXLVII/1
Ben mille volte ho detto, e il dico ognihora, CCXXIV/1
Ben mille volte il di meco m'adiro, CCXII/1
Ben ti mandò la donna mia per tempo, CCLXXXIII/2


        C
Candide rose, et voi ben nati fiori, CCLV/1
Carlo tu se pur debitor assai, CCCXCIX
Carlo tu vedi che la fe di Christo, CCCLXXX
Celeste è il sol, io son cosa mortale, CCLXXV/2
Ch'anchor ch'in fior de la mia vita sia, CCC/2
Ch'anchor ch'io veggia mille morti in lei, CCXCVII/2
Ch'anchor, ch'in fior de la mia vita sia, CCXLIX/2
Ch'il crederà ch'un laccio, LIV/2
Ch'il credera, perché giurando il dica, CC/1
Ch'il credera, se ben col ver lo scrivo, CLVI/1
Ch'il crederà; ch'a pena il credo io stesso, LIV/1
Ch'il dolorso stile, CCCXXXVII/2
Ch'il mio foco immortale, XXXIX/2
Ch'il vostro alto valor mi s'appresenta, LXV/2
Ch'in me non è più lena, C/2
Ch'in quel giorno, in quell'hora, et in quel punto, XXXVIII
Ch'in quello sol mio bene, CCXCI/2
Ch'in questo rozzo stile in cui vaneggio, CCCLIV/2
Ch'io ben vedrei su spesse, CLXXI/2
Ch'io giamai non potei, CCLX/2
Ch'io leggo spesso in l'uno, et l'altro Thosco, IX/2
Ch'io mi sentia nel core, CXLVII/2
Ch'io son lontano; et non saprei già dire, CLXXVI/2
Ch'un sol timor geloso, CCCXIX/2
Che ben mi fate voi si crudel guerra, CV/2

Che certo altro pensero, CCLIII/2
Che col sembiante suo leggiadro adorna, LXXXV/2
Che come in voi si trova, CCXLVIII/2
Che come sola havete, CCCXX/2
Che così grande è homai, et di tai tempre, XCII/2
Che credete voi far, donna, per fare, XXXIX/1
Che da che fui di quella luce prpivo, CXLVIII/2
Che da che i be vostri occhi mi lassaro, CLXXV/2
Che da che il vidi fu il mio foco tanto, CLXII/2
Che deggio io far, che mi consigli Amore, CCV/1
Che fuor d'ogni natura, CCVIII/2
Che gloria havrà tanta belta, ch'havete, LVI/1
Che i vaghi suoni, et quella chiara voce, XXIII/2
Che il foco è troppo homai, ch'il cor offende, CCXXXV/2
Che l'esser fredda, o calda, CCLXXXIX/2
Che l'impero, che havete, LXIII/2
Che la piaga mortale, CXLIII/2
Che le mie ardenti pene, CXXIV/2
Che nel più freddo, et più ghiacciato verno, CCXVIII/2
Che per cosa men bella, LXXX/2
Che più non può questa gelosa vita, CCCXVIII/2
Che può far il martire, CCLXXII/2
Che quando di voi scrivo, CXXV/2
Che quando penso à quella, CCLXXI/2
Che quando son più solo, CCCVII/2
Che quando vidi de le chiare stelle, CXIII/2
Che quanto v'amo più, tanto più indura, CCLXXXVI/2
Che s'io il potessi dir si come il sento, CXC/2
Che se ben di costei teco mi dolsi, CCCLX/2
Che se ben la stagione il mondo infiora, XXII/2
Che se cortese et pia, CCLXXXVII/2
Che se lasciar soffersi, CCLXXVI/2
Che sempre notte, e die, CII/2
Che sia se pur m'appresso, XX/2
Che solo il suo splendore, CCXXXIX/2
Che tanta è ben la noia,
Che tanta è ben la noia, XXXII/2, CLXXIV/2   [Duplicate poem]
Che tante doglie in me sento per vui, LVIII/2
Che val esser creata, CCXCIX/2
Che val esser nudrita, CCXCIX/1
Che val haver dal cielo, CLIII/2
Che vinto amor et rotto l'arco e i strali, CCCLXXI/2
Che voler voglio il vostro voler solo, XCVII/2
Chi puo accusar l'accesa voglia mia, CCXLI/2
Chi puo pensar veder morte pietosa, CCCLXIII/1
Chi solca il mar, in mar vita perde, CCCI/1
Chi vedesse la vita, CLXXXI/1
Chi vide mai, madonna, in un cor pio, CCCVII/1
Chi vuol veder fiorite, et fresche rose, LX/1
Chi vuol veder opra celeste, e rara, LXXIV/1
Cieco fanciullo, arcer alato, e ignudo, CCCXLVI/1
Com'havra fin la pena mia infinita?, XCIV/2
Com'havra vita Amor la vita mia, XCIV/1
Com'un soverchio ardire, LXIV/1

Come carbon al respirar d'i venti, CLXXXVII
Come ch'in chiaro sol guardo ben fiso, LIX/1
Come co'l balenar tona in un punto, CCLXXIV/1
Come consenti ahi ciel fuor del tuo stile, CLXXIII/2
Come l'alma Mancina alma felice, CCCLXXV/1
Come nel freddo ghiaccio, e in foco acceso, CCCLXII/1
Come sperar posso io, CCLXXXIV/2
Come sperar posso io, CCXVII/2
Con si cara dolcezza, XVIII/2
Con si famosa tromba, CCCXI/2
Con si vezzosa, et dolce tirannia, CCXCVII/1
Contra il cognato tuo, et Re di Franza, CDIX
Così cocente è il foco, XXXV/1
Così dal paradiso, CXII/2
Così grande è la doglia, et infinita, CXXXIV/1
Così il maggior mio danno, CLXVI/2
Così invaghiti homai son gli occhi miei, CCXIX/1
Così la giusta morte, CCCLXII/2
Così la stassi in la sua propria stanza, CCCLXXVIII/2
Così lassu tra l'anime beate, CCCLXXV/2
Così mi guida Amore, CXCI/1
Così pregiato è homai il sacro aspetto, CCCLIII/1
Così sono io mirando in le due stelle, LIX/2
Così trapasso il vero, CXCI/2


        D
Da che le gratie vostre, e i bei costumi, CCCXLVII/1
Da le più dolci parolette accorte, CCXLV/1
Da poi che piace a la fortuna mia, CXLIX/2
Da poi che su il fiorire, CCCLXV/1
Da quei belli occhi, che penar mi fanno, CXCIV/1
Da quel Dio vero il gran servor fu visto, CCLXVIII/2
Da un sol bel guardo, et da un vezzoso riso, CLXXXIV/1
Da una puro, honesto, et virtuoso amore, LXXXIII/1
Dapoi ch'amor con la divina imago, CI/1
Datemi triegua homai, CCCXVII
De l'alto mio desir sol fama aspetto, CCCLIII/2
Deggio sempre penar in questo inferno?, CCLI/1
Deggio sempre servire?, LXIX/2
Deh com'haver devrei di cio cordoglio, LI/2
Deh così fossi io solo in amar voi, CCCXX/1
Deh così potessi io, XXVII/1
Deh dite à lei, ch'homai per sua bontate, CCLV/2
Deh dite amore che lagrime fur quelle, CXIII/1
Deh dite homai con qual ragion consente, CCLXVII/2
Deh fate homai (che far io nol potrei), CXLVI/2
Deh fate homai, ch'in si lungo martire, LXVII/2
Deh fosse donna il vero, CCLIII/1
Deh fosse il ver madonna, CXLIII/1
Deh fosse il ver, che per ventura mia, CCLXXVIII/2
Deh fosse il vero, o spirito gentile, CCCXXXVII/1
Deh fosse ver ch'il duolo, LVIII/1
Deh maledetto sia quel riso, e il guardo, CLXXXIV/2

Deh morte tarda il tuo veloce corso, CCCLX/1
Deh non è questo quel leggiadro viso?, III/1
Deh non fu troppo, o mia fortuna trista, CXLVIII/1
Deh non mostrate Amore, CCII/1
Deh non v'incresca o donna del cor mio, CCCLXIX/1
Deh pensa homai, come morendo vivo, CCCXLVI/2
Deh perché il destin mio, CCCLIV/1
Deh perché non vedete alma ben nata, CCLXXXVIII/1
Deh Roma affrena affrena Roma alquanto, CCCLXXVIII/2
Deh sa signor mio caro, VI/2
Deh salvator da l'anime smarrite, CCXXXII/1
Deh sol de gliocchi miei almo, e sereno, CCIV/2
Deh vedi amor quant'è la voglia dura, CCC/1
Devreste Amor, voi, che vedete quanto, LIII/2
Di cio la morte incolpo, CCCLXVIII/2
Di quel divino Ottavio dir vorrei, CCCLXXXIV
Di quel Palavicino Sforza ardito, CCCLXXXVIII
Di rami, in rami, et poi di frondi in frondi, XIII/1
Di voi mi dolgo; et s'a ragion mi doglio, CCLXII/1
Di voi sempre mi doglio; e in questo Amore, XL/2
Dico ch'io penso, et voi non vi pensate, CCCXXI/2
Dico; ch'io vivo donna, CCXXVI/1
Dissi Madonna; io v'amo; et volsi dire, LXVI/1
Dolce nemica mia, CCVIII/1
Dolor de la mia doglia, CCIII/1
Dolor, s'il mio dolor altri non crede, CLXIII/1
Domenichi, s'amor fuor d'ogni tempra, CCXX/1
Donna, benche sia breve, XCIII
Donna crudel se pur desir havete, LII/1
Donna crudel, et tu spietato arcero, CCCXVI/1
Donna del ciel, s'in voi è la pietade, CCXXXIII/1
Donna gentil, si come udiste il canto, XXXII/1, CLXXIV/1
[Duplicate]
Donna gentil, un cor gentil si pasce, CCVI/2
Donna leggiadra, et bella, CLXV/1
Donna, quando il bel guardo, LXXXVIII/1
Donna, quando il desire, CCI/1
Donna, quando io vi guardo, CXLI/1
Donna quanto mi doglio, LI/1
Donna, s'il veder voi già mi fu tolto, CCCV/1
Donna s'io dissi, et se più volte dico, CCXCV/1
Donna s'io piango spesso, CCCXII/1
Donne, se la mia donna, LXXXI
Donna se voi vedeste, CCXLVIII/1
Donna spietate, et dura, CXXVIII/1, CCXLVII/1  [Duplicate]
Donne amorose, et belle, CCCLXVI/1
Dove lass'io quel si pregiato duce, CCCLXXXVI


     E
E i pensier miei son poi cotali, et tanti, CXXXVI/2
E il mio amoroso pianto, CCXLIV/2
E in quel pensier pensando io sol vorrei, XLIII/2
E possibil ch'amore, CCCXXVII/1
E possibil, ch'amore, CCXC/1

E possibil, ch'il duol i me stia tanto?, CXXXII/1
E possibil ch'il pianto, CXXXII/2
E possibil, ch'in voi sia gratia tanta, CCXXXVI/1
E se ben vien di fuore, CLXIX/2
Ecco che vede (et pur troppo per tempo), CCCLXX/2
Ecco i creato tuo Sforza gentile, CCCLXXXV
Egli è pur ver, come ch'il ver è vero, CCXLVI/1
Errai madonna, et il mio error fu poco, CXLII/1
Et ben direste poi, XXIV/2
Et benedetta sia vostra bellezza, CCLII/2
Et certo vi farei, CCCLXXV/2
Et che il sia ver, il ver hor si conprende, CXXVII/2
Et che poi penso a i vani miei desiri, CCLVII/2
Et che poi veggo le caste bellezze, XLIX/2
Et come il mio desir ogni altro excede, LXIV/2
Et con le accorte sue dolci parole, CCCII/2
Et con sue gratie farsi, CXXI/2
Et così amor in tutto à voi mi diede, CCCXLIII/2
Et così fermo, et saldo è il mio pensero, CVIII/2
Et così lieto vivo, CXXX/2
Et così spesso a me stesso m'involo, CCLXXIV/2
Et è l'ardir mio tanto, CLXXVIII/2
Et forse vi farei, CCCXXXIV/2
Et fra me dissi allhor mirando in quelle, CLXVIII/2
Et gli atti i sguardi, il riso, et le parole, CCXCVI/2
Et io che sempre più rallento il freno, CCCXLIV/2
Et io, che veggio i luminosi rai, I/2
Et io quando quel tuon via più risuona, XI/2
Et io so ben madonna, CCXXVI/2
Et Laura spira con si dolce gioia, XIII/2
Et maladico tutti i miei desiri, XCI/2
Et mille volte dissi, CCCXXII/2
Et mille volte sospirando dissi, CCCXXIV/2
Et parmi assai men mal dir la bugia, XCV/2
Et penso quanto è mal morir in culla, CCLXXIX/2
Et per fuggir il duol, di cui mi doglio, XXXVI/2
Et per maggio mio duolo, CIV/2
Et per virtù di sue luci divine, XV/2
Et perché so ch'in vano m'affatico, CLXXXII/2
Et poi scherzando tra l'amate frondi, CXXIII/2
Et pur al fin quando morir mi sento, CLII/2
Et pur di passo in passo, XXXIII/2
Et pur questa crudel fatal mia sorte, CCXCIV/2
Et pur tra morto, et vivo, X/2
Et pur veder non san questi occhi miei, CLXXVII/2
Et qual morte fù mai più dolce et pia, CCCLXV/2
Et quando credo le mie fiamme ardenti, XXXV/2
Et quando detto havrai quel, che più noce, CLXIII/2
Et quando più fra me vo ripensando, CXVII/2
Et quando son più fiso, LXXV/2
Et quante volte in quel sereno viso, CCXIX/2
Et quante volte poi, CXCIX/2
Et s'altro penser novo, CCLXXXII/2
Et s'in me grande è l'un, l'altro è maggiore, CCV/2

Et s'in me il vero per essempi espressi, CXCIV/2
Et s'io dicessi io non direi bugia, CXXXI/2, CCXLVI/2
[Duplicate]
Et s'io veggio un bel riso, CXI/2, CCXCIII/2  [Duplicate]
Et se già de la spene, CL/2
Et se girar poi veggo i sguardi altrove, CCCXXIX/2
Et se non fosse in me questa speranza, CIX/2
Et se quanto mia sei, CCCLVII/2
Et sento l'alma si giosa, et lieta, XLVI/2
Et si il viver m'incresce, XIV/2
Et sol ben si puo dir; perché sol voglio, CLVII/2
Et sospirando disse, CCCLXXVI/2
Et tu rapido Dio, ch'in questo tempo, CXXIX/2
Et veggo un van color, che lo dipinge, CLXXXIX/2
Et voi Donne leggiadre, CCXXXVIII/2
Et voi, poi che vedete, XXXIV/2
Et volentier morrei, CCXXV/2


F
Fate che tosto i moia, LII/2
Felice ben sono io, che in questa etade, LXXIV/2
Felice tomba che'l bel corpo ascondi, CCCLXXIV/1
Felice, aventuroso, almo paese, LXXXV/1
Forse che maraviglia il cor vi prende, CCLXIV/1
Fù già tempo ch'io vissi, CCCXXII/1


G
Gli altri grandi famosi imperatori, CD
Godete donna homai vostra beltate, CCCXLVIII/1


H
Hor che del ben sperato, CCXCVIII/1
Hor che l'error mio veggio, CCXXX/2
Hor che la pura, et candida colomba, CCCXI/1
Hor che sia poi, se a quello almo sembiante, LXXXVII/2
Hor che tornato è il sol de gli occhi miei, CLXXVIII/1
Hor con pietade ascolta, CCXXXII/2
Hor credo ben, ch'ogni cosa mortale, IX/1
Hor fosser ta, qua già le vidi prima, CCCXXV/2
Hor io posso ben dir alma ben nata, CCXXII/1
Hor la mia donna co suoi vaghi lumi, CCCLXI/2
Hor non più no, non più, crudel tiranno, CCCLXX/2
Hor provo ben, che più, che vero è il detto, CCLIV/1
Hor va sicuro; et mai pensar non dei, CCCXCVII
Hor vedesser il duol ch'ho nel corfisso, CLXXII/2
Hor vedi amor in qual pena m'hai messo, CLXXXV/2
Hor vedi amor in quanto error son messo, CII/1
Hor vedi Amor quanta è la gran dolcezza, XCII/1
Hor vedi Amor quanto è l'amor mio grande, LXXV/1
Hor vedi, amor, quanto è la voglia dura, CCXLIX/1
Hor veggio ben madonna, CLVII/1
Hor veggio ben, che voi tenete a gioco, LXVIII/1

Hor'è pur vero, come il vero è vero, CXXXI/1
Hora ch'il caldo estivo, XIX/1
Hora ch'il freddo ghiaccio, CCX/1
Hora ch'il sol'ad albergar col Tauro, XXII/1
Hora christiani, a che pensate voi, CCCLXXVII/2
Hora pensate quanto, CCCLXXIV/2


I

Il dico, et sallo amore, CCCLXIX/2
Il foco bel ch'in que belli occhi apparse, CLXII/1
Il prego il mio sol Dio, il mio Signore, CCCLXXI/2
Il tuo Almiraglio filgio di Nettuno, CCCLXXXIII
Il vidi pur, et per quella honestate, CCCXXVIII/2
Il vo pur dir, o genoroso Carlo, CDXII
Importuni pensier se lungo tempo, LXXVII/1
In quella odiosa stanza, CLXVII/2
In voi s'indura tanto, CCLXXIII/2
Incolparei ben io questi occhi miei, CXX/2
Io ben direi; che lor virtuti estreme, LXXVI/2
Io benedico il di, ch'il mio cor arse, CXCV/2
Io benedico mille volte quelli, CCCXXIX/1
Io con questi occhi la vittoria veggio, CCCXCII
Io consento al morir, poi che si piace, CCLXX/2
Io dico; ecco d'Amor le insidie nuove, XXXVII/2
Io direi ben, che quello, CCXI/2
Io dissi anchor; che troppo crudel sete, CCXCV/2
Io mi sento poi voi nel gran martire, XC/1
Io no'l vo dir; ma questo dir vorrei, CCCXLI/2
Io non havrei si dolorose pene, CCLXIII/2
Io non saprei mai dir perché mi doglia, XXXI/1
Io non sarei venuto, CLX/2
Io non so già come possibil sia, V/2
Io non vorrei più vita: et pur m'attrista, CXXXIV/2
Io penso; et co'l pensero, CCCXIII/1
Io penso tra me spesso, alma mia spene, CCLXXIX/1
Io per voi moio, e il mio morir vedete, CCXXIII/2
Io prego amor, ch'almeno, IV/2
Io prego il ciel, che l'ostinata voglia, CCCXLII/2
Io pur bramo, e vorrei, CLVIII/1
Io pur troppo amo; et del troppo s'avede, CXCVIII/2
Io pur troppo amo; il giuro; et per dio santo, CXCIII/2
Io scrivo il ver; et s'altri il ver non crede, CLVI/2
Io serro il pianto, et se pur come spero, CCLXXVII/2
Io sò ben ch'ardo, et sò che questo è vero, CCLXII/2
Io son di voi, del vostro honor colonna, CCCXXXII/2
Io son did vita privo, et di me stesso, CLXIV/2
Io son nel duol'homai si afflitto, et lasso, XXXIII/1
Io son tanto dolente, CCCXXXIV/1
Io son terreno, et sono houomo mortale, CLXXXIII/1
Io spero far un mi degno lavoro, XII/2
Io veggio chiara la tua forza intiera, CCCXCV
Io veggio tante gratie in quel bel viso, CCXL/1
Io veggio ben, ch'il mio gioir al verde, CCCXXIII/1

```
Io vidi in un sol die, CCCXXXVI/1
Io vive et non sò come viva in terra, CCCLVIII/2
Io vivo; et dir non so come sia vivo, CLXIV/1
Io vo fra me pensando almo mio bene, CXXXVII/1
Io vo fra me pensando almo mio sole, CLII/91
Io vo la notte al lume de la luna, CXVI/1
Io vo pensando pur come sia vero, XLIV/1
Io vorrei pur che quella, LVI/2
```

```
      L
L'alta speranza, ove nodrisco il core, CXXX/1
L'alto Marchese che l'honor sostene, CCCLXXXII
L'alto valor, che signoreggia in noi, I/1
L'un tiemmi l'alma in pene, et doglie estreme, LXXXIX/2
La donna mia non vuole, il posso dire, CCCXXX/2
La lingua se il peccato, et gli occhi miei, CCCL/2
La man non scrive più, la lingua tace, CCXCVIII/2
Lasciate donna homai tanta durezza, CXCVIII/1
Lasso che dir non posso, CCCXXXVIII/1
Lasso come potrò donnna giamai, CCCXXVI/1
Lasso, già quante volte, LXIX/1
Lasso, per che non fui come tu cieco, CIV/1
Laura gentil, che novamente spira, XV/1
Laura soave vita di mia vita, XVIII/1
Livia felice, se felice vive, CCCLXXII/1
Lo star lontan da voi donna m'ancide, CCCX/1
```

```
      M
M'attrista lo sperar; perché non viene, LXXIX/2
Ma a voi, ch'in me vedete, XXIX/2
Ma ch'il dira per me s'io nol so dire?, XXXI/2
Mà cotal gratia io non havrò giamai, CCCVI/2
Ma giunto presso ale bellezze estreme, XLII/2
Ma il ben certo lasciate per l'incerto, CCCLXXVI/2
Mà il Signor mio, che ascolta i dolor miei, CCCXXXVIII/2
Ma in voi come vedrò pieta giamai, CXLII/2
Ma infinita non fia tanta sciagura, CCCLI/2
Ma io vorrei pur sapere, XLVII/2
Ma l'accesa mia voglia, CCXXIV/2
Ma la dura durezza, CXIV/2
Ma la pieta natia, CCXXXI/2
Mà le vertuti, et sue gratie infinite, CCCLIX/2
Ma non bramo corona, VII/2
Ma non credete voi donna, che quelli, LXXI/2
Mà non vi lassa amore, CCLXXXVIII/2
Ma poi ch'ogni mio ben vien da lor sole, CLI/2
Mà poi quel giorno stesso udi novella, CCCXXXVI/2
Mà quando io cresi per mia morte uscire, CCCLXIV/2
Ma quando io veggo in più deserte piagge, CLXXX/2
Ma quando penso a quella, CCXII/2
Ma quando penso poi, CXXXVII/2
Mà quando sotto un puro, et bianco velo, CCXL/2
```

Nel cor mi cria una dolcezza tale, LXXXVIII/2
No'l veggo no, ne mai veder lo spero, CCCXXVII/2
No'l voglio palesar; ch'io non vorrei, CCCXXVI/2
Noi siam qui soli, et più che non credea, CCXIV/2
Non dico donna, il vero, XCV/1
Non dissi mal di voi, et nol direi, CCXXV/1
Non è più il tronco di speranza verde, CCCVIII/2
Non è più no quel tempo, CCCLXVII/2
Non è questa la bianca, et bella mano, III/2
Non già però mi sento, CXXXVIII/2
Non gite notte, e giorno consumando, LXXVII/2
Non havra mai vostra durezza forza, CCLXXII/1
Non pensar carlo che sia in tutto spenta, CCCXCIV
Non pensate crudel per gran dispetto, CV/1
Non sia chi pensi al mio cocente foco, CXXXIX/1
Non temer Carlo imperator invitio, CDI
Non v'adirate de le mie parole, CCCXXXI/2
Non v'adirate donna, CCLXIX/1
Non v'ammirate alma gentil, et bella, CCLXXI/1
Non v'ammirate poi, XCVI/2


         O                             [see also H]
O Bella donna, o donna bella bella, CXIX/1
O bella, et bianca man, o man soavem XLVIII/2
O bella man suor a le belle bella, XLVIII/1
O bellezze divine, o viso santo, LXXIII/2
O ben creata donna, et signorile, CCCLXXIII/1
O Carlo valoroso, o Carlo invito, CCCLXXIX/1
O cor felice mio hor vivi, et godi, LXX/2
O d'honestà colonna, a sacra dea, LXXXIV/1
O Dio il deggio dire?, CCCXXX/1
O Dio, per che non posso, CXC/1
O dolce et viva fiamma, CCCLXXI/1
O dolce mia nemica, CCCXLI/1
O Dolce servitù, dolce tormento, V/1
O dolci parolette, o dolce riso, CXLVI/1
O Donna al mondo rare, et di vertute, CCVII/1
O donna de le donne, o sol mio vivo, LXXXVII/1
O donna vana, hor più d'altri che mia, CCCXXIII/2
O drapicello del mio duol presago, CCLXXXIII/1
O felice chi puote, CCLX/1
O gloriosa impresa, alta, et divina, CCXLV/2
O Lauro mio gentile, VIII/2
O quanto, quanto debitor sarei, CXIX/2
O Re del ciel, che vedi in gran periglio, CDXIII
O Re del cielo, s'io te offesi mai, CCXXX/1
O sacro giorno se la sacra oliva, CCCLVIII/1
O sguardi irati, et voi caldi furori, CCLXVII/1
O sogno mio felice, o sogno grato, CCLXXVIII/1
O sole, ove è quel sole, CCXIV/1
O vita vita de la vita mia, CCCLV/1
O Voi, che havete in piccioletta barca, CXXIX/1
Occhi leggiadri, amorosetti, e gravi, LXI/1

Occhi miei lassi, hora che giunti sete, CXV/1
Occhi piangete, et tu rima dolente, CCCVIII/1
Ond'io ben vi ricordo alma gentile, CXCII/2
Ond'io che so la pena mia infinita, XCVIII/2
Ond'io ringratio amor, et sue facelle, XXX/2
Ond'io ringratio lui; ch'a tempo, et loco, LV/2
Onde io, che seguo amore, CCCI/2
Onde io rivolgo altrove il mio pensero, CCCXVI/2
Onde poi dico; a che servar più fede, LXVIII/2
Onde si bella se vostra persona, II/2


                              P
Pallida non, ma più che neve bianca, CXXI/1
Parer vorreste a i desir miei rubella, CCLXVI/2
Parmi veder il tuo real pensero, CDVI
Partito è ogni mio ben, partito è quello, CCCII/1
Passato ho valli, colli, poggi, et monti, CLXXVII/1
Pe'l viver vostro oprate ogni vertute, CCCLV/2
Pensate come vivo, CCCIV/2
Per far il bel più bello, II/1
Per far il mondo pien di maraviglia, LXXIII/1
Per far un bello intero, CXII/1
Per monti alpestri, solitari, et hermi, CLXXX/1
Per quanto in me discerno, CLIV/2
Per quei belli occhi, ove s'annida amore, CCCXXXIX/1
Per triomphar l'ingorda, et cieca morte, CCCLIX/1
Perché mi dolgo ognihor di voi si forte, L/2
Perché ne l'alto chiostro, CCCLVI/2
Perché quanto è il dolor, tanta è la vita, CCCLI/1
Però ch'il mio ha così largo campo, CCLIV/2
Però che da le gratie pellegrine, CCCLXXII/2
Però che dentro l'alma, CCXLIII/2
Però che gli occhi (ben che nol dica io), LVII/2
Però che l'amor mio, CLXXIX/2
Però che so ben io, che non direi, XLI/2
Però dolce mia spene, CCCXLIX/2
Piace a ciascun l'impresa d'oriente, CDV
Piacemi in voi veder quel, che pur veggio, LXXXVI/2
Piango la doglia mia, piango me stesso, CCCXII/2
Piansi gli affanni miei gaà pochi, et lievi, CCCXIV/1
Pien di timor, e di speranza insieme, LXXXIX/1
Poi ch'amor così vole, CXL/1
Poi che con gli occhi miei, CCLXXXIX/1
Poi che conosco et chiaramente veggio, CCCXLII/1
Poi che de lo mio stratio, IV/1
Poi che la vostra ingorda et crudel brama, CIII/1
Poi che per mille prove, LXXVIII/1
Poi che più dir non voglio, XCVII/1
Poi che si piace a la fatal mia stella, CCLIX/1
Poi che troppo alta è questa impresa et dura, LIII/1
Poi che voi sete quelli, LXI/2
Poi dico; ahi qual di me fu mai più fido, CLXI/2
Poi fra me dico; forse che l'eterna, CXXII/2

Pregate il figlio vostro unico, et vero, CCXXXIII/2
Prego Amor, che vi toglia, LXXII/2
Può tanto il tuo desir anima ardita, CLXXXVIII/1
Pur quando sento il foco in me mortale, CXLI/2
Pur se già stanco, et di canuto pelo, CCXX/2
Pur vivo sono; et credo ben, ch'in vita, CCCXXXIII/2


        Q
Qual amor fu già mai del mio più grande, CCLXX/1
Qual dolor in me fosse, alma mia spene, CCXCII/1
Qual fia che trovi la secura strada, CCCLXXIX/2
Qual fu giamai Imperato si degno, CDIV
Qual morte è più crudel de la mia morte, XCIX/1
Qual peregrin che già ramingo è gito, CCCLXXVIII/1
Qual più bel colpo far morte potea, CCCLXXVII/1
Qual sventurato mai, CLXXXVI/1
Qual'hora io penso a la fedel mia fede, CCLVII/1
Qualhora i veggo in que belli occhi sparse, CXCV/1
Quando ben miro in le serene stelle, CLI/1
Quando contemplo, et veggio, XXXVII/1
Quando dal caldo estivo, CLXX/1
Quando, il desir a riveder mi spinge, CLXXXIX/1
Quando il mio ardento foco, CCXLII/1
Quando in lo specchio rimirate fiso, CLV/1
Quando mi dolgo di quelli occhi belli, CL/1
Quando mi trovo in questa piaggia aprica, CCLXI/1
Quando ne la mia donna io penso, et guardo, CXXXV/1
Quando nel bel, fiorito, et verde aprile, CXXIII/1
Quando penso, ch'io son per altri privo, CCCXXXIII/1
Quando per farsi honore, CLIV/1
Quando per mia ventura, CCCXL/1
Quando più credo, che l'accesa fiamma, LXV/1
Quando più guardo fiso, CVIII/1
Quando più guardo le bellezze estreme, CCXXXVII/1
Quando più penso a l'aria del bel viso, XLIX/1
Quando più veggo ogni mia spene al verde, CVI/1
Quando sia mai che gratiosa, et pia, CCXXXI/2
Quando uscir veggio da quelli occhi belli, LVII/1
Quanto fareste a tua corona torto, CDII
Quanto il ciel adirato, XI/1
Quel, che col ciglio sol regge, et governa, CCCLXXXI
Quel, che dal venire virginal mio nacque, CCCLXXVII/1
Quel di, ch'uscir da i bei vostri occhi vidi, CLXVIII/1
Quel dì, che haveste sopra me l'impero, CCCXLIII/1
Quel Paol terzo che la chiesa regge, CDVIII
Quel Serpe dispietato l'ali spiega, CDXI
Quell'ardente desir, ch'Amore mi diede, XXI/1
Quella che vinta da le forze rie, CCCLXXVI/1
Questa dir si potra ben giusta guerra, CCCXCVIII
Questo è pur ver, et più vero ch'il vero, CLXXIII/1
Questo è pur ver, questo è pur ver madonna, CXXXVII/1

R
Raffrena homai quella ostinata voglia, CLXXXVIII/2
Rotte son le catene, e i nodi sciolti, CXLIV/1

S
S'a la stagion, ch'il freddo lascia adietro, CCXVII/1
S'à quel che lice e a quel che à far si dove, CCCLII/1
S'a un volger d'i belli occhi il sol s'oscura, CCLXXV/1
S'alcun verra che dica, o la chi giace, CCCLXXIV/2
S'altri con soni, et con soavi accenti, CCCLXI/1
S'amante fù giamai di sperar privo, CCXCI/1
S'error commesse la sfrenata lingua, CCCL/1
S'il Bembo, L'Aretino, il Molza, il Tasso, LXXVI/1
S'il casto petto de la mia nemica, CCXI/1
S'il gran poeta Thosco, et si famoso, VIII/1
S'il lungo pianto, che per gli occhi scoppia, CCCLXXVIII/1
S'il mi penser, che sempre in voi sol pensa, CXLV/1
S'il mio destin, mio fato, e la mia forte, L/1
S'il mio gran duol mi sforza, CCCXV/1
S'il non vedervi donna, CCCIV/1
S'il partir vostro ogni mio ben mi tolse, CCCIII/1
S'il timor, il sospetto, e i pensier rei, CCCXXVIII/1
S'in me, come esser suol, non è più ardita, CCCXVIII/1
S'io penso a le bellezze a parte a parte, XXXIV/1
S'io penso ne la vostra alma bellezza, XLIII/1
S'io veggio in altra donna una beltate, CXI/1, CCXCIII/1
[Duplicate]
S'un miracol d'amore, CCXV/1
S'un serpe è velenoso in fronte mostra, XLV/1
S'un troppo disiar madonna è quello, CCVI/1
Sallo anch'amor; ch'il mio secreto intende, CVII/2
Scoprite donna homai, scoprite quelle, CLIII/1
Scrivo quel che non veggio, CCLXIX/2
Se ben soverchio è il foco, CLXIX/1
Se con rispetto amai, et sempre vissi, CXCIX/1
Se far potessi quel, che far non posso, CCCLXXV/1
Se fuor d'ogni misura il mio cor arde, CVII/1
Se giorno, et notte mi consumo in pianto, CCCXXXI/1
Se in darmi doglia tanta, CCLXIII/1
Se infinita bellezza, CCLXXIII/1
Se l'amor mio fu simulato o vero, CCCLXXVI/1
Se l'amoroso stile, XII/1
Se l'anime perdute, CLXVII/1
Se la dura durezza, CCLXXXVI/1
Se la durezza in voi fosse men dura, CXIV/1
Se la fortezza in me fosse si forte, CCCXLV/1
Se la mia donna a mezzo giorno il sole, CCXXXVIII/1
Se la mia donna miro, XXX/1
Se la spietata morte acerba, et ria, CCCLVII/1
Se la vostra gentil e bianca mano, XLVI/1
Se lamentar augelli, CCLXXX/1
Se Laura, ch'esce da le dolce labbia, XX/1
Se le tormentate alme, CLXXII/1
Se mille volte il di per più mia doglia, CCLXXXIV/1

Se ne la vostra angelica bellezza, CLX/1
Se nel maggior mio sdegno, CCXLIII/1
Se nel più bel fiorir de la sua etade, CCCLXXII/1
Se non parlasse Amore, XLI/1
Se per amar vostra beltà infinita, CCLXXXII/1
Se per far nel mio cor, donna, infinita, LXXII/1
Se per morte finir, donna, potessi, CCCXIX/1
Se per voi piansi il san questi occhi miei, CCXXII/2
Se più non scrivo, et taccio, CCCLXVIII/1
Se potesse morir meco il desio, CLIX/1
Se quando guardo il bel sereno viso, CCL/1
Se quanto in voi si vede, LXXX/1
Se quel veglio barbato, iscalzo, e igniudo, CCLXVIII/1
Se quella alma gentil, alma ben nata, CCCLXXIX/1
Se quelle chiare luci, ardenti, et belle, CCCXXV/1
Se riveder i guardo, che m'incende, CCCXLIX/1
Se tanta leggiadria, CCXLI/1
Se tanto è il bel che copre, CCCLXXIII/2
Se troppo v'amo, et se'l mio amor è vero, CCVII/2
Se tutto il mondo, et Dio a cio ti chiama, CDVII
Se voi più bella d'ogni bella sete, CXCIII/1
Se voi vedeste come sete bella, XXIV/1
Seguendo vo la desperata via, CCIII/2
Segui dunque la sacra, et vera strada, CCCLXXIX/2
Sento dar menda a quella giusta morte, LXXXII/1
Sgombrate de la perti mie secrete, CXXVIII/2, CCXLVII/2
[Duplicate]
Sgombrate pensier vani, et noi sospiri, CCCLXVII/1
Si dolce è questo amor, ch'il cor m'assale, CLXXIX/1
Si gioioso mi fanno i dolor miei, CXXXIII
Si grande è la pieta, d'ha di me stesso, CLXXXV/1
Sia benedetta ogni amorosa voglia, CXXXIX/2
Sia benedetto amor, et quel desio, CCLII/1
Sia benedetto Amore, LV/1
Sia benedetto il di, che gli occhi apersi, CCLXXVI/1
Sia benedetto il giorno, CCXXXIX/1
Sia benedetto il tuo felice stato, LXXXIV/2
So ben che morte a voi non puo dar morte, CCCLVI/1
So bene il mio gioire, et Amor sallo, CCX/2
Sò ch'adirata dir spesso solete, CCL/2
So ch'il mio rozo, et amoroso stile, VII/1
Sol per cantar di quella alma gentile, CCCIII/2
Sol per dar fine a tanti miei martiri, CCXCIV/1
Sol per veder il vostra, et mio desire, CIII/2
Sola se stessa, et nulla altra somiglia, CXXXV/2
Sotto silentio in queste rime passo, CCCXC
Spesso fù detto, et io più volte il dissi, CCCIX/1


    T
Taccio il mio foco, et pur tacendo il core, CXL/2
Tante son le mie pene, XCI/1
Tanti fonti in un giorno, et tanti rivi, CCXXVIII/1
Tanto co i lieti suoni, et dolci canti, XXIII/1
Tanto è il mio duol intenso, XXXVI/1

Temendo hor morte, et hor sperando vita, CCCLXIV/1
Tolti sono i pensieri, e i van desiri, CXLIV/2
Tradito son da quel, che più mi fido, CCCXIV/2
Tu fortunato ardito, e valoroso, CDIII
Tu puoi ben morte gir alta, et superba, CCCLXXIII/1
Tu vedi in fatto don Ferrando armato, CCCLXXXVII


U
Uccisa hai pur crudel, uccisa hai quella, CCCLXXIII/2
Un si grande direi, CCXIII/2
Uson quei dolci amorosi sospiri, XIX/2


V
Vana legge d'Amore, LXXIX/1
Vana speranza, in cui sperar solia, CXCVI/1
Veder potria come in un punto gielo, CLXXXI/2
Vedi il valente Conte Torniello, CCCLXXXIX
Vedovi il cor si desto a ogni vertute, LXXXVI/1
Ver è, ch'io dissi che spietata sete, CCLXXXI/2
Ver è che ben direi, CCCXIII/2
Ver'e ch'ogni gran sir convien fidarsi, CCCXCVI
Veramente, Madonna, e gli è pur vero, CCXXXIV/1
Veramente madonnna io dico il vero, CIX/1
Vergine santa a voi piangendo vegno, CCXXXI/1
Vi innamorate si de la bellezza, CLV/2
Vide Thomaso; et poi che veduto hebbe, XXIX/1
Vile sarebbe l'animosa Hispagna, CCCXCIII
Virginia, hor che fra noi non si ritrova, CXVIII/1
Virginia, io vo pensando, CXVII/1
Visto hò più volte in un soffiar di vento, CCCXLIV/1
Vivo d'un guardo; e un guardo sol m'ancide, XCVIII/1
Vivo presente a quei belli occhi vostri, LXXI/1
Voi, che vedete, amor, la doglia mia, CCLIX/2
Voi, che vedete in fronte al mio bel sole, XCVI/1
Voi di lontano andate, e in vista ardita, CCXXIX/2
Voi di mia vita havete in mano il freno, CLXV/2
Voi mi stratiateò; e anchor non v'accorgete, CCIX/2
Voi no'l direte mai, che dishonore, CCXCII/2
Voi sguardi, et risi pur date à ciascuno, CCCXXXV/2
Voi sopra voi il vostro impero havete, CCLXV/2
Volgi cor lasso i penser nostri altrove, CXX/1
Vorrei donna crudel, che quante volte, CLXXI/1
Vorrei si pronta haver la lingua in dire, XLII/1
Vostra vertù non è, ma di quei lampi, CCXXVII/2

# VII.
## Giovanni Della Casa
### *Rime*

A

A questa breve e nubilosa luce, LXIII/2
Affliger che per voi la vita piagne, III/1
Amor, i' piango, e ben fu rio destino, XLV/1
Amor, per lo tuo calle a morte vassi, IV/1
Anzi 'l dolce aer puro e questa luce, LXIV/2
Arsi; e non pur la verde stagion fresca, XXXII/1


B

Bella fera e gentil mi punse il seno, XII/2
Ben debb'io paventar quelle crude armi, XXXII/2
Ben foste voi per l'armi e 'l foco elette, XX/1
Ben lo prego io ch'attentamente apprenda, XXXIX/2
Ben mi scorgea quel dì crudele stella, XLI/1
Ben pote ella sparire a me dinanzi, XLIV/2
Ben veggo io, Tiziano, in forme nove, XXXIII/1


C

Cangiai con gran mio duol contrada e parte, XIV/1
Canzon, tra speme e doglia, XLVI/7
Certo ben son quei due begli occhi degni, XXVIII/1
Ch'io pur m'inganno, e 'n quelle acerbe luci, XLV/4
Che 'l su propio tesoro in altri apprezza, LX/2
Che parlo? o chi m'inganna? A tanta sete, XLV/7
Ciò con tutto 'l mio cor vo cercand'io, XXII/2
Come doglia fin qui fu meco e pianto, X/2
Come fuggir per selva ombrosa e folta, XLVI/1
Come splende valor per ch'uom nol fasci, XLVIII/1
Come vago augelletto fuggir sòle, XL/1
Correggio, che per pro mai né per danno, LIX/1
Così deluso il cor più volte e punto, V/2
Cura, che di timor ti nutri e cresci, VIII/1
Curi le paci sue chi vede Marte, L/1


D

D'ignobil selva. Dunque i versi, ond'io, LIII/2
Danno (né di tentarlo ho già baldanza), IX/1
Deh chi 'l bel volto in breve carta ha chiuso?, XXXIV/2
Di là, dove per ostro e pompa e oro, LXI/2
Doglia che vaga donna al cor n'apporte, LVII/1
Dolci son le quadrella one'Amor punge, X/1
Donne, voi che l'amaro e 'l dolce tempo, XLVI/4
Dunque dovevi tu spirto sì fero, XVI/2


E

E 'l dolce riso ov'era il mio refugio, VII/2
E 'n pianto mi ripose e 'n vita acerba, XXV/2
E de' leggiadri membri anco mi lagno, XXIX/2
E fo come augellin campato il visco, XIX/2
E io son preso ed è 'l carcer aperto, XV/2

E per far anco il mio pentir più amaro, XLVII/3
E perché in te dal sangue non discorda, LVIII/2
E più mi fora onor volgerlo altrove, I/2
E poi ch'a mortal rischio è gita invano, XVII/2
"E questa man d'avorio tersa e bianca, XXIV/2
E vero che 'l cielo orni e privilegi, LIX/2
Ella sen fugge, e ne' begli occhi suoi, XLVI/2
Errai gran tempo, e del camino incerto, XLVII/1


F

Fallace mondo, che d'amaro cibo, LXI/4
Feroce spirto un tempo ebbi e guerrero, LII/1
Forse (e ben romper suol fortuna rea, XLV/6
Fuor di man di tiranno a giusto regnno, XIII/1


G

Già in prezioso cibo o 'n gonna d'oro, LXI/7
Già lessi, e or conosco in me, sì come, LXII/1
Già nel mio duol non pote Amor quetarmi, XXI/1
Già non mi cal s'in tanta preda parte, XLV/8
Già non potrete voi per fuggir lunge, XLII/1
Già vincitor di gloriosa guerra, LXI/6
Gioia e mercede, e non ira e tormento, XXVII/1
Gli occhi sereni e 'l dolce sguardo onesto, V/1


I

Il mio di voi penser fido o soave, II/2
Il tuo candido fil tosto le amare, XII/1
Io che l'età solea viver nel fango, XVII/1
Io, come ville augel scende a poca esca, LXI/3
Io mi vivea d'amara gioia e bene, VII/1
Ivi senza riposo i giorni mena, VIII/2


L

L'altero nido, ov'io sì lieto albergo, XXXV/1
La bella greca, onde 'l pastor ideo, XXXVI/1
La spoglia il mondo mira. Or non s'arresta, LII/2
Lasso, e ben femmi e assetato e 'nfermo, XLV/5
Lasso: e soviemmi d'Esaco, che l'ali, LXII/2
Le bionde chiome, ov'anco intrica e prende, XXXI/1
Le braccia di pietà, ch'io veggio ancora, LXV/1
Le chiome d'or, ch'Amor solea mostrarmi, XXX/1
Le nubi e 'l gielo e queste nevi sole, XXXII/6


M

Ma io come potrò l'interna parte, XXXIII/2
Ma io rassembro pur sublime augello, XLIX/2
Ma la nemica mia perché non piaga, XL/2
Ma lasso me, per le deserte arene, XXXII/3

Ma perch'Amor consiglio non apprezza, XXXII/7
Ma s'io sommetto a novo incarco l'alma, XXIII/2
Ma volse il penser mio folle credenza, XLVII/6
Mansueto odio spero e pregion pia, XXVII/2
Meco di voi si gloria: ed è ben degno, XXXV/2
Mendico e nudo piango, e de' miei danni, LV/1
Mentre fra valli paludose e ime, XXVI/1
Misero: e degno è ben ch'ei frema e arda, LVI/2


        N
Né di me, credo , o del tuo fido e saggio, XLVIII/2
Né quale ingegno è 'n voi colto e ferace, XXII/1
Né, quello estinto, men riluce poi, XXXI/2
Né taccio ove talor questi occhi vaghi, XLVI/3
Né verno allentar pò d'alpestri monti, XXXVIII/2
Nel duro assalto, ove feroce e franco, VI/1
Nessun lieto giamai, né 'n sua ventura, XXIV/1
Nova mi nacque in prima al cor vaghezza, XLVII/2
Novo arboscello a i verdi boschi accrebbe, XXXVI/2
Nulla da voi fin qui me vene aita, III/2


        O
O dolce selva solitaria, amica, LXIII/1
O fera voglia, che ne rodi e pasci, XVIII/2
O fortunato chi sen gio sotterra, XLV/3
O rivi o fonti o fiumi o faggi o querce, LXI/5
O sonno, o de la queta, umida, ombrosa, LIV/1
O vedess'io cangiato in dura selce, XLVI/6
O verdi poggi, o selve ombrose e folte, XLIII/2
Onde m'assal vergogna e duol, qualora, XXVI/2
Or piagni in negra veste, orba e dolente, XXXVII/1
Or pompa e ostro e or fontana ed elce, LVI/1
Ov'è 'l silenzio che 'l dì fugge e 'l lume?, LIV/2
Ove il sonno talor tregua m'adduce, VI/2


        P
Per poter poi, quando sì rio tal volta, IX/2
Però che gli occhi alletta e 'l cor recide, LVII/2
Però che da lei sola ogni mio fato, XXI/2
Picciola fiamma assai lunge riluce, XLVII/7
Pietosa tige il cielo ad amar diemmi, XLVI/5
Poco il mondo già mai t'infuse o tinse, XLIX/1
Poi ch'ogni esperta, ogni spedita mano, I/1
Poi che sì dolce è 'l colpo ond'i' languisco, XXVIII/2
Portato da destrier che fren non have, XLII/2
Pur come foglia che col vento sale, LI/2


        Q
Qual chiuso albergo in solitario bosco, XLV/2
Qual chiuso in orto suol purpureo fiore, XXX/2

Qual dura quercia in selva antica, od elce, XLI/2
Qual peregrin, se rimembranza il punge, XLVII/5
Quando in questo caduco manto e frale, L/2
Quel vago prigioniero peregrino, XXXIX/1
Quel vero Amor dunque mi guidi e scorga, XLVII/4
Quella che del mio mal cura non prende, XV/1
Quella che lieta del mortal mio duolo, XLIV/1
Quella leggiadra Colonnese, e saggia, LV/2
Questa vita mortal, che 'n una o 'n due, LXIV/1
Questa, angel novo fatta, al ciel sen vola, XXXVII/2


      R
Rendimi il vigor mio, che gli anni avari, XXXII/5
Ricca gente e beata ne' primi anni, LXI/2
Rigido già di bella donnna aspetto, XXXII/4


      S
S'egli averrà che quel ch'io scrivo e detto, LX/1
S'io vissi cieco, e grave fallo indegno, XVIII/1
Sagge, soave, angeliche parole, XI/1
Sì cocente penser nel cor mi siede, II/1
Sì lieta acess'io l'alma, e d'ogni parte, LI/1
Signor fuggito più turbato aggiunge, XIV/2
Signor mio caro, il mondo avaro e stolto, LVIII/1
Soccorri, Amor, al mio novo periglio, XXIX/1
Sol per vaghezza del bel nome chiaro, XX/2
Solea per boschi il dì fontana o spero, XXV/1
Son queste, Amor, le vaghe trecce bionde, XXXIV/1
Sotto 'l gran fascio de' miei primi danni, XXIII/1
Sperando, Amor, da te salute in vano, XIX/1
Squarciato è 'l vel, che tolse a gli occhi interni, LXV/2


      T
Tal che, s'i' non m'inganno, un picciol varco, IV/2
Tempo ben fora omai, stolto mio core, XVI/1
Tolsemi antico bene invidia nova, XIII/2


      V
Vago augelletto da le verdi piume, XXXVIII/1
Varchi, Ippocrene il nobil cigno alberga, LIII/1
Vivo mio scoglio e selce alpestra e dura, XLIII/1
Voi d'Amor gloria sète unica, e 'nseme, XI/2